The Illustrated Guide to Social Science Research

This accessible and engaging textbook helps students to get to grips with key concepts, issues, and practices in social science research through the use of fun and informative illustrations and examples.

Written and illustrated by an experienced teacher of research methods in the social sciences, each chapter explains research concepts while using everyday examples and illustrations to make applied research comprehensive to students. It explains the step-by-step process for carrying out research through a range of topics and approaches, including survey research, research ethics, sampling, and experimental research. Chapters also include learning objectives, class activities, key terms, helpful hints, and suggestions for further reading.

This book will be essential reading for any undergraduate research methodology class in the social sciences.

Divya Sharma is Professor of Justice and Law Administration at Western Connecticut State University, CT, USA. She holds a Ph.D. in Sociology and Master's degrees in Sociology and Criminal Justice. Her research interests include informal banking systems, visual criminology, cultural communication, and white-collar crimes. She has collected data in India, Kenya, and the United States. She specializes in program and policy evaluation, survey and field research, and research ethics concerning non-western and cross-cultural settings and digital data. She has developed and taught a wide range of graduate and undergraduate courses in criminal justice, homeland security, and sociology, and has extensive experience in supervising student research projects involving primary and secondary data. She is the author of the textbook *Fundamentals of Criminology* (2019), and editor of *Ethics, Ethnocentrism and Social Science Research* (2021).

The Illustrated Guide to Social Science Research

Divya Sharma

LONDON AND NEW YORK

Designed cover image: Divya Sharma

First published 2025

by Routledge
4 Park Square, Milton Park, Abingdon, Oxon OX14 4RN

and by Routledge
605 Third Avenue, New York, NY 10158

Routledge is an imprint of the Taylor & Francis Group, an informa business

© 2025 Divya Sharma

The right of Divya Sharma to be identified as author of this work has been asserted in accordance with sections 77 and 78 of the Copyright, Designs and Patents Act 1988.

All rights reserved. No part of this book may be reprinted or reproduced or utilised in any form or by any electronic, mechanical, or other means, now known or hereafter invented, including photocopying and recording, or in any information storage or retrieval system, without permission in writing from the publishers.

Trademark notice: Product or corporate names may be trademarks or registered trademarks, and are used only for identification and explanation without intent to infringe.

British Library Cataloguing-in-Publication Data
A catalogue record for this book is available from the British Library

ISBN: 978-1-032-32379-4 (hbk)
ISBN: 978-1-032-32377-0 (pbk)
ISBN: 978-1-003-31473-8 (ebk)

DOI: 10.4324/9781003314738

Typeset in ScalaSans
by Deanta Global Publishing Services, Chennai, India

Contents

List of Boxes	ix
List of Figures	x
Acknowledgments	xiii

Introduction — 1

1 Research Methods: An Overview — 6
Introduction — 6
Types of Research – What Can You Do With Research? — 9
Errors in Reasoning — 15
Community-collaborative approach — 19
Cultural analytics — 19
Generalization, Causal, and Measurement Validity and Authenticity — 20
Longitudinal and Cross-Sectional Research Designs — 25
Further Reading — 28
Key Terms — 28
Class Activity — 29
Works Cited — 29

2 Research Steps — 31
Introduction — 31
Quantitative and Qualitative Research Methods — 33
Research Question — 34
Literature Review — 39
Search Tips and Tricks — 41

	Public Databases	44
	News Sources	45
	CRAAP test	46
	Annotated Bibliography	48
	Reading an Article (and making sense of it!)	50
	Theoretical Framework	51
	Research Steps	55
	Could My Research Proposal be Rejected?	56
	Further Reading	59
	Key Terms	59
	Class Activity	60
	Works Cited	60
3	**Research Ethics**	**62**
	Introduction	62
	The Tuskegee Experiment	63
	The Tearoom Trade Experiment	64
	The Milgram Experiment	64
	The Stanford Prison Experiment	65
	Institutional Review Board	66
	Ethical Guidelines	68
	Ethics Abroad	74
	Digital Data and Ethics	76
	Funded Research	78
	Further Reading	79
	Key Terms	79
	Class Activity	80
	Works Cited	80
4	**Defining and Measuring Concepts**	**82**
	Introduction	82
	Concept	83
	The Chicago (Ilinois) Alternative Policing Strategy	84
	Weed and Seed program	84
	Levels of Measurement	86
	Further Reading	91
	Key Terms	91
	Class Activity	91
	Works Cited	92
5	**Sampling**	**93**
	Introduction	93
	Sample Planning	97

	Probability and Non-Probability Methods	101
	Probability Sampling Methods	102
	Non-probability Sampling Methods	107
	Sampling error	111
	Key Terms	113
	Class Activity	113
	Works Cited	113
6	**Collecting Primary Data: Survey Research Methods**	**115**
	Introduction	115
	National Crime Victimization Survey	116
	Monitoring The Future Survey	118
	Types of Surveys	119
	Questions – Format and Considerations	128
	Further Reading	137
	Key Terms	137
	Class Activity	137
	Works Cited	137
7	**Collecting Primary Data: Experiment Research Methods**	**139**
	Introduction	139
	The Minneapolis Domestic Violence Experiment (MDVE)	143
	A Class Divided Experiment, 1970	144
	Zimbardo's Experiment on Vandalism, 1969	145
	Conditions of Causality	147
	Types of Experiments	150
	Classical Experiment	151
	Quasi-experiments	152
	Factorial Survey … or Experiment	152
	Validity and Generalizability in Experiments	154
	Ethical Considerations in Experiments	155
	Further Reading	158
	Key Terms	158
	Class Activity	158
	Works Cited	159
8	**Collecting Primary Data – Qualitative Methods: Focus Groups, Observation, Intensive Interviews**	**160**
	Introduction	161
	Qualitative research	161
	Focus Groups	161
	Focus Groups – Generalizability	166
	Focus Groups – Ethics	166

	Planning for Observation and Intensive Interviews	168
	Observation	169
	Types of Observation	170
	A Quick Word on Technology	173
	Intensive Interviews	175
	Qualitative Research – Visual Digital Data	178
	Further Reading	184
	Key Terms	184
	Class Activity	184
	Works Cited	185
9	**Data Organization, Report Writing, and Presentation**	**187**
	Introduction	187
	Data Organization	188
	Data Analysis	191
	Data Ethics	193
	Report Writing	194
	Format and Structure	194
	Presenting Findings	198
	Further Reading	201
	Key Terms	201
	Class Activity	201
	Work Cited	202
	Glossary	*203*
	Index	*228*

Boxes

BOX 1.1	Sentencing Goals or Philosophies/Goals of Punishment	8
BOX 1.2	Example of Reductionist and Ethnocentric Errors	19
BOX 1.3	National Crime Victimization Survey	25
BOX 1.4	Impact of Drug Courts on Recidivism and Cost	27
BOX 2.1	Policy Questions	38
BOX 2.2	The CRAAP Test	46
BOX 2.3	Quantifying Qualitative Data	57
BOX 2.4	Minneapolis Domestic Violence Experiment	58
BOX 3.1	University of Illinois Missed Warning Signs	63
BOX 3.2	Sample Consent form	69
BOX 6.1	National Crime Victimization Survey (NCVS) Methodology	117
BOX 7.1	Experiment on Distracted Driving	140
BOX 7.2	Computational Simulation of Visual Distraction Effects on Car Drivers' Situation Awareness	141
BOX 7.3	The Consequences of Race for Police Officers' Responses to Criminal Suspects	142
BOX 7.4	The MDVE Methodology	143
BOX 8.1	Murphy's Law	173
BOX 8.2	Study on Women in Outlaw Motorcycle Gangs	174
BOX 8.3	Quantitative Analysis of Qualitative Data	182

Figures

Figure 0.1	My Cat	xiii
Figure I.1	Research Journey	4
Figure 1.1	Types of Research	10
Figure 1.2	Where to Start?	11
Figure 1.3	Descriptive Research	12
Figure 1.4	Evaluation Research	14
Figure 1.5	Overgeneralization	16
Figure 1.6	Confirmation Bias	17
Figure 1.7	Errors in Reasoning	18
Figure 1.8	Main Goals of Social Science Research	20
Figure 1.9	Causal Validity	21
Figure 2.1	Research Proposal	32
Figure 2.2	Research Methods	34
Figure 2.3	Show Me the Question	35
Figure 2.4	Good Research Question	37
Figure 2.5	Literature Review	40
Figure 2.6	Boolean Operators	42
Figure 2.7	The Librarian	43
Figure 2.8	Show Me the Money	48
Figure 2.9	Citation Loop	49
Figure 2.10	Plagiarism	50
Figure 2.11	Theory, Hypothesis, Opinion	52
Figure 2.12	Research Steps	55
Figure 3.1	Power Dynamics and Voluntary Participation	67

Figure 3.2	Ethical Guidelines	69
Figure 3.3	Ethnocentrism	75
Figure 4.1	Concept – Fear of Crime	83
Figure 4.2	Physical Incivilities	85
Figure 4.3	Levels of Measurement	86
Figure 4.4	Ordinal Level – Pepper Hotness Test	88
Figure 4.5	Interquartile Range	88
Figure 5.1	Sampling	94
Figure 5.2	Sample for Blood Work	95
Figure 5.3	Census	95
Figure 5.4	Census not Possible and Census not Needed	96
Figure 5.5	Where to Start	97
Figure 5.6	Sampling Methods	101
Figure 5.7	Simple Random Sampling	102
Figure 5.8	Random Selection Error	103
Figure 5.9	GPS	104
Figure 5.10	Stratified Random Sampling	106
Figure 5.11	Non-probability Sampling Methods	107
Figure 5.12	Availability Sampling	108
Figure 5.13	Purposive Sampling	109
Figure 5.14	Snowball Sampling	110
Figure 5.15	I Never Get Picked in Any Sample!	112
Figure 6.1	Types of Surveys	119
Figure 6.2	Phone Surveys	123
Figure 6.3	Skip Pattern	124
Figure 6.4	You've Got Mail!	126
Figure 6.5	Double-negative	133
Figure 6.6	Uniform Style in Survey	135
Figure 7.1	Nothing Can Distract me!	140
Figure 7.2	False Correlation	145
Figure 7.3	What Would You Do?	146
Figure 7.4	Causal Explanations	147
Figure 7.5	Time Order	149
Figure 7.6	Classical Experiment	151
Figure 7.7	Factorial Designs	153
Figure 8.1	RRR	162
Figure 8.2	Incentives	164
Figure 8.3	Effective Moderator	165
Figure 8.4	Conflict of Interest	167
Figure 8.5	Focus Groups	168
Figure 8.6	Observation and Intensive Interviews – Basic Steps	169
Figure 8.7	Covert Observation	170
Figure 8.8	Reactive Effect	172

Figure 8.9	No Generalizability	177
Figure 8.10	Emojis	180
Figure 8.11	Quantitative Data and Qualitative Data	183
Figure 9.1	Organizing Data	189
Figure 9.2	Pie Chart	190
Figure 9.3	If It's Online ...	191
Figure 9.4	Multiple Regression	192
Figure 9.5	Generalizability	194
Figure 9.6	Title Page	195
Figure 9.7	Be Prepared	200
Figure 9.8	Research Journey	202

Acknowledgments

I would like to thank my mom for her unparalleled support in everything that I do. She takes immense pride in all my efforts and accomplishments and cheers me on no matter what. She always gets me to see the brighter side of things. A huge thanks to my sister for her love, sense of humor, and generosity. Her unreal belief that I'll succeed at almost everything is exactly what gets me in trouble, but also encourages me to keep exploring, trying, and learning. As always, Papa's memory inspires me, and his blessings, integrity, and *mantra* of happiness continue to guide me. He would have been happy and surprised to see how far I have come from the days of drawing the same cat in the whole drawing book one summer vacation after another.

Figure 0.1 My Cat

I am forever grateful to Professor Peter Jones for his selfless support, guidance, and encouragement throughout my professional journey of over two decades in the United States. A big shout out to Pat for her unwavering support. She's been a wonderful friend and I cherish all our chats, laughs, tennis matches (I won them all), and get-togethers over the years. A huge thanks to Ms. Helen for playing thousands of drawing games with me that must have germinated the idea for an illustrated guide. She embodies kindness and fun in equal measure. Above all, they keep it real!

Last but certainly not least, I want to thank Chris Parry at Routledge for his immense patience and guidance. His kind reminders and support kept me on track and helped me to complete this project. Thank you

Introduction

We have extensive personal, social, and professional experiences. We also have access to information about almost everything around the world. From the research perspective, information, opinions, and experiences are only a starting point. An experience, interaction, and observation may also raise curiosity to study an issue or topic. However, we need to develop a scientific temperament and use research tools to study any topic systematically, objectively, and empirically. Many may feel nervous about taking a research methods course because they may have heard that it is all about math and statistics. Some may feel that they do not need to know about research methods as they will not be doing any research themselves. For starters, leave all such preset notions about research at the start of the semester.

Now, some skills come naturally to us while others are acquired. To acquire any new skill, one has to be willing to learn. Therefore, as we *start* learning about research methods, it is fine to be nervous and not know everything – or much of anything – about social science research methods. If you knew everything, you would not be taking this course! All that we need is a willingness to learn while knowing that we cannot learn everything. Yet, we will continue to learn something all through our lives. That mindset toward learning will go a long way in grasping the need and purpose of research. From buying the latest mobile phone to deciding whom to hire to repair windows, we do some form of rudimentary research all the time. When studying topics on social science, we expand that canvas and use several quantitative and qualitative research methods.

This guide will help you to understand the basic reasons to do research, how to do research, and how to navigate what may seem like a daunting academic and social space. Treat this guide as a GPS or a roadmap, but also pay attention to the surroundings and use your critical thinking skills. Research tools are effective only if the people using them are aware of what they are studying, why, and how.

The research skills acquired during the research methods course go beyond getting a passing grade. The skills will be useful for anyone advancing to a graduate program and exploring research assistantships or jobs. It will help to develop an ability to cut through the clutter by taking one piece of the puzzle and fixing it while being aware of the larger picture. Every law, policy, or program has certain objectives. Through research, you will begin to understand what works, what needs to improve, and how it can be improved. We need research to understand what programs need more funds, what new training the employees would benefit from, what new courses and programs students should take while keeping in mind the job market, and so on. Evaluating existing literature not only expands one's understanding of complex topics and lays the foundation to study them further, but also enhances critical thinking, writing, and communication skills. Students working on research projects, particularly involving primary data, can also explore publishing their work in student journals, present at conferences, and show it off on their resume!

Each chapter in this guide will introduce the key research concepts. It is best to select a topic of interest and develop a research proposal following the steps as explained. Illustrations are used to explain concepts as well as to catch the reader's attention. For most students in undergraduate programs, this guide would be more than adequate to grasp the basic research concepts and process. However, this guide can be supplemented with other articles and book chapters on particular research topics, especially for detailed statistical analysis that is generally covered in a separate course. At the undergraduate level, as my students do an in-depth literature review or some may collect data using surveys, I use additional resources on those aspects of research. At the graduate level, one would need a more detailed research methods book, and this guide can be used for a refresher or supplemental read.

Chapter 1 begins with a discussion of the importance of research in criminology, criminal justice, and sociology. It explains the main types of research, including descriptive, explanatory, generative, and evaluative. It explains common mistakes that researchers may make at any stage of research and why it is important to guard against them. These errors can be made even while doing a literature review or using secondary data. Some of the common mistakes explained in this chapter are overgeneralization, illogical reasoning, hypothesis myopia, confirmation bias, normalcy bias, and so on. This is followed by a discussion on causal validity and measurement validity. The chapter concludes with a brief discussion on authenticity, longitudinal research, and cross-sectional research.

Chapter 2 begins with an overview of research methods for quantitative and qualitative data, known more commonly as quantitative and qualitative research methods. The chapter explains the research process, including what makes for a good research question, and how to go about finding answers to research questions. The chapter gives an overview of how to search databases, find relevant sources, and conduct a literature review. It explains step-by-step the inductive and deductive research strategies and how and when to use them, data collection, analysis, and findings. In explaining the research process, the chapter introduces the research concepts of hypothesis, theory, grounded theory, and independent and dependent variables in applied social science research. It concludes with a discussion on good planning, willingness to learn, and enjoying the research process.

Chapter 3 provides a brief history of ethics in social science research. It explains the key ethical guidelines such as ensuring voluntary participation, causing no harm to subjects, maintaining confidentiality and anonymity, disclosing the researcher's identity, and ensuring that the benefits of the research outweigh the risks. It also explores challenges while conducting research abroad, in cross-cultural settings, or unfamiliar settings, the problem of helicopter researchers, the ethics of funding, and so on. The chapter explains dilemmas and challenges in both qualitative and quantitative research methods. Chapter 4 explains the process of defining abstract concepts and identifying measurable indicators for the same. It explains the importance of selecting the most suitable research method, and levels of measurement for different types of variables.

Chapter 5 explains the significance, purpose, and methods of taking a sample from the population or setting that the researcher wants to study. It begins with discussing the basic steps and issues to consider before deciding on which sampling method to use. The chapter walks the reader through the process of drawing samples using probability methods of simple, systematic, stratified, and cluster sampling. Among the non-probability sampling methods, the chapter explains the significance and process of availability, quota, purposive, snowball, and theoretical sampling methods. The reader will not only learn the steps involved in using these sampling methods but also when and why to use which method. The chapter concludes with a note on sampling error and the need to keep doing research.

Chapter 6 explains the quantitative research method of designing and using surveys. It explains different types of surveys, the preconditions or settings where they could be used, and the strengths and limitations of each

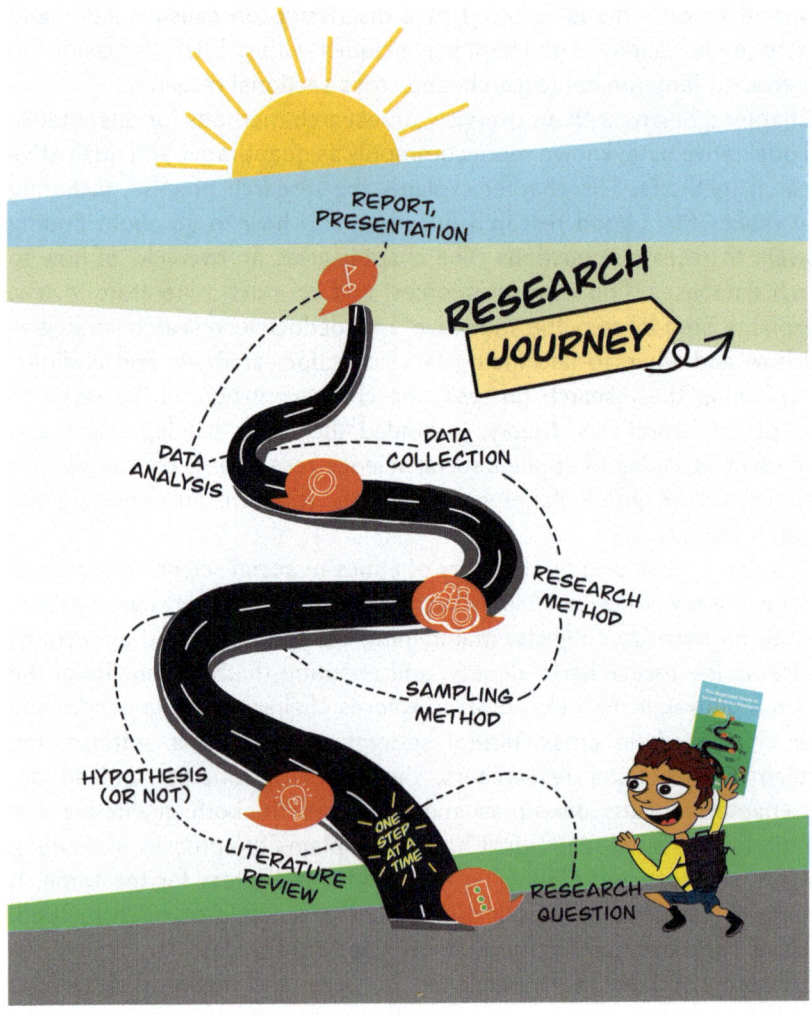

Figure I.1 Research Journey

type of survey. The chapter explains survey research methods with reference to validity, generalizability, and ethics. Chapter 7 explains the quantitative research method of designing and using experiments. It explains classical and quasi-experiments, the potential preconditions or settings where they could be used, and the strengths and limitations of each method. The chapter explains criteria for causal explanation, and experimental research methods with reference to validity, generalizability, and ethics.

Chapter 8 explains the qualitative research methods of designing and using focus groups, observation, and intensive interviews. It explains different qualitative methods, the preconditions or settings where they could be used, and the strengths and limitations of each method. The chapter explains issues of validity, generalizability, and ethics in relation to each qualitative method. Chapter 9 explains data organization, data analysis, and data ethics surrounding interpretation and presentation. It includes a brief discussion on data manipulation through images, graphs, colors, and so on. The chapter explains the step-by-step process of report writing and presentation.

Knowing these basic aspects of research would be enough to get you started on your journey of systematic examination of issues in criminal justice, criminology, and sociology. Never hesitate to ask questions to your professors teaching research methods courses, and those involved in doing research themselves. Essentially, all research is not as complicated as it has been made out to be. Start with a simple project with a small sample size. Design a project that requires you to follow the basic research steps. Once you get the hang of it, you will be able to carry out research with a larger sample or examine more complex topics. Remember not to try to understand and solve everything about the whole world in one research project! Instead, select just one tiny aspect of the larger issue and examine it. Of course, do not collect any data without getting all the approvals from the Institutional Review Board. Above all, do not try to memorize all the research terms and concepts. Instead, understand their meaning and application. Take one step at a time. Be systematic. Document everything. Ask. Read. Think. Re-read. Take a break. Continue. All the best!

As you use this illustrated guide, feel free to send me some feedback on what else you would like to see in it, or what helped you in your understanding of research methods in social sciences.

Divya Sharma
sharmad@wcsu.edu

chapter 1

Research Methods
An Overview

This chapter begins with a discussion of the importance of research in criminology, criminal justice, and sociology. It explains the main types of research including descriptive, explanatory, generative, and evaluative. It then explains common mistakes that researchers may make at any stage of research and why it is important to guard against them. Some of the common mistakes explained in this chapter are overgeneralization, illogical reasoning, hypothesis myopia, confirmation bias, normalcy bias, and so on. It is followed by a discussion on causal validity and measurement validity. The chapter concludes with a brief discussion on authenticity, longitudinal research, and cross-sectional research.

After this chapter, students will be able to understand and explain:

- The types of social science research
- The common mistakes that researchers make
- Generalization, causal validity, and measurement validity
- Authenticity in social science research
- Longitudinal and cross-sectional research approaches

Introduction

Research can be seen as a way of learning or finding out information about the research subject. It may be to understand a social problem, identify its causes, and make or evaluate a policy or law about it. It could be focused on an individual, group, organization, processes, systems, and so on. The core aim is to reach valid conclusions. Different topics or research subjects require different approaches, samples, methods, and data to study them. The very basic research steps are identifying the research subject, collecting data about it, and analyzing and presenting it. The data may be primary or secondary, and quantitative or qualitative. The sampling methods may be probability or non-probability. The research methods may be quantitative or qualitative. The research subject may be individuals, groups, or organizations. You may be able to plan for every aspect of the research, or you may not. You may test a hypothesis(es) drawn from a theory(ies), or start from collecting data and then theorize it. Research helps to describe, explain correlations, make predictions, compare, explore, evaluate, and so on. There are many studies on practically every topic in social science. Replicating some of the previously done research is as meaningful as studying something new. This chapter gives an overview of all these aspects of research and these are explained in detail in subsequent chapters.

We all have opinions, but we do not always know the basis of our opinions. Research helps us, among other things, to deconstruct opinions and work with tangible facts, evidence, and logic. It is all the more critical to recognize the importance of research in the age of social media, where one receives information from every corner all day long without always checking the veracity of the information. After all, for policies to be effective, they should be rooted in findings made through systematic research and not just opinions and hearsay.

Most professionals in social sciences, including criminal justice, either consume or produce research. You are already consuming a lot of research as a student when reading journal articles, books, technical reports, and so on. You have not read everything on every topic that you are writing about in your coursework, but as you read, you gain more perspective. You may also read conflicting information, and start to debate what holds more weight and logic, or what applies better to a particular setting. As you learn more from existing information, you may also be tempted to collect more information. That is research – examining the existing literature and collecting more information or data to further analyze. One cannot make policies aimed at everything from **rehabilitation, incapacitation, deterrence**, and **retribution** to reform based on personal feelings or public sentiment around the election season. For example, if you want to study whether a particular deaddiction program works better for non-violent drug offenders as compared to imprisonment, you will need to design a research project that examines multiple hypotheses, gather evidence, and see which hypothesis is empirically supported.

BOX 1.1 – Sentencing Goals or Philosophies/Goals of Punishment

Retribution – This is the oldest sentencing goal. It is based on the concept of *lex talinois* or the law of retaliation. It argues that the punishment should match the crime. This type of punishment is an end in itself. The death penalty is most commonly used as an example of retribution.

Deterrence – This is considered the first systematic effort by Bentham and Beccaria to understand the purpose of punishment. The theory of deterrence assumes that humans are rational, have free will, and serve self-interest. If the benefit of committing a crime is more than the risk or cost of committing a crime, they will commit crimes. Therefore, the purpose of punishment should be to create deterrence. It should be carried out in a way that increases the harm or the risk while reducing the potential benefit. **Specific deterrence** can be measured through the recidivism rates – did the punishment deter the punished offender from reoffending? **General deterrence** can be measured through overall crime rates – did the punishment for certain offenses reduce the overall crime in that area? For punishment to create deterrence, it should be certain, swift, and proportionate to the crime.

Rehabilitation – This sentencing goal is rooted in the medical model that views crime as a disease. That means that some people may get better (stop offending/reoffending) sooner, while others may take longer. Therefore, the criminal justice response cannot be one size fits all, and instead, the punishment or the response should be tailored to the offense, offenders, and situational and background factors. It recognizes that free will is not absolute and may be impacted by duress, abuse, intoxication, mental illness, environment, and so on. For example, if a drug dealer is also an addict himself, the system's response needs to have room for treatment programs.

Incapacitation – This aims to incapacitate the offenders for a specific time by removing them from society, thus removing the opportunity to commit a crime. Incarceration is one of the most common ways to achieve the goal of incapacitation.

Restorative Justice – This is the newest sentencing goal and is generally combined with one of the other goals, particularly rehabilitation or deterrence. It aims to restore the offender, victim, and society to a pre-crime state (Braithwaite, 1989).

Lawmakers and practitioners have to understand what policies are or could be effective for what kinds of crimes and offenders, what programs are needed for victims, how to run community-based programs, how to strengthen and deliver social support services, and so on. Everyone may have an opinion about any topic, but not every opinion is based on thorough, current, and valid research. Opinions have value as these are rooted in personal experiences and views. They may be good conversation starters. They may also be unique to individuals placed in certain situations that are difficult to replicate. They may motivate someone to further examine the issue that they have heard of, experienced, or thought about. To understand behavior, address social issues, or make effective policies, one needs to systematically and empirically study the topic at hand and explore opinions, evidence, and literature, understand local needs and resources, and find solutions. Not every research would involve all these elements. For instance, one study may be used only to describe the nature and prevalence of online shopping during the holiday season, while another may evaluate police training in detecting **e-tailing fraud**.

Types of Research – What Can You Do With Research?

Before moving any further, let's discuss what you can do with research. This will help you to understand different types of research. Many studies, if not most, involve multiple types of research. For example, in a research paper, one may start with the description of informal banking systems, their meanings, types, *modus operandi*, and extent, while also evaluating a specific law in the United States, India, China, or anywhere else in dealing with informal banking systems. **Descriptive, evaluative, exploratory, applied,** analytical, **explanatory, deductive, inductive, predictive, qualitative**, and **quantitative** are just some of the types of research or research terms that you would come across.

When you think of a type of research, think of its purpose – that is, what is it that you want to do with research?

> **Helpful Hint** – As we examine different types of research, think of what topic you would like to study. It is easier to understand the research concepts and their relevance when we can apply them to real-world situations. Therefore, as you read, think of a topic and try to apply these research concepts and see if you can develop a sound proposal one step at a time.

> **Caution**: Do not collect any data until your research proposal has been examined by your professor and approved by the appropriate Institutional Review Board or the Ethics Committee. This is explained in detail in Chapter 3.

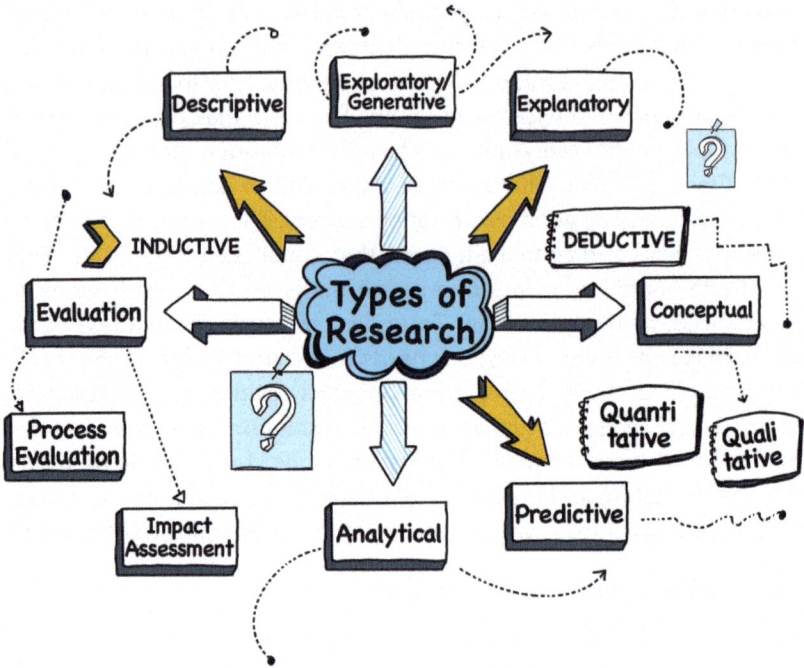

Figure 1.1 Types of Research

You may not see yourself as a researcher as yet, but

a) You have been doing research, however rudimentary. For instance, when you shop for a new pair of shoes and look for the best bargain across websites, or try to find more information about the lawnmower that you want to buy, that is research*ing*. It has limited applicability and utility, but it is still research.

b) You just have to think of a general topic right now, such as distracted driving, gun violence, political corruption, **Ponzi schemes**, gardening habits, time spent on social media, road safety, juvenile justice, bias in news media, and so on. For inspiration, think of the other courses that you have taken in your major and the topics discussed. You can also talk to your friends or fellow students and exchange ideas. The inspiration may also come from anything that you watch on television or online. On any given day, you are exposed to innumerable ideas and images about umpteen topics. See if you can tap into that reservoir.

The first step is to identify what type of research you want to do. Is your aim to simply describe the social issue or identify the reasons why it is so, or maybe both, and more? Let's have a look at the types of research.

Figure 1.2 Where to Start?

Descriptive research – This describes the subject of the study. The more descriptive and detailed the information, the better the understanding of what the setting, event, and population entail, what to analyze further about it, and how to analyze it. Most commonly it aims to answer the question of 'what'. *What percentage of people eat oranges for lunch in your office? What has the rate of domestic violence been in your city in the past five years? How many people played tennis at the local community center last weekend?* Though the last question is phrased using 'how', note that it produces descriptive information. The descriptive information can be used to identify patterns, dominant values, common themes, and norms. It can give reasonable insight into what can be predicted to happen in that setting if the circumstances do not change much.

Exploratory research – Exploratory research, also called **generative research**, is often used to gain an understanding of a setting, phenomena, concepts, or events that may not be clearly defined. They may carry subjective meanings and manifest differently for different people. For example, two people may be afraid of crime, but how it impacts their lives or what steps they take to address it may be very different. As it focuses on how people

research methods

Descriptive Research

Figure 1.3 Descriptive Research

interpret their behaviors and environment, it is also known as **ethnological** research.

Many concepts that have not been previously studied or have been studied in a manner that does not address various dimensions or more recent developments would benefit from starting with an exploratory approach. It is also very useful when one tries to understand different settings or behaviors and attitudes in different cultures. For example, justice, punishment, freedom of speech, feminism, economic victimization, social development, happiness, and so on would have different meanings and indicators even within a country, but there are all the more differences across cultures and countries.

Many studies on victims of violence and conflict also use an exploratory approach. This can be used to gain an in-depth understanding of any field such as offenders, social media influencers, law enforcement officers, traveling nurses, and so on. *How has the crime in the neighborhood impacted your business? How are the community and police relations in your neighborhood? How stressed do you feel about traveling alone? How does social media create echo chambers? What are your thoughts on capital punishment?* Though the last question is phrased using 'what', note that it produces exploratory information.

Explanatory research – Explanatory or **correlation** research aims to connect different ideas to explain the cause and effect. It explains causal relationships between variables. It essentially answers the question of 'why'. In criminology and sociology, students learn about many theories that explain behavior at micro and macro levels. *Why do individuals commit crimes? Why do groups of people get together and commit crimes? Why do certain locations have higher crime than others? Why does social media result in more discord in democratic countries than in theocratic and authoritarian regimes? Why do people drink and drive? Why is there an increase in online bullying? What is the correlation between poverty and residential mobility?* As you would note, the answers (data collection) to all these questions would generate explanatory data. It aims to identify correlations among variables. Many factors result in crime; causal relations help to identify which factors have a stronger correlation with crime and which ones have a weaker correlation.

Evaluation research – Evaluation research refers to a systematic inquiry aimed at evaluating a program, policy, or law. It is also used to study user experiences about a particular product or service. It aims at evaluating a very specific set of needs and goals with the objectives of assessment and improvement. It would help to study cost-effectiveness, quality control, the strengths and weaknesses of a program, and so on. It has two main goals – whether the program is implemented as planned (**process evaluation**), and whether the program has the desired outcome (**impact evaluation**). *Has Meta effectively addressed the privacy concerns of Facebook users in its latest policy update? How did the Rockefeller laws result in prison overcrowding in New York? Was the Gang Resistance Education And Training program in Bridgeport (Connecticut) effective in guiding young people to avoid gangs, alcohol, and substance abuse?* Similar questions can be developed to evaluate community programs, victim-support services, deaddiction programs, educational programs behind bars, and so on. It is important to identify a particular program, policy, law, product, or service and then evaluate it. One should avoid trying to study all community policing programs in a general manner, and instead evaluate a specific program in a particular setting. This requires reading about the program, then reviewing literature about it (specific program or community policing in general), then developing hypotheses or research questions, and so on.

In evaluative research, the researcher may come across a program that is implemented as planned but does not have the desired outcome, and vice-versa. Evaluation of both process and impact can help researchers to identify the gaps or weak links and specifically address them instead of trying to overhaul everything or maintain the status quo. For example, a deaddiction program may be working better for women than men, the in-patient program may be working better than an out-patient program, a program may be successful in reducing recidivism for drug abuse but may be struggling to retain patients, or the evaluation may show a need

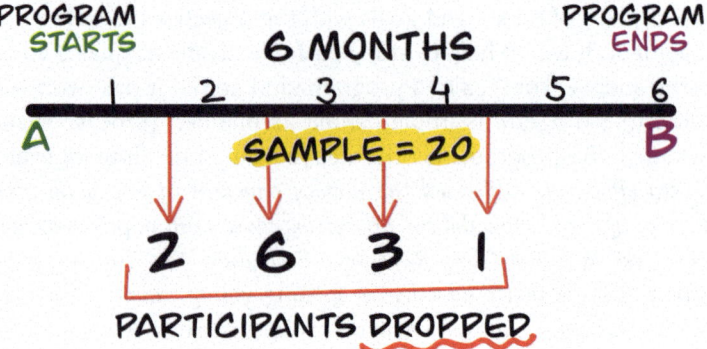

Figure 1.4 Evaluation Research

for better training for those involved in implementing the program, and so on.

After evaluation, a decision can be made whether the policy, law, or program is achieving its stated objectives and should continue as is, should be modified, or should be scrapped altogether and replaced with a new program. Having conducted an evaluation would also give enough information about what to avoid doing in the new program. In social sciences, many programs are funded by local, state, and federal governments and need to show success to continue to receive funds. It is always beneficial to carry out evaluative research before any policy, law, or program is implemented, but, as one can know its real impact only after it is enacted, it is important to keep evaluating it once implemented.

The above four types of research are the most common. There are many other categories, types, and subtypes of research or even different labels for the same types of research, but these should be enough to get you started. Most research projects would include more than one type of research if not all four, and more.

> **Helpful Hint:** At this point, you should have a general topic that you would like to examine and some early discussions about what type of research would you like to do. If more than one student selects the same topic, talk to your professor to work as a team and develop a research proposal to include more than one type of research.

Errors in Reasoning

It is common to make certain mistakes, and they can occur at any stage of research – planning, reviewing the literature, collecting data, analyzing data, and writing a report. If you are aware of these common errors, it will be relatively easier to identify and guard against them. Here are a few common errors that one should be mindful of while engaging in social science research. There may also be overlap among some of them. These errors can be made even while doing a literature review, using secondary data, or collecting primary data.

Overgeneralization – This is the tendency to look at a small sample or a handful of cases and assume that it applies to a much larger population. Some of the common reasons for this are inadequate sample size, sample misrepresentation, and personal biases, among others. Many people may watch a news item, documentary, or movie or read an editorial or an article and overgeneralize it to cultures, groups, and so on, and that is an error.

Figure 1.5 Overgeneralization

Hypothesis myopia – This is also called **selective observation**, where one only looks at the information relevant to one's preset ideas and beliefs. The information in such an instance may not be incorrect, but it is partial or skewed and thus would result in faulty assumptions. It may also result in overgeneralizations as one may selectively pick only one type of respondent or set of information as it fits one's proposed hypothesis, but then apply those assumptions to the whole setting. Selective observation may also come about through the way that we frame questions. People tend to ask leading questions or ask questions only about one aspect of the issue.

This does not mean that one has to study all aspects, all the time – not expected, not possible! But researchers have to acknowledge that they are only studying one specific aspect of the setting or the issue, and therefore, should not overgeneralize it.

Confirmation bias – This is another logical fallacy where one selectively searches, interprets, and documents only the information that suits one's beliefs.

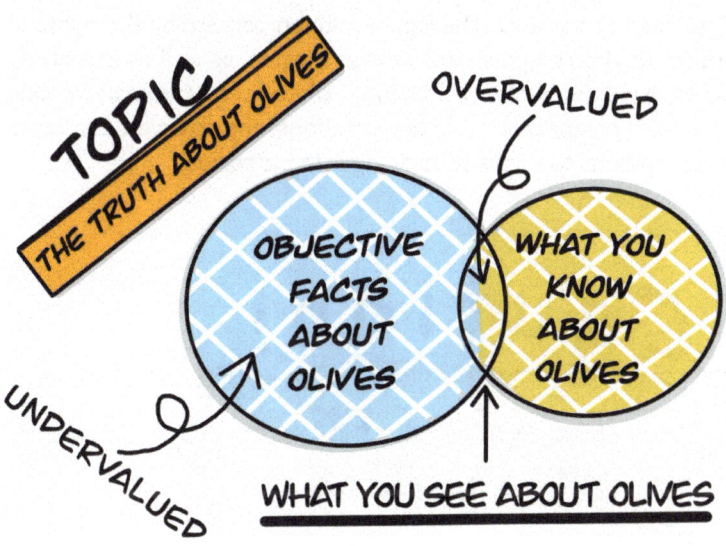

Figure 1.6   Confirmation Bias

Anecdotal fallacy – This refers to the use of personal experiences as evidence for the topic of study. Individuals have limited experiences, but to conduct a scientific study, one needs to study and reason systematically. The anecdotal fallacy also creates an empathy gap, as one seems to struggle to understand anything beyond what one has personally experienced.

Normalcy bias – This comes from a state of mental paralysis where one ignores the imminent grave danger and does not believe that it could happen. A researcher may work with preset ideas and ignore the actual seriousness or reality despite the evidence. They may focus on the aspect of the issue that they are comfortable dealing with and develop and examine the question and evidence in that preset framework only, while ignoring its more serious aspects.

research methods

Illogical reasoning – This error occurs when the very basis of an argument or information is illogical. For example, many tend to believe anything trending on social media is factual! The **Slippery Slope** is a type of **logical fallacy** where one believes that a single event would result in a chain of events in the future. Many conspiracy theorists thrive on it. The **Straw Man Argument** and **Ad hominem** are other common logical fallacies.

Neophobia – The fear of change or anything new can make researchers resistant to change. People may be set in their ways and used to certain systems and practices, and may not feel the need to disturb the status quo. Many may quietly follow orders and do what they are told to do. However, for any change to occur, including legal evolution, one needs to keep doing research, identify and study socioeconomic changes and their impact on society, and so on. New policies, laws, and programs may be needed, while some previous ones may need to be modified or stopped. The legal evolution concerning the rights of racial minorities, children's rights, and women's rights, as well as identifying and addressing legal loopholes concerning white-collar criminals, online bullying, outsourced businesses, labor law violations, and so on are examples of how the laws continue to evolve with changes in the society.

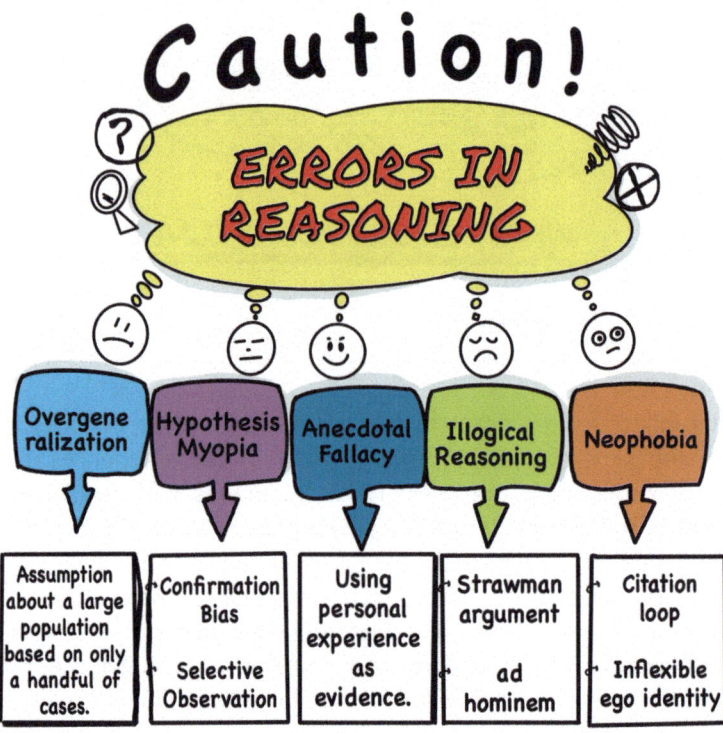

Figure 1.7   Errors in Reasoning

It is also important to guard against the **citation loop**, where one keeps framing the issue using previously used sources, authors, and perspectives. This is increasingly being criticized when Westerners study topics in Asian and African continents predominantly from the Western or Eurocentric perspective. In many spheres of history, criminology, politics, Indology, and economics, there is concern about ego-based commitments where researchers struggle to change the views that they have held for decades. These concerns encourage using a **community-collaborative approach** to avoid these errors and learn new or previously ignored perspectives.

BOX 1.2 – Example of Reductionist and Ethnocentric Errors

"Edwina Thompson (2007) refers to a paper (Sharma, 2006) on the informal banking systems of hawala and hundi and states that the *current* Indian literature tends to separate local financial practices from hawala in Pakistan and Afghanistan that are tainted with a brush of terrorism. However, the passage that Thompson refers to explains hawala practices in India only, and that too prior to the 1940s: Pakistan was created in 1947 (Sharma, 2019, p. 10). Additionally, a large number of people who use hawala in India are not Muslims or do not use it due to religious factors. "Any Indian police officer, scholar, investigator, or journalist would have clarified these facts about religion and history. On Thompson's part, it could be a simple error in judgment, or worse, it could reflect the reductionist way of looking at the [Indian] subcontinent through conflict and/or religious lens. Either way, it affects perceptions, understanding, and actual policies. While conducting research in cross-cultural settings, it is beneficial to understand the larger sociocultural and historical contexts or collaborate with the local experts" (Sharma, 2019, p. 10).

Social science research does not assume or mandate the researcher to not have any opinions and emotions. It does, however, require that one should be able to set aside personal preferences, values, emotions, and biases while doing research and should systematically and objectively observe and present findings.

Cultural analytics – This is a useful tool in social sciences and humanities that can help to avoid some of the above-mentioned errors. It helps to identify what is a pattern or a regular occurrence – something that happens all the time or is happening quite frequently – as against what is an individual experience, an outlier, or a one-time occurrence. Depending on the purpose of the study, it can help to identify deviations as well. Alternatively, outlier analysis can specifically focus on identifying abnormal observations in data. Do not discard the outliers though. They can be very useful and reflect the weak points, the potential for growth, the point of change in patterns, reasons for negative feedback from customers, and thus areas that need improvement, and so on. The key here is to know what is an outlier and what is not, and to frame questions and draw conclusions accordingly.

As you have selected a topic of interest, at this point, with guidance from the professor, start to discuss what opinions you have about it and if you can identify the basis for those opinions. In the process, you will begin to realize what perhaps you do not know about the topic, or if you do not know how you have reached a particular opinion.

> **Helpful Hint:** It is good to ask, 'could I be wrong?' 'Am I open to learning?' 'Am I making assumptions or ignoring evidence as it challenges my long-held beliefs about people, cultures, systems, and so on?' Keep asking these questions to yourself.

Generalization, Causal, and Measurement Validity and Authenticity

The main goals of social science research are generalization, causal validity, measurement validity, and authenticity.

Unlike in mathematics, where 2 plus 2 is always 4, there is less predictability and more uncertainty in social science. It is not always possible for people to

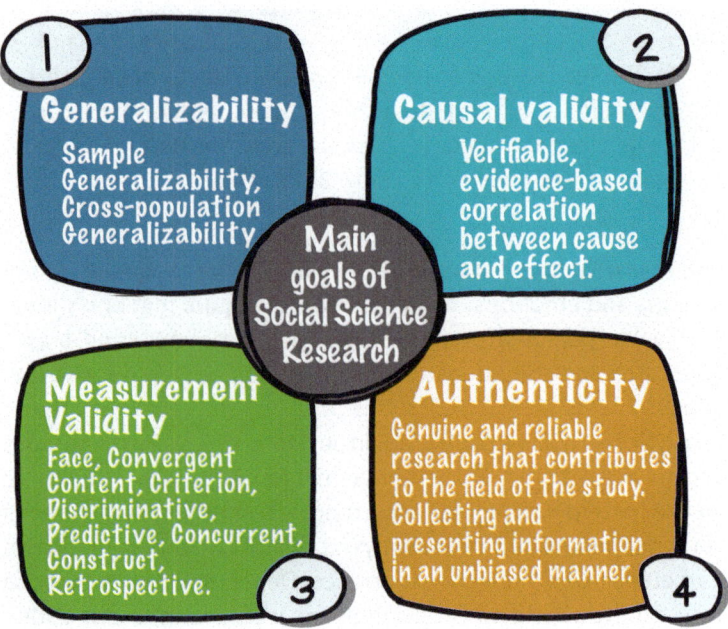

Figure 1.8   Main Goals of Social Science Research

20 research methods

predict how they will act when placed in certain situations. Long-term predictions are more difficult than short-term predictions. Predictions in diverse settings with multiple forces at play are more difficult than predictions about relatively stable homogenous settings. At its core, human nature is dynamic and complex. It is not possible to achieve absolute validity and generalizability in any social science study. However, one tries to achieve it as much as possible, while also identifying where it is not possible to generalize findings and for what reasons.

Generalization – Also known as generalizability, this is the ability to generalize findings from a sample to the larger population from where the sample is taken. Unless they were dealing with very small populations or had a boatload of money, researchers would not conduct a **census**. Instead, they would take a sample, study the sample, and then generalize the findings to the population. This is known as **sample generalizability**. Researchers may also apply their findings to another similar population or setting though they did not take a direct sample from it. This is called **cross-population generalization**. If the two settings are not similar or comparable, it is best to take separate samples from both populations and try to achieve sample generalizability in different settings.

Causal validity – This refers to the ability to establish a verifiable, evidence-based correlation between cause and effect. The cause is the **independent variable** and the effect is the **dependent variable**. Though it is commonly referred to as a causal explanation, it does not imply absolute cause and effect. Some factors may have a stronger correlation than others. For example, there are many reasons why people steal, including need, opportunity, habit, and thrill. These four factors would vary in strength of correlation.

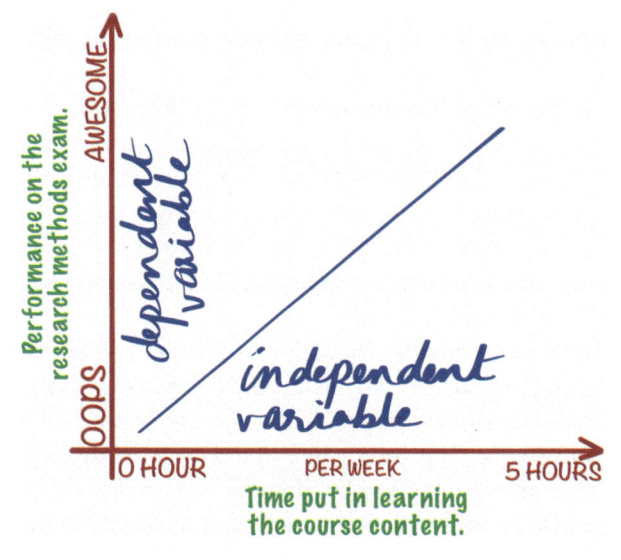

Figure 1.9   Causal Validity

Measurement validity – This refers to the reliability and validity of the tool of data collection. The researcher will select a method or tool of data collection that is best suited for the study. For example, one can subjectively guess the speed of a car, but a speedometer would be its valid measure. Similarly, it is easy to ask questions about demographic information such as age, gender, race, and so on, but asking someone about their shoplifting habits, that too in a group setting, may not be the best way to collect reliable information. In terms of power dynamics, it is best not to ask employees to share their thoughts on the work conditions and environment in front of the employer, and so on. Though there are many types of measurement validity, the following should be more than enough for this research methods course. As you read about the types of measurement validity, remember that it is about the validity of the research method or the tool of data collection.

Face validity – This is a judgment-based method where one is sure that on its surface, the measure correctly measures what it is intended to measure. It is easy to make such a judgment or establish face validity when the concept is simple and clearly defined. The research method would have face validity if, on its face, it appears to be appropriate for the sample and the research question. For example, one can ask employees in an office how much water they drink in a day. The question is simple, and it is easy to ask questions on this topic. However, one cannot email surveys to human traffickers active in the field! For that topic, that method would not be appropriate.

Content validity – This assesses whether or not all aspects of the subject can be measured using the research method that one has selected. It relates to fully understanding the concept and having the appropriate method(s) to study it. One often gathers a comprehensive understanding of the concept through a literature review. It helps to understand various aspects of the concepts, how they have been studied, the findings, and so on. For example, by reviewing the literature, one may note that domestic violence has many dimensions, including physical, psychological, emotional, financial, and so on. One may also note that there are more studies on female victims of domestic violence than male victims of the same. This broader understanding of the topic could guide how to further study the topic. If one is not clear about what to study, it is difficult to pick a method to measure it or decide how to study it.

Construct validity – This is achieved when the variables or factors explained in a study are logically strung together. It establishes the correlation among variables and systematically explains the cause(s) and effect(s) in a broader context or theoretical framework. The researcher would have to develop multiple scales to measure correlations among different sets of variables. Construct validity is an estimate of how well the method measures various items or dimensions identified in content.

Criterion validity – This requires testing one measure against the other and assessing the results of both to see how similar or dissimilar they are. For example, if a driver is speeding and jumping lanes, a police officer may stop him. The driver reeks of alcohol and also fails the walk-and-turn test. The officer may make a judgment that the driver is drunk. A Blood Alcohol Concentration test can confirm the same by measuring the level of alcohol in the blood.

This type of validity can also be useful when developing new programs, tests, training modules, and so on, based on the previous measure. For example, an organization running a program for senior citizens about how to protect their information against online and phone scams can evaluate what works and what needs to be improved upon in the existing program, and then develop a new program bearing in mind the previous assessment tool or knowledge base. It would give the stakeholders – including program managers – more confidence in the new program.

Criterion validity is further divided into predictive, concurrent, convergent, retrospective, and discriminant validity, but for this course, it is more than enough to have a general understanding of criterion validity.

Despite the many technical terms, the most important criterion is to understand what to study and how to study, to remain aware of the research question at all times, and to actively guard against common mistakes in reasoning. While considering measurement validity, the researcher must also consider measurement reliability. It is possible to have a reliable but invalid measure.

Therefore, one also needs to ensure that the measure is not producing data that is consistently incorrect. Guarding against mistakes in reasoning at all stages of research and selecting the method that best suits the research question, setting, and sample are important. The two most common ways to establish measurement reliability are **test-retest reliability** and **inter-rater** or **inter-observer reliability**. Test-retest reliability can be achieved by measuring the phenomenon twice (or more), and if the results are similar, the measure can be considered reliable. Inter-rater reliability can be achieved by having more than one researcher study and interpret the findings. Several studies (Maxfield and Widom, 1996; West and Farrington, 1977) establish the usefulness of inter-rater reliability in establishing consistency or uniformity in designing and carrying out research.

The researchers should also aim to be authentic in their recording and analysis of data. **Authenticity** refers to genuine and reliable research that contributes to the field of study. It includes collecting and presenting information in an unbiased manner. It is important to present the views of the research subjects without tainting them with personal ideologies or filtering information as per preset views. Though there are no absolute validity and generalizability, one can be authentic in presenting the findings – that is, recognize the limitations of the study, gaps, and scope while presenting it. It requires a certain humility on the part of the researcher to not be in awe of their own work and to recognize that:

- Despite one's best efforts, one may not understand certain aspects of the setting.
- The data should be recorded without making inferences based on personal judgments and expectations.
- Some people may be underrepresented in the sample. It is important to note this while analyzing data and report writing as well.
- The study may be influenced by the gatekeepers' perspective. It may result in bias, skewed perception, or limited information. It is important to recognize this as it would affect validity and generalizability. There may be a language barrier or cultural nuances that one missed, and so on.
- **Ethnocentrism** may compromise authenticity.
  - For one of my research projects, I met the director of the Universal Just Action Society based in Jodhpur, India. The director informed me that in the past, a few researchers had visited to interview Hindu and Sikh refugees from Pakistan seeking shelter and citizenship in India, but then published whatever *they* wanted to publish. It made some of the respondents wary of outsiders, including researchers and journalists. That is, the authentic views and experiences of the respondents did not fit the preset frameworks within which the researchers may have been working.
- Some researchers may also feel compelled by the ideological framework of their funding sources, may have to present a particular view to get their works published in one or the other forum, or have a sense of superiority about *their* understanding of the different settings, human behavior, conflict, crime, justice, or so on. Any of these factors may result in researchers making errors – intentionally, unwittingly, or habitually. Walker (1994) argues that in criminal justice for many people, ideological biases – across the political spectrum – trump facts. All these factors impact the authentic collection, interpretation, or reporting of information.

> **Helpful Hint:** Measurement validity is about choosing the appropriate research method to study your research question. At this point, as we have not studied research methods, do not start selecting a research method for your research proposal. But when we discuss various methods such as surveys, focus groups, and so on, it would be good to revisit this section to see if the method that your research proposal includes would be the best to study the topic that you have selected.

Longitudinal and Cross-Sectional Research Designs

Research can use longitudinal data or cross-sectional data. In a **longitudinal study**, the researcher would analyze data from or about the same individuals over time to closely examine correlations. This helps to determine patterns over time, understand developmental trends, and assist in more accurate predictions, and it has strong internal validity. For example, if a judge has the option to assign treatment or prison time for a particular offense, evaluation of data over time can show which approach worked better for whom and why by studying offender characteristics and situational factors. Depending on the research method, longitudinal studies may produce qualitative or quantitative data. The downside or limitation of a longitudinal design is that it is time-consuming and because of this, the sample may become contaminated over time. Respondents may drop out of the study, move away, and feel disinterested. Such research designs would have a smaller sample to begin with, and the change in the sample size and composition would further impact the study's generalizability. For example, all women may drop out of the sample after 3 years while the study is planned for 14 years. In that case, along with the sample size, the sample composition is also changed. Cohort, panel, and record linkage are the most commonly used longitudinal research designs.

BOX 1.3 – National Crime Victimization Survey

"The NCVS identifies repeat victims through the collection of separate incident reports for each victimization reported during the interview period as well as its classification of series victimizations. Series victimizations are incidents that occurred six or more times during the recall period (the preceding 6 months), are similar to each other in detail, and whose details are indistinguishable to the respondent (Planty, 2007). Researchers also have used the NCVS as a longitudinal dataset to examine repeat victimizations across interview periods (Ybarra and Lohr, 2002; Dugan, 1999). A few limitations arise with these uses of the NCVS to study repeat victims. With regard to series victims, only a small amount of information is collected about series victimizations, which makes it difficult to ascertain the association between the incidents. Additional questions or a supplement could investigate the interdependence of these victimizations as well as the factors that may contribute to the persistence of the victimization (Cantor & Lynch, 2000). Using the NCVS longitudinally also has limits. One particular issue is the fact

> that the NCVS is a survey of households and does not follow individual respondents who move. Repeat victims may be more likely to move and fail to be included in subsequent interviews" (Addington, 2008, p. 3).
>
> "…While researchers have used the NCVS as a longitudinal dataset (Ybarra and Lohr, 2002; Dugan, 1999), the survey does not follow mobile respondents. As such, substantial changes to the current NCVS design would be required to study this group of victims. Creating a longitudinal crime survey is not a new idea. This possibility was considered as part of the NCS redesign (Biderman and Lynch, 1991). One alternative to completely changing to a longitudinal design is to follow a sample of individuals. Such a format would permit highly mobile individuals to be studied within a primarily household survey format. During the redesign discussions, BJS suggested the possibility of a supplement that would follow a subset of respondents (Biderman and Lynch, 1991). This supplement was never pursued" (Addington, 2008, p. 4).

In a **cross-sectional study**, the researcher would collect data from the sample at one point in time and analyze it. It helps to study numerous variables in a short amount of time that may need immediate attention. For example, with a sudden increase in the opioid crisis, health workers may not have the luxury of studying this increase for over a decade before coming up with a response. Similarly, if there is any major crisis such as a terrorist attack, pandemic, tsunami, and so on, one does not have the time to study its various aspects long-term before coming up with any solutions as there is a need for almost immediate assistance to those impacted. Thus, cross-sectional studies would help to identify those impacted, the nature of the immediate impact, what is needed, and so on. It is a snapshot of the setting or people at a given point in time. However, as these studies collect data at one point in time, it is important to keep evaluating any policies based on this design as the needs and challenges evolve.

A cross-sectional study is also known as a **transverse study** or **prevalence study**. Just as the longitudinal studies, cross-sectional studies can also use quantitative or qualitative methods. Cross-sectional studies also allow for a larger sample and thus carry stronger generalizability, however, as they collect data at one point in time, they do not have strong predictability, and they cannot establish long-term trends. For several topics, researchers use both longitudinal and cross-sectional approaches. A researcher may study the immediate risks of flooding in an area and address immediate needs while also continuing to examine the risks over a longer time.

Studies on the same topic would produce different results often due to different samples, research designs, and settings, but above all, due to human nature. It is a humbling fact to remember and serves as a reminder to keep evaluating programs, policies, and laws. For example, deterrence and retribution used to be more common sentencing goals until there was more research on the psychological and biological factors of crime and victimization. It created room for rehabilitation as a sentencing goal (Box 1.1). Drug courts are an example of a criminal justice response aimed at rehabilitation.

BOX 1.4 – Impact of Drug Courts on Recidivism and Cost

"Lower recidivism. Using retrospective data, researchers in several studies found that drug courts reduced recidivism among program participants in contrast to comparable probationers. For example, one study found that within a two-year follow-up period, the felony re-arrest rate decreased from 40 percent before the drug court to 12 percent after the drug court started in one county, and the felony re-arrest rate decreased from 50 percent to 35 percent in another county.

In an unprecedented longitudinal study that accumulated recidivism and cost analyses of drug court cohorts over 10 years, NIJ researchers found that drug courts may lower recidivism rates (re-arrests) and significantly lower costs. They used data from a primarily pre-plea adult drug court in Portland, Oregon, to track 6,500 offenders who participated in the Multnomah County Drug Court between 1991 and 2001. Re-arrests were lower five years or more later compared to re-arrests for similar drug offenders within the same county.

The researchers also found, however, that the drug courts' impact on recidivism varied by year as a result of changes in programming and judge assignments over time. Reductions in recidivism ranged from 17 to 26 percent.

Lower costs. Compared to traditional criminal justice system processing, treatment and other investment costs averaged $1,392 lower per drug court participant. Reduced recidivism and other long-term program outcomes resulted in public savings of $6,744 on average per participant (or $12,218 if victimization costs are included).

> Factors for success. Although general research findings are that drug courts can reduce recidivism and promote other positive outcomes such as cost savings, several factors affect a drug court program's success:
>
> - Proper assessment and treatment.
> - The role assumed by the judge and the nature of offender interactions with the judge.
> - Other variable influences such as drug use trends, staff turnover and resource allocation." ("Do Drug Courts," 2008).

When done systematically, social science research can result in a better understanding of human behavior, needs, and dynamics. It can help to explain the frameworks or contexts within which behaviors develop and take shape. It can allow us to build a large knowledge base, answer conflicting ideas in theories, develop better policies, make adequate institutional changes, and plan better for various challenges and changes.

Further Reading

Drug Courts: The Second Decade. Special Report, NIJ. U.S. Department of Justice. Retrieved from https://www.ojp.gov/pdffiles1/nij/211081.pdf

Key Terms

Anecdotal fallacy
Authenticity
Causal validity
Census
Citation loop
Community-collaborative approach
Confirmation bias
Content validity
Construct validity
Correlation
Criterion validity
Cross-sectional research
Cultural analytics
Dependent variable
Descriptive research
Deterrence
E-tailing fraud
Ethnological research
Evaluative research
Explanatory research
Face validity
General deterrence
Generalizability
Generative research
Hypothesis myopia
Illogical reasoning
Impact assessment
Incapacitation
Independent variable
Inter-observer reliability
Inter-rater reliability
lex talinois
Logical fallacy
Longitudinal research
Measurement validity
Neophobia
Normalcy bias
Overgeneralization
Ponzi schemes
Prevalence study
Primary data
Process evaluation
Qualitative research
Quantitative research
Recidivism

Rehabilitation	Secondary data	Test-retest method
Reliability	Selective observation	Transverse study
Restorative justice	Slippery slope	
Retribution	Specific deterrence	

Class Activity

The instructor can ask students to bring a copy of a newspaper or printout of two or three articles from an online news portal. Specify the timeline, such as the past one or two weeks, and the length of the article. Ask students to read one article at a time and make note of what type of information it contains. It will help to clarify the differences as well as the overlapping nature of different types of research. To make it even more interesting, give the same article to every three to four students and ask them to individually examine it for the type of information that it provides. It would help to see what aspects of the same information different students focus on and what observations they make.

Works Cited

Addington, Lynn A. 2008. *Current Issues in Victimization Research and the NCVS's Ability to Study Them.* Bureau of Justice Statistics. Retrieved from https://bjs.ojp.gov/sites/g/files/xyckuh236/files/media/document/addington.pdf

Biderman, A., and J.P. Lynch. 1991. *Understanding Crime Incidence Statistics: Why the UCR Diverges from the NCS.* New York: Springer.

Braithwaite, John. 1989. *Crime, Shame and Reintegration.* New York: Cambridge University Press.

Cantor, D., and J.P. Lynch. 2000. "Self-Report Surveys as Measures of Crime and Criminal Victimization." In D. Duffee, D. McDowall, L.G. Mazerolle, and S.D. Mastrofski (eds.), *Criminal Justice 2000: Measurement and Analysis of Crime and Justice.* Washington, DC: National Institute of Justice.

"Do Drug Courts Work? Findings From Drug Court Research." 2008. National Institute of Justice. Retrieved from https://nij.ojp.gov/topics/articles/do-drug-courts-work-findings-drug-court-research

Dugan, L. 1999. "The Effect of Criminal Victimization on a Household's Moving Decision." *Criminology,* Vol.37(4), pp. 903–930.

Maxfield, Michael G., and Cathy Spatz Widom. 1996. "The Cycle of Violence: Revisited Six Years Later." *Archives of Pediatrics and Adolescent Medicine,* Vol.150(4), pp. 390–395.

Planty, M. 2007. "Series Victimizations and Divergence." In J.P. Lynch and L.A. Addington (co-editors). *Understanding Crime Statistics: Revisiting the Divergence of the NCVS and UCR* (pp. 156–182). Cambridge: Cambridge University Press.

Sharma, Divya. 2006. "Historical Traces of Hundi, Sociocultural Understading and Criminal Abuses of Hawala." *The International Criminal Justice Review*, Vol.16(2), pp. 99–121.

Sharma, Divya. 2019. *Fundamental of Criminology*. San Diego, CA: Cognella.

Thompson, Edwina. 2007. "Misplaced Blame: Islam, Terrorism and the Origins of Hawala." In A. von Bogdandy and R. Wolfrum (eds.), *Yearbook of United States Law*, Max Planck. Volume 11, pp. 279–305. Leiden: Brill.

Walker, Samuel. 1994. *Sense and Nonsense About Crime and Drugs: A Policy Guide*. 3rd ed. Belmont, CA: Wadsworth.

West, Donald J., and David P. Farrington. 1977. *The Delinquent Way of Life*. London: Heinemann

Ybarra, L.M.R., and S.L. Lohr. 2002. "Estimates of Repeat Victimization Using the National Crime Victimization Survey." *Journal of Quantitative Criminology*, Vol.18(1), pp. 1–21.

chapter 2

Research Steps

This chapter begins with an overview of research methods for quantitative and qualitative data, known more commonly as quantitative and qualitative research methods. The chapter explains the research process, including what makes for a good research question, and how to go about finding answers to research questions. The chapter gives an overview of how to search databases, find relevant sources, and conduct a literature review. It explains step by step the inductive and deductive research strategies and how and when to use them, data collection, analysis, and findings. In explaining the research process, the chapter introduces the research concepts of hypothesis, theory, grounded theory, and independent and dependent variables in applied social science research. It concludes with a discussion on good planning, willingness to learn, and enjoying the research process.

After this chapter, students will be able to understand and explain all key aspects of the research process:

- Developing a research question
- Searching databases, finding relevant sources, and conducting a literature review
- Selecting the relevant research strategy – inductive and deductive
- Understanding the research concepts of theory, hypothesis, and independent and dependent variables
- Collecting and analyzing data

Introduction

For any type of research, one needs to develop a research proposal. This is a blueprint of what you will study, why, and how. It is one thing to have a thought about a research topic or question in mind; it brings more clarity once you start putting it down on paper. Developing a research proposal helps one to plan every step of the research, including identifying what sampling and research methods to use, what ethical dilemmas may arise, how to get a sample, and so on. Generally, a research proposal consists of:

Title page, introduction, aims and objectives, literature review, hypothesis, methodology, ethical considerations, timeline, budget (if applicable), works cited, and, endnotes (if applicable). Most proposals now include an abstract as well.

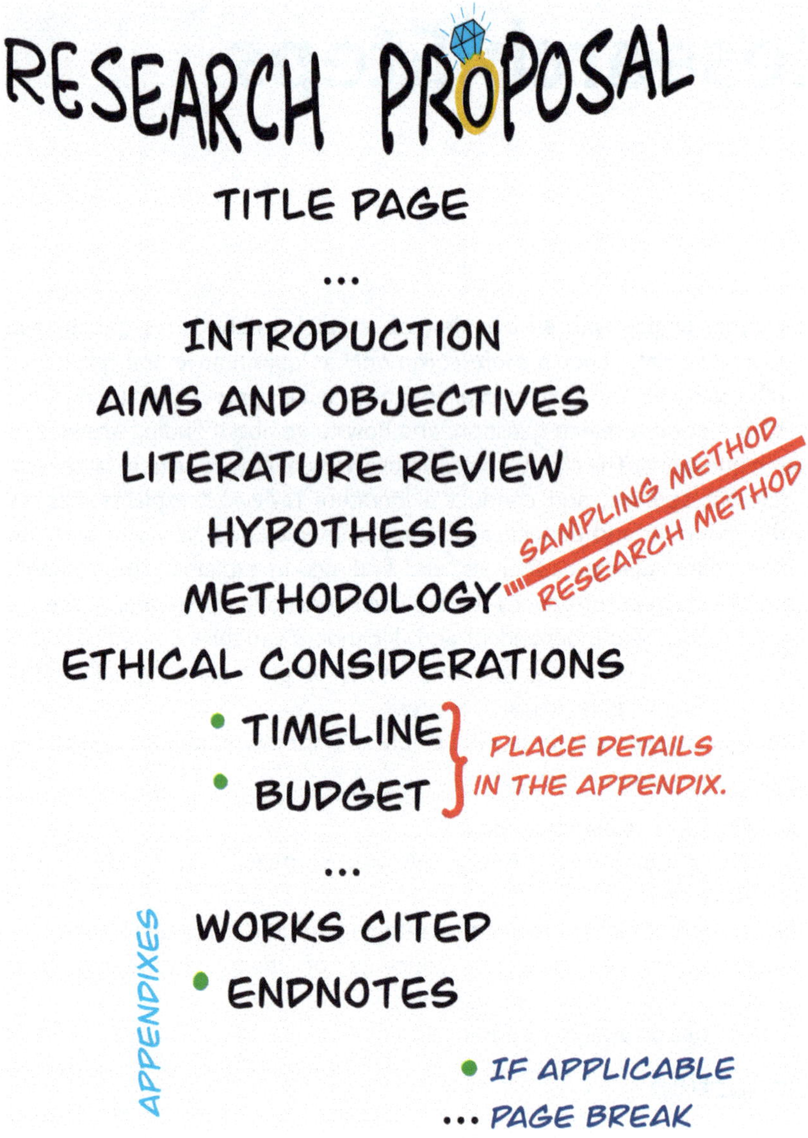

RESEARCH PROPOSAL

TITLE PAGE

...

INTRODUCTION

AIMS AND OBJECTIVES

LITERATURE REVIEW

HYPOTHESIS

METHODOLOGY — SAMPLING METHOD / RESEARCH METHOD

ETHICAL CONSIDERATIONS

- TIMELINE ⎫
- BUDGET ⎬ PLACE DETAILS IN THE APPENDIX.

...

WORKS CITED
- ENDNOTES

APPENDIXES

• IF APPLICABLE
... PAGE BREAK

Figure 2.1 Research Proposal

The complete research report would also include the findings, analysis and discussion, recommendations (if applicable), and concluding comments. In the final report, you will also note if anything did not go as planned or if some of the outcomes were not along the expected lines. Generally, a research report consists of:

Title page, abstract, introduction, aims and objectives, literature review, hypothesis, methodology, ethical considerations, timeline, budget (if applicable), findings, analysis and discussion, recommendations (if applicable), concluding comments, tables and charts (if applicable), works cited, and endnotes (if applicable).

That is, the report would show how you achieved what you had proposed to achieve in the proposal. For example, in a research proposal, you would write about potential ethical considerations, and in the research report, you would include how you addressed them. In a research proposal, you would contextualize your research question by explaining theoretical and methodological aspects in other sources (literature review), and in the research report, you would show how you proved or made those theoretical connections in your work while adding new information. We will talk more about this toward the end of this guide. For now, let's get back to quantitative and qualitative methods.

Sometimes there may not be enough literature available to propose a concise hypothesis. In that case, you can propose a research question. These issues are discussed in detail later in this chapter. For now, note that research methods can be divided into two general categories: quantitative and qualitative methods.

Quantitative and Qualitative Research Methods

As the names suggest, quantitative methods produce quantitative data, and qualitative research methods produce qualitative data. Surveys and experiments are quantitative research methods. Further, there are several types of surveys and experiments that the researcher can choose from. Observation, focus groups, and intensive interviews are considered qualitative methods. Observation also provides various roles that a researcher can choose from. More often than not, if researchers are studying a topic about which they can plan (almost) everything ahead of time, review relevant literature, and propose a specific hypothesis(es), they are likely to use quantitative methods. For some topics, researchers may not know what kind of sample they may find or where, what kind of questions to ask, or there just is not enough information available to develop a specific hypothesis, and so on. In that case, they may prefer to use qualitative methods. Each research method has strengths and limitations that will become clear as we go over specific methods later in this guide.

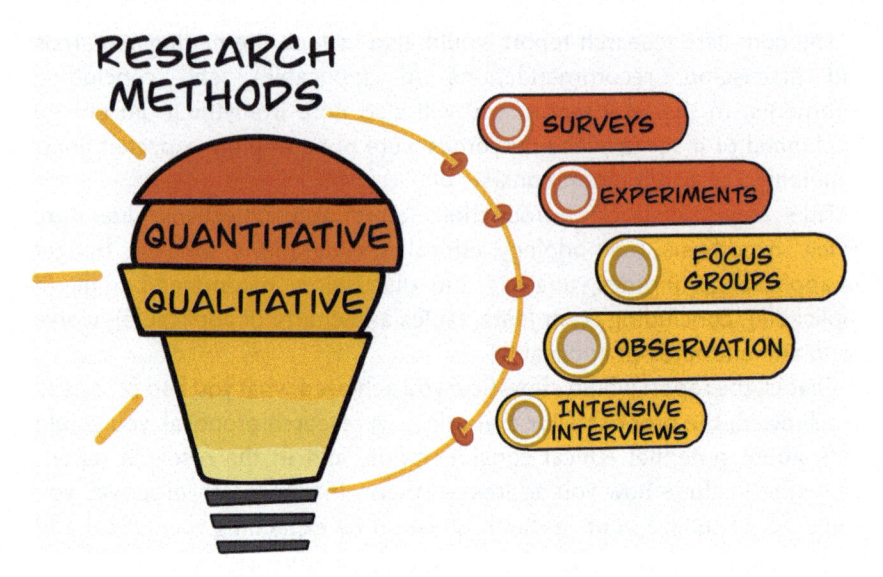

Figure 2.2 Research Methods

Epistemology is the philosophy of knowledge that deals with what we know, how we know it, and by what methods in a discipline. In social sciences, among other things, we study social constructs including crime, justice, and punishment. Without venturing deep into philosophical ideas and concepts, we will squarely focus on **deductive** (rationalism) and **inductive** (empiricism) approaches. Rationalism builds on the knowledge gained by objective reasoning, evidence, and experience. Empiricism refers to gaining knowledge through observation and experience. In examining research steps in this chapter, we will discuss *almost* all that you need to know about quantitative and qualitative methods in this course. Understanding these key research concepts and steps will also guide you to walk through the specific research methods such as experiments, surveys, observations, focus groups, and so on discussed later in the guide.

Research Question

In research methods courses in graduate and many undergraduate programs, students will demonstrate their understanding of the research process that is best reflected through developing a research project. Many undergraduate programs have research methods and capstone courses that students take in their senior year. In the research methods course, students often develop a research proposal, and in the capstone course, they may use primary or secondary data to examine the research question, draw conclusions, write a report, and present findings. At the graduate level, most students work on a research project spanning two or more semesters. This chapter explains the basic steps that can be used to design a research project for many topics in the social sciences. These can be further refined under the supervision of the professor to best fit the research question under study.

In any research project, one needs to consider the following:

- What to study
- Why study it
- How to study it
- How to manage the resources to study it. As a student, the biggest resource is time, and you would need to develop a timeline for the project.

Sometimes a clear research question may magically appear in your head, but more often than not, it will take time and active thinking.

Figure 2.3 Show Me the Question

The search for a research question may begin with what it is that you are interested in, something that you watched on the news, or something that you find fascinating or feel concerned about. It may be something that people in your neighborhood, school, or work complain about. I remember a student once proposed to study the duration of the flashing lights for pedestrian crossing on campus. It was a simple project but required the student to walk through all the research steps – the question and its relevance, sample, research methods, data collection, data analysis, and report writing.

> **Helpful Hint:** Ask your professor if you can select a research topic that can be studied on campus. It can be a short survey asking for opinions on an issue of interest for the whole campus. You could consider including students, faculty, and staff in your sample. It will also make you think about how to take a representative sample.

You will need to get the proposal approved by the Institutional Review Board or Ethics Committee. Collecting data on an actual topic, no matter how simple, would help you to gain a more realistic understanding of the research steps instead of only reading about how to do research. It may seem daunting at first, but it is a more rewarding learning process.

While working on any research project for the first time, you will need to first identify a general topic and then identify a specific research question that you want to examine. The more specific the question, the easier (relatively speaking) it would be to stay focused. For example, instead of proposing to evaluate the complete USA PATRIOT Act, 2001 (Uniting and Strengthening America by Providing Appropriate Tools Required to Intercept and Obstruct Terrorism), it is advised to check its list of contents and select a provision or a section that can be effectively studied within the given resources – time, money, and research staff. Again, for an undergraduate research project, most students would probably be working alone under the supervision of a professor, may not have research funds, and would be taking a few other courses as well. Therefore, keep it simple.

A good research question should be

- **Focused** – Do not try to find answers to every aspect of every problem in one research project. The research question should be clear and focused.
- **Relevant** – Consider developing a question that adds to the knowledge base, addresses conflicting ideas in theories or adds to understanding, or answers a policy question. Though you can study topics far and wide today, it is even more relevant if you can identify a topic in the local community and study it.
- **Researchable** – Identify clearly what needs to be measured and how, examine how to make concepts measurable, what variables and information would show effectiveness, where and how to find information, and so on.
- **Feasible** – Be realistic about the available resources, including time. Most professors would also prescribe a word or page limit.

Figure 2.4 Good Research Question

Therefore, it is important to develop a research question that can be adequately addressed in the given time. If the research work involves primary data collection, one needs to set aside enough time for approval by the Institutional Review Board or Ethics Committee. You will need to work with your professor to select the most suitable sampling and research methods as these will directly tie into the feasibility of your project.

research steps   37

To develop a good research question, start with a broad topic of interest, followed by preliminary research about the topic. That is, read about the topic to understand it in a bit more detail. Then identify the potential gaps, or what aspect of it you would like to research further. These steps would help to develop a clear question. It is possible to come up with multiple questions. However, when doing research for the first time, do not get tempted, and select one very specific question only.

> ### BOX 2.1 – Policy Questions
>
> Finigan, Carey, and Cox (2007) designed a study "to look at the operations and outcomes of a single drug court in Multnomah County (Portland, Oregon) over a 10-year period of court operations through examining the entire population of drug court-eligible offenders over that period" (p. 9). The researchers did not take a sample for their evaluation and instead examined the entire population. Here are the policy questions that they examined (p. II, III, IV).
>
> 1. What is the overall impact of the Multnomah County Drug Court on criminal recidivism?
> 2. Does the drug court show consistent levels of success in reducing re-arrest for each year of the 10-year period?
> 3. Do internal or external changes affecting policies and procedures of the court affect its success or failure?
> 4. Do changes in judicial leadership affect the success of the drug court?
>   4a: Do judges differ in their success in reducing re-arrests?
>   4b: Do eras where multiple judges are conducting the drug court do worse than eras in which only a single judge is operating the program?
>   4c: Did the drug court improve its success rate over time? Did later judges do better than earlier judges?
>   4d: Do judges improve with experience? Did judges who had multiple eras improve their success rate in the second era?
> 5. Did the Multnomah County Drug Court save taxpayer resources compared to the costs of traditional court processing?
>
> (Finigan, Carey, and Cox, 2007, p. II to IV)

Closely examine the clarity and specificity of the policy questions in Box 2.1. The way that they are phrased gives a clear indicator as to what the researcher needs to collect data on. It also informs the reader of what the study addresses.

Here is an example of developing a specific research question.

The general topic: White-Collar Crimes. That is a broad topic. The first step is to identify the type of white-collar crime you want to study. For this example, let's say that you are interested in studying Ponzi schemes. If so, you need to identify possible questions, problems, sub-problems, or sub-topics related to Ponzi schemes.

- Examine the trends over the past 10 years in setting X.
- Identify specific law(s) dealing with Ponzi schemes: differential implementation of the law, legal evolution, gaps in the law, and so on.
- Victims of Ponzi schemes – identify different aspects of victimization such as financial, social, emotional, and so on.
- Investigative challenges for law enforcement – training, tools, issues surrounding underreporting and non-reporting.
- Applying theories of white-collar crimes to Ponzi schemes – theoretical framework, gaps, and so on.
- Public perception and attitudes toward victims and offenders involved in Ponzi schemes.

You can think of many more! You do not have to examine each of these questions. Once again, talk to your professor, share what interests you the most, and see what specific question(s) you can address within the given timeline. It is also possible to refine your question(s) after doing the literature review.

Literature Review

Approach the literature review as leading from more general information about the topic to a very specific question and/or hypothesis. It involves four main categories – broad topic or background, research categories, studies more closely relevant to your research question, and the hypothesis. At the very least, a literature review serves a two-fold purpose:

a) Learning about the topic, including how others have studied it, findings, and directions for future research, including yours.
b) Developing a sound hypothesis as it is rooted in the 'education' about the topic – a hypothesis is an educated guess.

While reviewing the literature, keep an open mind and search for as much information as possible, but also remain aware of any variables that may be of interest to your study, such as gender, race, income, age, and so on. While reading, make note of any articles that include these variables. It will help to further refine the research question and the hypotheses. Though one may have read Tweets, watched videos, and generally have heard of the topic that they are interested in researching, for a systematic study, one needs to read scholarly sources and tap into more sources of information. That treasure trove would be the databases that one can generally access through the school library. These databases contain millions of sources, and it can seem challenging to find relevant information.

Finding the Relevant Literature

Finding relevant and valid information takes time. We live in the age of data clutter, politely known as the information age. On many topics in social sciences, there is no shortage of information; the challenge is to

Figure 2.5 Literature Review

find information or sources that are relevant to your project. If you have cultivated a reading habit, that's great, and it will be useful as you start doing the literature review. But you do not have to read every book in the library or every source online. You need to know where to search for what kind of sources, and how to search.

Libraries

University or college libraries house a huge number of sources. Libraries are often part of the larger network of libraries in the region and beyond. You will be able to find what book, video, journal, or any other source is available in your institution's library and what it can borrow for you, how much time it would take, and for how long you can keep it. You can also check the local or public libraries for local topics.

Increasingly – more so in some countries or regions than others – libraries have electronic databases that make the search process easier and much less time-consuming. The electronic databases can be searched using key terms. Some of the most common databases accessible through the school library are EBSCO, ProQuest, JSTOR, LexisNexis, Scopus (Elsevier), Criminal Justice Database (ProQuest), Legal Collection, Congressional Publications (ProQuest), and so on. The main page of the library contains a complete list of databases and journals. You can also search journals as classified by discipline.

Search Tips and Tricks

- To avoid repetition, make a list of keywords that you are using to search for information.
- Use **Boolean operators** – AND, OR, NOT, AND NOT, using quotation marks " ", and parentheses ( ). These help to expand or limit database searches.
- Using truncation symbols, such as an asterisk (*), can help to broaden research results.
- Search more than one database.
- Use search filters to set the date of publication, location, peer-review, dissertations, full-text, language, and so on.
- When searching for information on a specific policy, law, or program, do not hesitate to start with a basic Google search. Enter the full title of the policy, law, or program and location, such as state, if applicable.
- Specificity helps. For example, instead of using keywords such as *drug laws*, specific results can be found by using keywords such as *drug laws*

BOOLEAN OPERATORS

HARE AND TORTOISE — BOTH

HARE OR TORTOISE — EITHER

HARE NOT TORTOISE — JUST ONE

TORTOISE NOT HARE — JUST ONE

Figure 2.6   Boolean Operators

in Connecticut. Even more specific results can be found by using the exact titles such as *Rockefeller drug laws in New York, Michigan 650-Lifer Law*, and so on.

- One may not be able to evaluate every provision in a law or every aspect of a policy or program in one research paper. It is best to read the law, policy, or program in totality and identify the provision(s) of interest.
- Do not hesitate to contact research librarians. They have supernatural powers when it comes to finding sources across libraries. Check the university or college website for how to contact them.
- The librarians will also guide you if they can get you a resource from another library.
- Do not procrastinate. It is especially important when you contact the research librarian or your professor. When they guide you in finding information, you will need to still read, think, and write! Therefore, start research early.

Figure 2.7 The Librarian

> **Helpful Hint:** searchFAST is a useful tool to generate keywords or search terms for your topic. "Enter any search term and click search to begin. The initial search is a keyword search across all facets. The interface has an autosuggest feature, which displays headings as you type that you may want to select for your search. After the initial search, options to refine the search will be available" ("searchFast," p.2).
>
> searchFAST, https://fast.oclc.org/searchfast/

Public Databases

Many databases are open source or available to the public without any payment or subscription. Here's a list of a few websites that students and scholars can access to study a variety of topics in criminal justice in the United States.

- You can access the Uniform Crime Reports on the Federal Bureau of Investigation website https://www.fbi.gov/services/cjis/ucr.
- Monitoring The Future survey findings are available on the National Institute on Drug Abuse website at https://www.fbi.gov/services/cjis/ucr.
- The National Crime Victimization Survey results are available on the Bureau of Justice Statistics https://bjs.ojp.gov/data-collection/ncvs.
- The General Social Survey by the NORC is also available online at https://gss.norc.org/.
- National Criminal Justice Reference Service (NCJRS) https://www.ojp.gov/ncjrs/new-ojp-resources
- Bureau of Justice Statistics (BJS) https://bjs.ojp.gov/. The BJS also contains the Working Paper Series https://bjs.ojp.gov/working-paper-series
- Federal Bureau of Prisons https://www.bop.gov/about/statistics/

The Global Terrorism Database https://www.start.umd.edu/gtd/ is "an open-source database including information on terrorist events around the world from 1970 through 2020 (with additional annual updates planned for the future). Unlike many other event databases, the GTD includes systematic data on domestic as well as transnational and international terrorist incidents that have occurred during this time period and now includes more than 200,000 cases" (Overview of the GTD, n.d.).

Researchers can also access country-specific data, but there may be gaps as the data may not be tabulated the same way across countries, or the data may not be available online. They can also access reports about various topics around the world from the United Nations and its affiliate websites and the European Union. Many websites, including universities, contain working papers categorized by department or discipline. Along with reports and data, the United Nations Office on Drugs and Crime also contains a working paper series at https://www.unodc.org/ropan/en/working-paper-series/working-paper-series.html

- United Nations, https://www.un.org/en/
- European Commission Publications, https://commission.europa.eu/publications_en

- International Monetary Fund, data, https://www.imf.org/en/Data You can also access regional economic reports, annual reports, country reports, and so on. https://www.imf.org/en/Publications
- WorldCat is a global catalog of millions of books, magazines, music, videos, photos, audiobooks, articles, and so on. https://www.worldcat.org/
- Open Library is an editable library catalog that aims at creating one webpage for every book ever published, https://openlibrary.org/
- Along with ProQuest Dissertations and Theses, you can also use Open Access Theses and Dissertations at https://oatd.org/.

> **Helpful Hint:** Though many researchers use online sources, it is always good to remember the digital divide by region, country, topic, and language. Remembering this at all stages of research will help to guard against errors in reasoning.

News Sources

Though many databases are available on government, agency, and organization websites, one should be careful while accessing all open sources. For instance, news media is a good source of information on a wide variety of topics, but one needs to maintain a very critical stance due to the preferred line of commentary of newspapers, news channels, and other similar sources. Though, generally speaking, news sources may not manufacture information, there may still be errors, bias through omission, selective observation, edited or cropped photographs, and framing of narratives. Journalists are often seen as writing the first draft of history, but remember that they are not mere stenographers – they take a position on various topics that they write about. Ideally, they should be transparent about it. Just as researchers select their topics of interest, so do journalists. However, in doing so, they should neither demonize what they do not cover, nor commit the errors like overgeneralization, illogical reasoning, and so on. In the age of social media, one image can be shared around the world without much context, follow-up, or checking of its veracity. Similar to researchers, journalists will also only find what they are looking for. The **Baader–Meinhof phenomenon** can be used to explain this cognitive bias about one's tendency to observe or notice something more often and to wrongly believe that it occurs more often than it actually does.

The bottom line is to not rely on any one type of source to collect information. The more sources that one uses, and the more variety of sources that one uses, the better the understanding of the topic will be as one looks to frame the question. However, one does not have to study all aspects of the issue – but to avoid misconceptions and overgeneralizations, it is critical to be specific about what aspect(s) is being studied and later present findings within that context only.

While using news sources, you should be mindful of generalizability based on one case or even ten cases. If there is no or limited generalizability, it does not mean that the source cannot be used – it is useful as a case study as long as the same is specified. The one good thing is that unlike journals and other scholarly sources, newspapers, news portals, and news channels (television and radio) are open to the public and thus easy to scrutinize. Many social scientists carry out **content analysis** including by using news sources. Content analysis is a study of structured and unstructured information including text, photos, videos, and so on. Researchers generally focus on a list of keywords and examine content to identify patterns or trends.

> **Helpful Hint:** If you are struggling to pick a topic relevant to your local community, reading a local newspaper would be a good start. Many news stories also help to put a face to the topics of crime, justice, and victimization.

In the previous chapter, you have been introduced to some of the mistakes that researchers make. You need to remember them even when searching for and using sources. No database is complete or completely devoid of bias and gaps. It is always advisable to get information from multiple sources. Before deciding to use any source, you need to evaluate its usefulness and reliability for your research topic. Though there is no one way to find the 'perfect' information, in academia you can evaluate a source using the **CRAAP test** – Currency, Relevance, Authority, Accuracy, and Purpose. This was developed by Sarah Blakeslee (2004) and her team at the Meriam Library at the University of California, Chico.

Box 2.2 – The CRAAP Test

Currency

- What is the publication date (print or digital)?
- Is the information outdated or has it been revised?
- Is the newer information available?

Relevance

- Who is the target audience of the source? (General public, lawyers, experts, and so on)
- Does it serve your needs? – Can you relate it to your topic? Is it helpful for your assignment?

Authority

- Who is the author, editor, content creator, or publisher? Examine their credentials, experience, and organizational affiliations.
- Is the author or content creator an expert in their field?

Accuracy

- Is the information supported by evidence – reliable, truthful, and accurate?
- Is it a peer-reviewed source, news article, blog, newsletter, film, or documentary? Has the information been reviewed by other professionals?

Purpose

- Is the information aimed at persuading, informing, or entertaining? What is the intent of the author?
- Is there obvious propaganda, a biased point of view, or prejudice? What does it clearly exclude? Does it present other viewpoints?
- Is it based on opinion and conjecture or does it contain factual information?
- Does it use neutral and unbiased opinions or make an emotional appeal?
- How does it compare to other source(s) on the same topic?

Most databases that you access through the school library require an annual subscription that the school pays for. While using Google Scholar, you will be able to see what resources are available in full without a fee and what requires payment.

When connected through the school network and logged in, the same resources can be accessed in full as long as the school subscribes to them.

When accessing journals independently, there may be a certain fee for each article. However, there are many Open Access journals available online free of cost. Many conference papers, dissertations, graduate theses, and working papers may be available online as well without any payment wall.

Figure 2.8 Show Me the Money

> **Helpful Hint:** Now that you have learned about how to search databases, start looking for sources on the research topic that you have selected. It will help you to decide whether to use a deductive or inductive approach.

Annotated Bibliography

Think of an **annotated bibliography** as gathering almost all the ingredients before cooking a meal. Having all the ingredients makes the process less cumbersome and helps in staying focused. An annotated bibliography is a list of sources available on the topic of research and contains a short paragraph about each source. It is especially helpful to create it while searching for sources and before writing the paper. Having a snapshot of each source makes it easy to organize information and construct an argument.

If you find an excellent article or book that covers all aspects of your research topic, look at its bibliography to see what other sources you can read. However, guard against the **citation loop**, where one only reproduces the already published work and adds little to no new value or perspective. There is also the limitation of the same sources being cited by a vast majority of subsequent researchers and scholars and the hesitation to move out of the loop or explore new ideas. It is important to contextualize ideas and learn about previous works, but it is also important to create new and original knowledge. It is even more important to guard against the citation loop when the research topic is about a different culture, country, religion, and so on. A vast majority of resources used in Western academia, including in social sciences, are written from a Eurocentric perspective and have linguistic limitations as well. It is important to recognize if one is framing the argument in preset echo chambers or if one may need to explore more sources in different languages, which in turn may include collaborating with researchers or scholars in other settings. This topic is further explored in Chapter 8.

> **Helpful Hint:** Ask your research professors if they would be willing to review the annotated bibliography before you start writing the literature review for your research proposal.

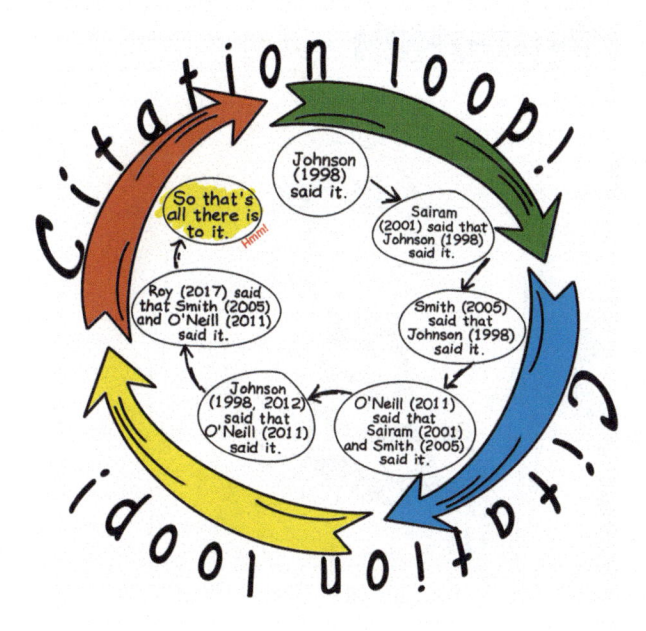

Figure 2.9   Citation Loop

Reading an Article (and making sense of it!)

It can seem daunting to read a journal article for the first time. It is best to start by reading the abstract and introduction, and the concluding remarks or the last section. It gives the reader a general idea about the topic. Then read a couple of paragraphs or a page at a time and start making notes on it by writing very brief comments in the page margins, and circling or highlighting the key points. That is, get the gist of the information and write it down. It allows one to summarize the key points and makes it easy to then use that information while writing one's own research paper.

> **Caution:** All summarized and paraphrased material should be cited as per the academic writing style required for the paper that you are working on. Some of the commonly used styles are the American Psychological Association (APA), Modern Language Association (MLA), Chicago Manual of Style (CMS), and so on.

The APA Style, https://apastyle.apa.org/
The MLA Style, https://style.mla.org/
The CMS Style, https://www.chicagomanualofstyle.org/home.html

Figure 2.10 Plagiarism

Theoretical Framework

While reviewing the literature, identify the relevant theories. Maintaining an interest in a theory adds immense value to one's work and helps root the hypotheses into a larger theoretical framework. In criminology and sociology, students learn about numerous theories including social disorganization theory, broken windows theory, deterrence theory, differential association theory, symbolic interactionism theory, labeling theory, functionalism, rational choice, routine activities theory, and so on. It is also fine to note conflicting ideas in theories and assess what your proposed research work would build on or address.

A **theory** is a systematic study of facts based on evidence and helps to explain things – behaviors, systems, processes, cultures, and so on. Among others, Turner (2002) views theories as containing concepts, variables, and statements or fundamental assertions. Here are a few theories that students would learn about in criminology. While reading various theories, remember that a) correlation is not the same as causation, and b) no single variable can predict criminality. Theories do not justify crime or blame victims, they help to explain it and potentially guide people, social and criminal justice organizations, and lawmakers on how to best respond to it.

- In the 18th century, Jeremy Bentham and Cesare Beccaria's works on the purpose of punishment led to the development of classical thought in criminology. This explains crime as a result of free will, rational choice, and hedonism. It argues that people have free will, they are rational, and they make choices that are beneficial to them. If the act of crime includes less risk and more benefit, less pain and more pleasure, the individual will choose to commit the crime.
  - Classical thought led to the development of deterrence theory that argues that the goal of punishment is to create deterrence, and, to achieve that goal or for punishment to be effective, it must be certain, proportionate to the crime, and swift.
- Clifford R. Shaw and Henry D. McKay's Social Disorganization theory (1942) proposes that the physical and environmental factors are correlated with crime. That is, certain areas punctuated with a breakdown of social institutions would invite more crime, as it creates social and physical incivilities. It argues that the neighborhoods with higher residential mobility, high population density, more heterogeneity (ethnic diversity), and higher poverty and unemployment are at risk of higher crime and victimization. The

• THEORY • HYPOTHESIS • OPINION

Figure 2.11 Theory, Hypothesis, Opinion

outward mobility toward suburban areas sees less crime, while inner city areas witness a higher crime rate.
- James Q. Wilson and George L. Kelling's Broken Windows theory (1982) argues that visible signs of physical decay and social or behavioral disorder when left unattended can invite more serious crime. It argues that neglect reflects people's attitude toward the environment or neighborhood and creates and invites further disorder and crime.
- Robert K. Merton's theory of Anomie (1938) argues that people aspire to achieve culturally approved goals, but due to their different positions in the social structure, they do not have access to the same culturally approved means. The gap between the goals and the means results in cultural strain. They adapt to goals and means through conformity, innovation, ritualism, retreatism, and rebellion.
- Edwin Sutherland's Differential Association theory (1939) proposes that criminal behavior is learned like any other behavior through shared values, attitudes, frequency, and techniques. It applies to street crimes as well as white-collar crimes.

- Howard Becker's Labeling theory (1963) proposes that the criminal justice system processes individuals in a way that erodes all of their identity except the crime that they have been convicted of. Upon their release, offenders carry only that label, and society views them through that lens only. The criminal label thus becomes a self-fulfilling prophecy, resulting in higher recidivism rates.
- Ronald V. Clarke and Derek B. Cornish's Rational Choice theory (1985) is classified as a neoclassical theory. It adopts the utilitarian view of free will, rational choice, and self-interest. To explain criminal behavior, it uses the principle of economic utility, according to which people make choices based on maximizing profit and minimizing cost. It contends that decision-making is rooted in getting a higher degree of satisfaction or pleasure. Similar to Sutherland's Differential Association theory, it is extensively used to also examine white-collar crimes.
- Marcus Felson and Lawrence E. Cohen's Routine Activities theory (1979) provides a spatiotemporal explanation of crime. During their routine activities, victims and offenders may converge in time and space, which results in crime due to three elements: a motivated offender, a suitable victim, and the absence of an adequate guardian. It is also classified as a neoclassical theory.

Hypothesis

A hypothesis is often defined as an educated guess. The literature review is the 'education' that one needs to develop a sound hypothesis. The hypothesis is a tentative statement that specifies an association between independent and dependent variables that the researcher aims to prove, or in some cases, disprove. The literature review can also be used to develop a research question that may not contain a precise hypothesis but shows the gaps in research that the researcher aims to address in their work. Reviewing the existing literature helps one to become familiar with the topic, how it has been studied, what the findings have been, what areas of the topic are underexplored, and how and why to study it further. A research study may include more than one hypothesis, and a hypothesis may include more than one independent and dependent variable.

Hypothesis

- Clearly explain what the research expects to find.
- You will need to ensure that the hypothesis is measurable (check the discussion on concepts in Chapter 4). It involves defining abstract concepts and identifying indicators that help to measure those concepts.
- Identify independent and dependent variables.

- An independent variable is the one that impacts the other variable (dependent). Change in the independent variable results in change or variation in the dependent variable. The independent variable is the cause, and the dependent variable is the effect or the outcome.

Before moving further, identify independent and dependent variables in the following statements.

1. An increase in unemployment results in an increase in poverty.
2. Social cohesion is increased by greater residential stability.
3. Spending more than two hours a day on social media is likely to increase headaches.
4. The mandatory arrest of the abusive spouse on the spot is likely to reduce recidivism rates for domestic violence.
5. The sooner I start to work on my research project, the less stressed I will be about its deadline.

The above hypothetical statements also show the **direction of association** between variables – that is, whether there is an inverse or negative relation between variables or a positive relation. When the value of one variable increases and the other decreases, it is called a **negative** or **inverse correlation**. Contrary to this, when the increase (or decrease) in the value of one variable results in an increase (or decrease) in the value of the other variable, it is called a **positive correlation** or association. Using the same above-listed statements, identify which shows a positive correlation and which shows a negative correlation. In a statistics course, you will also learn about the strength of association or multiple correlates (strong and weak).

> **Helpful Hint:** A very thorough literature review would help you to develop confidence in your proposed hypothesis. It will also help to determine whether you have enough information to propose a hypothesis or not.

Researchers may do research not just to prove a hypothesis, but also to disprove a hypothesis or challenge theoretical propositions. For example, in his theory of Atavism, Cesare Lombroso argued that criminals have different physiological traits than non-criminals. Goring (1913) compared the physiological traits of over 2,000 criminals with non-criminals and disproved such a proposition.

A **deductive approach** involves deducing or extrapolating a specific hypothesis from a theory, collecting data, and analyzing the findings to see if the hypothesis is proven.

If, despite your best efforts, you cannot find enough literature on a topic, talk to your professor and consider using an **inductive approach**. This does not involve precise hypothesis testing. It starts with a specific question or an observation, followed by data collection and data analysis. While analyzing data, the researcher will pay close attention to see if any patterns or themes emerge that could lead to a **grounded theory** – a theory grounded in the data collected in the study.

Research Steps

Figure 2.12   Research Steps

One can use primary or secondary data. **Primary data** is collected by researchers themselves, while **secondary data** already exists – that is, others have collected it for various studies or databases and the researcher can use it. Before collecting data, the researcher has to decide about the sampling and research methods as well as ethical considerations based on the sample, access to the setting, method of data collection, and so on. Each of these decisions would also impact the generalizability of the study. Probability sampling methods would allow for stronger generalizability than non-probability methods. However, for certain settings and research questions, using non-probability methods may be the only way to go forward. For example, when trying to understand the non-reporting of domestic violence in a certain setting, the researcher, criminal justice professional, or social worker may not know the exact population (people who did not report domestic violence), and thus would not be able to use a probability method to draw a sample. The different types of sampling methods, preconditions, processes, strengths, and limitations are explained in Chapter 5.

The research topics, settings, and respondents would present different ethical concerns about how and where to collect data, whether one has direct access to the research subjects, and so on. Different research methods would pose different ethical dilemmas. This topic is discussed in detail in Chapter 3. In most cases of hypothesis testing, it is convenient to plan everything ahead of time as there is ample information about the topic, and therefore, one can use the **quantitative methods** of surveys and experiments.

Could My Research Proposal be Rejected?

Working with a professor who has expertise in teaching research methods and doing research themselves would help to minimize the likelihood of the proposal being rejected. It is always good to have a timeline for developing a proposal as each of the aspects involved is time-consuming. Sometimes just selecting a good research question may take time. Finding the relevant sources for the literature review, reading and analyzing, and then writing is always demanding. Having enough time to critically evaluate each part of the research proposal helps to identify any errors or gaps early on. However, here are a few reasons why a research proposal may get rejected:

- Relevance – The proposal did not establish the need for the research. It is not deemed relevant or necessary.
- Logic – The literature review lacks a logical thread. The question is not framed with reference to the sources analyzed. The important theories on the topic are not analyzed. The research problem is proposed on the basis of emotion, ideology, or conjecture.
- Feasibility – The proposal has too many objectives that cannot be studied within the given timeframe or other resources.
- Methods – The proposed sampling or research method is impractical or not adequate for the proposed research question. It may not be possible to access the sample/respondents.
- Focused – The aims, objectives, question, method, or any other aspect is unclear or vague. There is no clear focus.

There could be more reasons as well. The process of rejection is still good learning and tells us what to avoid or what to add when we submit the next proposal.

After the proposal is approved, including by the Institutional Review Board or Ethics Committee (Chapter 3), you will collect data, analyze it, draw conclusions, and write a report.

Software programs such as SPSS (Statistical Package for Social Sciences) make it easy to analyze quantified data. However, when one starts with data collection or carries out inductive research, it is convenient to use **qualitative methods** of observation, intensive interviews, and focus groups. Software programs such as Atlas.ti and HyperRESEARCH make it relatively easy to organize and analyze qualitative data. One can quantify qualitative data in a simple Excel file that can then be used for more in-depth analysis through software programs. It is useful when one does not know the length and breadth of the information that one may find and thus cannot create all categories or identify all variables and their values ahead of time.

BOX 2.3 – Quantifying Qualitative Data

In one of the research projects, I was examining case files of financial transactions that involved violating banking rules by using informal money transfer systems or were under investigation for money laundering and unaccounted money (untaxed, bribery, and so on.). I would examine one file at a time and start creating categories of variables as I came across them.

The first category of interest may be the country and it may contain different values such as India, the United States, Australia, France, and so on. I would add these values as I came across them while examining files. The next category may be the amount of money, and I would enter the different amounts as I came across them in each file.

Another category would be the direction of the transaction, followed by the month of transactions, the rate of interest charged, and so on. In sum, I could create categories and subcategories to classify and organize data as needed without having full knowledge of all variables and their values ahead of time.

Though **content analysis** is more widely used for qualitative research, depending on the research question and approach, it can be quantitative as well. All these methods are explained in detail in Chapters 6 (survey research), 7 (experiments), and 8 (qualitative methods).

Analysis and generalizations

After data collection, the researcher needs to analyze data, run cross-tabulations, identify strong and weak correlations, identify generalizations, patterns, or commonalities, and draw inferences. If evaluating a policy, law, or program, the study should also include policy implications and recommendations. These are the basic steps of doing any research. The Minneapolis Domestic Violence Experiment is a good example that contains the above-explained research steps, and you will read about it in detail in Chapter 7. Box 2.4 contains a short summary of the research design from the original study.

> ## BOX 2.4 – Minneapolis Domestic Violence Experiment
>
> Sherman and Berk (1984) worked with the Minneapolis Police Department to evaluate the most effective police response to domestic violence calls. They designed an experiment to study the impact of a) arrest, b) sending the suspect away for 8 hours, and c) advice or counseling on reducing the recidivism rates. Drawing from the deterrence theory, it attempted to study the potential deterrence in relation to the three variables – arrest, separation, and counseling. It included only misdemeanor (simple domestic assault) cases. The police officers who participated in the experiment were asked to randomly pick one of the three responses when they responded to the calls that met the experiment's criteria. The sample size was 330. After the initial data collection phase was completed, a follow-up was done after 6 months to examine if there was a repeat offense. It included checking the official records as well as interviews with the previous victims. The study concluded that the recidivism rate was the lowest for the arrest at only 13 percent. That is, arresting the suspect was the most effective way to lower the repeat offense of domestic violence (Sherman and Berk, 1984).
>
> These are just the basic steps. In Chapter 7, you will learn more about this experiment and the potential errors in the implementation of what looked like a very good research design on paper.

In a more recent study, Allen, Ash, and Anderson (2022) examined who finds media violence funny and what it indicates. They carried out two cross-sectional survey studies and had samples of 215 and 178, respectively. The study found that men who enjoyed media violence may have dark personalities. They were more prone to moral disengagement and sadism, and took delight in other people's misfortune. It is important to note a few items when analyzing research findings to avoid common mistakes in reasoning, as explained in Chapter 1. First, it would be incorrect to assume that everyone who laughs at violence in media has a dark personality. Second, as noted earlier, human beings are not like mathematics – these are correlations and not absolute causes. Therefore, to make a reliable and valid connection between the independent and dependent variables in such a study, one may need to also examine the exposure to media violence at an early age and its continuation over time, and if that impacts one's personality. It does give an interesting insight into developmental psychology, similar to many other studies on this topic. It could be useful in guiding future research with a larger sample, though. The study cannot be generalized to a large population either, as the sample size was small and only included undergraduate students in psychology at one university (a large midwestern university in the United States). The authors acknowledge these limitations regarding causality and generalizability. Most importantly, the authors recognize that there may be other factors "associated with finding humor in media violence" (Allen et al., 2022, p. 45). It is possible to read the key findings of this study on a news portal or social media posts, but to have an understanding of the complete picture, it is always suggested to find the original study and examine it for its methodology, year, location, sample, limitations, and so on. Many researchers themselves would caution the reader about methodological limitations and larger applications, as done in this study. It is a good reminder for your own research work as well.

Many undergraduate research methods courses may only involve developing a research proposal, while some may involve collecting data, writing a report, and presenting the findings as well. Nonetheless, even in undergraduate courses, students will read various journal articles and studies and should be able to identify the step-by-step process of doing scientific research using the material explained in this chapter.

Further Reading

searchFAST, Faceted Application of Subject Terminology, https://www.oclc.org/research/areas/data-science/fast.html

Key Terms

Annotated bibliography
Baader–Meinhof phenomenon
Boolean operators
Citation loop
Content analysis
CRAAP test
Deductive approach
Dependent variable
EBSCO
General Social Survey
Global Terrorism Database
Grounded theory
HyperRESEARCH
Hypothesis
Independent variable
Inductive approach
JSTOR
LexisNexis
Literature review

Minneapolis Domestic Violence Experiment	Negative correlation	Secondary data
	Positive correlation	SPSS
Monitoring The Future survey	Primary data	Theory
	ProQUEST	Uniform Crime Reports
National Crime Victimization Survey	Qualitative methods	
	Quantitative methods	

Class Activity

Organize students into teams of two or three members. Assign research topics by group. Students should identify three articles per group and create a CRAAP test worksheet. Discuss in class.

Useful links:

- Tips from experts: http://www.istl.org/18-winter/tips2.html (Lewis, 2018)
- Is your source CRAAP tested, https://guides.library.illinoisstate.edu/ld.php?content_id=14672390

Works Cited

Allen, J. J., S. M. Ash, and C. A. Anderson. 2022. "Who Finds Media Violence Funny? Testing the Effects of Media Violence Exposure and Dark Personality Traits." *Psychology of Popular Media*, Vol.11(1), pp. 35–46.

Becker, Howard. 1963. *Outsiders: Studies in the Sociology of Deviance*. New York: Macmillan.

Blakeslee, Sarah. 2004. "The CRAAP Test." *LOEX Quarterly*, Vol. 31(3), Article 4.

Clarke, Ronald V., and Derek B. Cornish. 1985. "Modeling Offenders' Decisions: A Framework for Research and Policy." In *Crime and Justice: An Annual Review of Research*, Vol. 6, edited by M. Tonry and N. Morris, pp. 147–185. Chicago, IL: University of Chicago Press.

Cohen, Lawrence E., and Marcus Felson. 1979. "Social Change and Crime Rate Trends: A Routine Activities Approach." *American Sociological Review*, Vol.44, pp. 588–608.

Finigan, Michael W., Shannon M. Carey, and Anton Cox. 2007. "Impact of a Mature Drug Court Over 10 Years of Operation: Recidivism and Costs (Final Report)." Office of Research and Evaluation, National Institute of Justice. Retrieved from https://www.ojp.gov/pdffiles1/nij/grants/219225.pdf

Goring, Charles. 1913. *The English Convict: A Statistical Study*. London: H.M. Stationery Office.

"Is Your Source CRAAP Tested?" Illinois State University Library. Retrieved from https://guides.library.illinoisstate.edu/ld.php?content_id=14672390

Kelling, George L., and James Q. Wilson. 1982. "Broken Windows: The Police and Neighborhood Safety." *Atlantic*, March. Retrieved from https://www.theatlantic.com/magazine/archive/1982/03/broken-windows/304465/

Lewis, Abbey B. 2018. "What Does Bad Information Look Like? Using the CRAAP Test for Evaluating Substandard Resources." Issues in Science and Technology Librarianship, Winter 2018. Retrieved from http://www.istl.org/18-winter/tips2.html

Merton, Robert. 1938. "Social Structure and Anomie." *American Sociological Review*, Vol.3(5), pp. 672–682.

"Monitoring The Future." National Institute on Drug Abuse. Retrieved from https://nida.nih.gov/research-topics/trends-statistics/monitoring-future

"Overview of the GTD. Global Terrorism Database." The University of Maryland. Retrieved from https://www.start.umd.edu/gtd/about/

"searchFast, About searchFast." Retrieved from https://fast.oclc.org/searchfast/

Shaw, C.R., and H.D. McKay (eds.). 1942. *Juvenile Delinquency and Urban Areas*. Chicago, IL: Chicago University Press.

Sherman, Lawrence W., and Richard A. Berk. 1984. "The Minneapolis Domestic Violence Experiment. Police Foundation Reports." April. Retrieved from https://www.policinginstitute.org/wp-content/uploads/2015/07/Sherman-et-al.-1984-The-Minneapolis-Domestic-Violence-Experiment.pdf

Sutherland, Edwin H. 1939. *Principles of Criminology*. 3rd ed. Philadelphia, PA: Lippincott.

Turner, Jonathan H. 2002. *The Structure of Sociology Theory*. 7th ed. Belmont, CA: Wadsworth.

chapter 3

Research Ethics

This chapter provides a brief history of ethics in social science research. It explains the key ethical guidelines such as ensuring voluntary participation, causing no harm to subjects, maintaining confidentiality and anonymity, disclosing the researcher's identity, and ensuring that the benefits of the research outweigh the risks. It also explores challenges while conducting research abroad or in unfamiliar settings, the problem of helicopter researchers, ethics of funding, and so on. The chapter explains dilemmas and challenges in both qualitative and quantitative research methods.

After this chapter, students will be able to understand and explain:

- The role of ethics in research
- Ethical guidelines for researchers
- Ethical issues when collecting data in foreign settings
- Ethics concerning digital data

Introduction

Social science research involves a myriad of ethical considerations. Whenever you collect data from or about human beings, you have to ensure that it is collected with their consent, does not bring any harm to them, is recorded with honesty and authenticity, and so on. It reflects integrity on the part of the researcher. Failure to adhere to ethical guidelines results in getting discredited, causing harm to the actual subject matter, and possibly involving legal penalties.

> **BOX 3.1 – University of Illinois Missed Warning Signs**
>
> "For a year, the University of Illinois at Chicago has downplayed its shortcomings in overseeing the work of a prominent child psychiatrist who violated research protocols and put vulnerable children with bipolar disorder at risk.
>
> But documents newly obtained by ProPublica Illinois show that UIC acknowledged to federal officials that it had missed several warning signs that Dr. Mani Pavuluri's clinical trial on lithium had gone off track, eventually requiring the university to pay an unprecedented $3.1 million penalty to the federal government.
>
> UIC's Institutional Review Board, the committee responsible for protecting research subjects, improperly fast-tracked approval of Pavuluri's clinical trial, didn't catch serious omissions from the consent forms parents had to sign and allowed children to enroll in the study even though they weren't eligible, the documents show.
>
> The IRB's shortcomings violated federal regulations meant to protect human subjects, putting it in "serious non-compliance," according to one of five letters from UIC officials to the federal government the university turned over to ProPublica Illinois after a nearly yearlong appeal for the documents under open records laws" (Cohen, 2019).

There is a dark history of unethical and outright criminal abuse of certain populations in the name of research.

The Tuskegee Experiment

From 1932 to 1972, the US Public Health Service (USPHS) in collaboration with the Tuskegee Institute carried out a study on the impact of untreated syphilis on African-American males. Out of the 600 men included in the sample, 399 were infected with syphilis without their informed consent. The participants were told that they were receiving treatment for "bad blood" – a term used for syphilis, anemia, and fatigue. In return for their participation, the participants received "free medical exams, free meals, and burial insurance" (The Tuskegee Timeline). By 1943, penicillin was widely available, but it was not given to the participants in the study. After 40 years, following a news report about the study, the "Assistant Secretary for Health and Scientific Affairs appointed an Ad Hoc Advisory Panel" finally concluded that it was a grossly unethical study. Following that, the USPHS was asked to provide treatment to all participants and their families affected by the disease. Two years after this, a class-action lawsuit for $10 million was settled out of court. "In 1997, President Bill Clinton issued a formal apology for the study" (The Tuskegee Timeline). The study has been criticized for the intentional and continuous harm caused to the subjects, no real benefits of the research given that the treatment was available, and the lack of informed consent.

The Tearoom Trade Experiment

From 1965 to 1968, Robert Allan Humphreys carried out a study about men having sexual encounters with anonymous men in public restrooms. It was published in 1970. Humphreys visited many tearooms in New York City and volunteered himself to be the lookout guy while men engaged in sex. He made note of the sounds coming from the stalls and also the license plate numbers of their vehicles. With the assistance of some police officers, he tracked them down and showed up at their home to conduct an interview. It is considered one of the most unethical studies particularly due to the lack of voluntary participation, the harm caused to the subjects, and the deception involved.

The Milgram Experiment

In his 1961 experiment, Stanley Milgram wanted to study why ordinary people obey authority often without question even when it is illegitimate or harmful to follow orders. During the Nazi trials, 'just following orders' was a common defense that many tried to use. In the experiment, the respondents (men in the age group of 20–50 years), in the role of a 'teacher', agreed to teach word combinations to the 'learner'. If the 'learner' made an error, the 'teacher' could administer an electric shock. With each error, the intensity of the electric shocks would increase. The machine was clearly labeled, from 'Slight Shock' to 'Danger: Severe Shock', for the 'teacher' to see the intensity of the shocks being administered. The 'learner' was part of the research staff (a confederate) and the machine was phony – the sounds of getting an electric shock were pre-recorded and played as the 'teacher' chose to give an electric shock. The volts ranged from 15 to 450. The only authority figure was Milgram himself in a mere lab coat. Of the subjects, 65 percent inflicted the highest shock. Milgram summarized the results in an article, 'The Perils of Obedience'.

The experiment was criticized for causing emotional harm to the subjects (the 'teachers'). It was argued that despite the benefits of the experiment,

Milgram should have noted the stress that it was causing to some subjects as they began to get nervous, tense, and anxious and to shake, sweat, and so on. Milgram countered this as more than 80 percent of the respondents had expressed that they had a positive experience and were 'glad' or 'very glad' that they participated in the experiment.

The Stanford Prison Experiment

In 1971, Phil Zimbardo designed an experiment on the psychological study of prison life that involved examining the effect of role-playing, labeling, and social expectations. He turned the basement of the psychology department at Standford University into a prison. The volunteers were randomly divided into groups of prisoners and guards. The guards wore uniforms and mirrored glasses, and they were told not to physically abuse prisoners. The prisoners wore a loose dress as a uniform, had a padlock around an ankle, and had stocking caps to reflect shaved heads ("Stanford Prison Experiment.").

The interactions between the guards and prisons became dehumanizing, aggressive, and hostile in a very short time. Three prisoners were released after 4 days only as they were too traumatized to continue. The experiment was designed to last for 14 days but was terminated after 6 days due to the emotional, mental, and psychological distress that it was causing. Zimbardo notes that he was too engrossed in the experiment to recognize it until another faculty member saw the proceedings and was appalled ("Stanford Prison Experiment.").

Over the years, various government agencies, private organizations, hospitals, religious groups, and academic institutions have sanctioned questionable practices in the name of research.

- The Walter E. Fernald State School, Waltham, Massachusetts was involved in medical experiments on children. It was involved in notorious radiation experiments in the field of mental retardation. From the 1940s to the 1950s, teenage boys were used in radiation studies sponsored by the Atomic Entergy Commission (Boissoneault, 2017). The volunteers were told that they were 'volunteering' to join a science club. The experiments were jointly conducted by Harvard and the Massachusetts Institute of Technology (Yemma, 1997). In 1995, a class-action lawsuit was filed. In 1998, MIT and Quaker agreed to pay $1.85 million to the victims (Yemma, 1997).
- In the 1950s, the now-defunct Atomic Energy Commission sanctioned a controversial research project at the University of Chicago. Known as the 'Chicago Baby Project', it involved cremating newly deceased infants and analyzing residual radioactive material in their ashes.

Official reports noted that most likely the parents' permission was not sought, nor they were notified that their children's ashes were used in an experiment (Lee, 1995; Schneider, 1994).
- Harmful experiments were often carried out on the poor or 'charity patients' – researchers believed that they were doing respondents a favor as they were poor and, during the experiment, they would get free food (MacPheran, 1995).
- In 1946, Tulane University carried out a series of radiation experiments at New Orleans Charity Hospital under the United States War Department grant, the forerunner of the Defense Department. The experiment was carried out on 300 patients, mostly black women. They were injected with radiation equivalent to up to 100 chest X-rays in one experiment (Allen, 1994). In 1994, a former member of the Tulane research team portrayed the experiment as a blessing to the 'lucky' subjects; the 'researchers would say they loved us as they got the most attention' (Allen, 1994).

In the past, prisoners have been used as subjects by the cosmetic and pharmaceutical industries. The outcast environment allowed for abuses to continue without any hesitation. These subjects are considered economical and do not have a laundry list of demands (Mitford, 1973). In 1975, James Downey, a former state prisoner in Oklahoma, testified at a United States Senate hearing on human experimentation. He had participated in a 30-day program designed to test a new drug for liver ailments (Mintz and Cohen, 1976). He was told that it carried no side effects. Later he learned that he was suffering from drug-induced hepatitis (Mintz and Cohen, 1976).

Medical, political, and economic institutions have exploited the poor for various reasons. Though there is more regulation in Western countries about it now, people in many other parts of the world are still exploited due to a lack of oversight. In the same vein, much needs to be done when researchers collect data in communities and cultures other than those they are part of.

The fact that many of these examples are well-documented reflects that it was an accepted or sanctioned norm rather than an anomaly or an error. As sociolegal and cultural sensibilities evolved, such practices were identified as being unethical, including many that have now been recognized as criminal.

Institutional Review Board

While doing any research, it is important to recognize the power dynamics involved. For example, the researcher may know prison staff and could ask them to hand out surveys to inmates, but that is a clear violation of ethics as the inmates would have little option to refuse due to the power equation. Similarly, one may have a friend who works in a rehabilitation center for juveniles. Asking one's friend to share information that they are privy to due to their position in the organization is unethical or could also be illegal. It does not mean that these populations cannot be studied.

POWER DYNAMICS AND VOLUNTARY PARTICIPATION

Figure 3.1   Power Dynamics and Voluntary Participation

The key is to recognize the power equations and conflict of interest, emotional and physical vulnerabilities, access to information, and so on, and then develop a research proposal that does not violate or abuse such access, get all the required approvals and permissions, and *then* engage in the data collection. In this regard, the American Psychological Association has developed five key guidelines that researchers should follow. The Institutional Review Board (IRB) or Ethics Committee would review, suggest changes, or approve the research proposal before one can collect data.

research ethics

There may be more than one IRB involved in the process. One of my research projects involved collecting data about the Youth Development Unit program at the Garner Correctional Institution in Newtown, Connecticut. It required submitting the research proposal to two IRBs – at the university where I worked, and at the Connecticut Department of Correction, Wethersfield, Connecticut. I also had to complete the Collaborative Institutional Training Initiative (CITI Program) training.

- American Psychological Association, https://www.apa.org/monitor/jan03/principles
- CITI Program, https://about.citiprogram.org/

The IRB evaluates the proposal in terms of what is a sample and how it will be accessed; how and where the data will be collected; how, where, and for how long the data would be stored; potential risks to the respondents and how they have been addressed; and so on. Therefore, if you are planning to collect primary data, you will need to work with your professor to ensure that you complete the IRB training and have enough time to submit and revise or modify the proposal as needed. The IRB approval is time-bound and researchers need to contact the IRB again to seek an extension.

> **Helpful Hint**: Even if the coursework does not require primary data collection, students can work with their professor to develop a research proposal for hypothetical scenarios, and invite a guest speaker from the institution's IRB to discuss, critically evaluate, and refine the proposals in class.

Ethical Guidelines

The five general ethical guidelines can be summarized as follows:

1. **Voluntary participation and informed consent**: The respondents should participate in the study of their free will and should be free to leave the study at any time without any repercussion or explanation.
   - Each respondent should sign the consent form that summarizes the ethical guidelines and how the researcher will abide by them. It also contains the contact information of the researcher. The respondents get a copy of the consent form. When a study involves minors, parents or legal guardians should sign the consent form.
   - Ethically, there should be no deception involved in collecting data. However, in many experiments, research subjects are put under certain conditions to see how they would act. In submitting their application to the IRB, the researchers would need to present information on

Ethical Guidelines

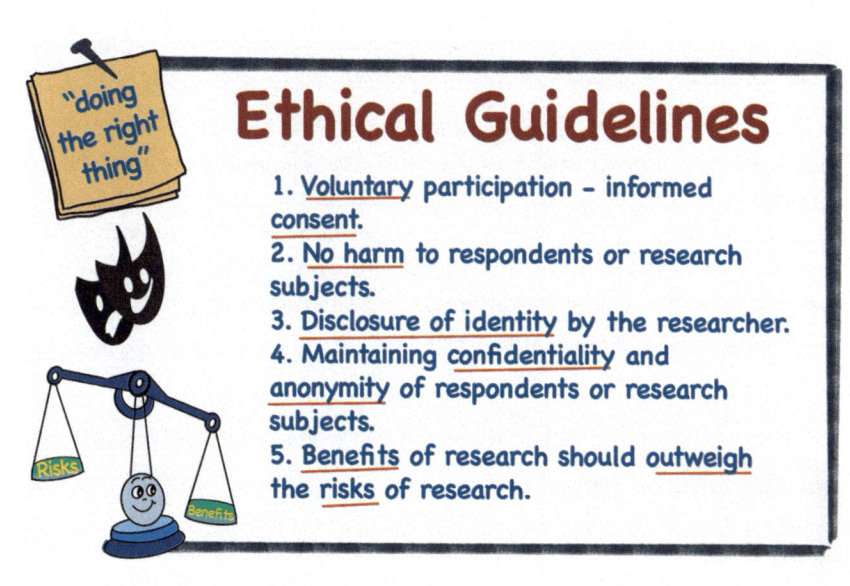

1. **Voluntary** participation - informed **consent**.
2. **No harm** to respondents or research subjects.
3. **Disclosure of identity** by the researcher.
4. Maintaining **confidentiality** and **anonymity** of respondents or research subjects.
5. **Benefits** of research should **outweigh** the **risks** of research.

Figure 3.2 Ethical Guidelines

what kind of deception may be involved, and why. They would also need to consider if there is another way to carry out the research without involving deception. If a study involves any level of deception, the consent form would also need to include a statement that the *deception may be involved*. After the experiment, or any other method that is used, is completed, the researcher should **debrief** the subjects about the deception involved in the study. The researcher should explain the purpose, intervention, and related behavioral outcomes and stressors to the research subjects. If needed, provide additional help and do follow-ups to ensure that there is no negative impact of the study on the participants.

The following is a sample consent form. Depending on the purpose and structure of your study, it may be longer or shorter. Work with your professor to create a consent form for your proposed work.

BOX 3.2 – Sample Consent form

Informed consent form

Age: You should be 18 years or older to participate in this study. If you are under 18 years old, you have been selected in error and should not participate in this study.

Introduction:

You are being asked to participate in a research study. Please read this document carefully as your free and informed consent is required for participation. This document informs you about the study, conveys that your participation is voluntary, explains risks and benefits, and informs you that you can choose to participate, refuse to participate, or stop participating at any time without requiring an explanation. You can ask any questions to the researcher(s).

Study title:

Researcher and title:

Affiliation:

Contact:

Study: You are being asked to participate in a research study on [research topic and question]. You have been selected to participate because you are a [reason; it could also be a random selection based on location, affiliation, etc.]. From this study, the researchers hope to learn about the [main issue].

Voluntary participation: Taking part in this study is completely voluntary. You may skip any questions that you do not want to answer. You may stop participating in the study at any time. You are not required to give me any explanation for refusing to participate in this study.

Confidentiality: No personally identifiable information about the people involved in the study will be collected, shared, or published in any forum. The findings presented in the paper will not include any information that will make it possible to identify you.

Data: The data will be stored in a locked facility and only I and [co-researcher, research assistant, and so on] would have access to it. [If you are getting data electronically, include a statement on how it would be kept secure]. The completed questionnaires will be destroyed after the data has been organized, coded, and analyzed. I anticipate that to be within [months/years] of data collection. The data will be used for a research paper that will be presented at [class/conferences/online/etc.].

The paper will be submitted for publication in a [newspaper/journal/book/etc.]

Risks and benefits: There is a concern that you may feel uncomfortable answering questions about [list any stressors]. Therefore, please remember that you are free to stop participating at any point in time. You will also be reminded to not answer any question/s that you are not comfortable answering. [If applicable, include helpline number for counseling, etc.]

Compensation: You will not receive any compensation for your time. [If research subjects are compensated for their time, then note the same here]

If you have questions: The researcher conducting this study is [name]. Please ask any questions you have now. If you have questions later, you may contact [name] at [phone, email]. If you have any questions or concerns regarding your rights as a subject in this study, you may contact the Institutional Review Board (IRB) at [phone, email, website].

If you agree to participate in this study, please sign the consent form and complete the questionnaire [research tool for data collection].

You will be given a copy of this form to keep for your records.

Statement of consent: I have read the above information, and have received answers to any questions I asked. I consent to take part in the study.

Your Signature _____ Date _____

Your Name (printed) _____

Signature of the person obtaining consent _____
Date _____

The printed name of the person obtaining consent _____
Date _____

This consent form will be kept by the researcher for [months/years] beyond the end of the study.

If you plan to use a recording device – audio or video – or take manual notes in person, you should include that also in the consent form:

> In addition to agreeing to participate, I also consent to researchers taking notes using [recording device/pen and paper/laptop].

If there are no foreseeable risks associated with the participation, then you can write that in the section for risks and benefits. If you have contacted research subjects by email and they will be sending the completed survey or reply by email, make a note in the consent form.

> The data will be linked to your email address. It will be used only to track participation and send a reminder. The IP addresses will not be recorded. The email addresses will be deleted at the end of data collection and before data analysis.

2. **No harm to subjects:** The researcher is required to identify if there is any potential harm to subjects and address it in the IRB proposal. The harm could be physical, psychological, or emotional. In some instances, it could also be economic. The researcher also needs to maintain the dignity and privacy of subjects. In the Standford Prison experiment explained earlier in the chapter, some of the subjects playing the role of the prison guards became abusive, and some of the subjects playing the role of the inmates became anxious and stressed and started to cry. The power of the situational factors was such that the 'prisoners' forgot that they could just walk out of the experiment at any time. The researcher should have been able to see the harm and stopped the experiment immediately, but it took another professor to notice the abuse that led Zimbardo to call off the experiment.
   - The researcher should also identify if collecting information in certain settings could pose a risk to the respondent. For example, asking employees about work conditions while they are at work surrounded by other employees or supervisor(s) is not the best approach. Therefore, care must be taken to identify the location of data collection as much as the method of data collection.
   - Though most can identify potential harm in experiments, intensive interviews, and covert observation, researchers using a survey method may also face the dilemma of potential harm to subjects. For example, surveys about a wide range of topics such as domestic abuse, drug overdose, job loss, online bullying, and so on may be

emotionally upsetting or cause distress and anxiety. The IRB may suggest including information for a helpline on the consent form for the respondents to seek any assistance.
- You will also want to identify the potential gain for the respondents. For example, if the study is on a new deaddiction program or provides tools to protect against online scams, you can establish the benefit for the respondents as well.

3. **Disclose identity:** The researcher should disclose their identity to the research subject so that the information is shared with an understanding of who is collecting data and for what purpose. However, it may not be possible if a researcher chooses the role of covert participation (qualitative method). This would also involve deception. This is also common in investigative journalism.
   - The BBC documentary *The Secret Policeman* reveals racism in the police service. The journalist, Mark Daly, was undercover. Though the documentary resulted in resignations and disciplinary actions against certain police officers, it was also criticized for deception and not sharing information sooner with the police so that corrective measures could be taken ("Police hit back," 2003). Though one often hears about the undercover work by police officers, and often by journalists as well, ethical requirements for social science researchers are far more stringent, and each proposal needs to be carefully and thoroughly vetted by the IRB before collecting any data.

4. **Confidentiality and anonymity of research subjects:** The researcher should maintain complete privacy of the research subjects at all stages – recruitment, data collection, data storing, data analysis, dissemination of findings, and disposal of records. **Administrative safeguards** should be in place to identify who can or cannot access the data. **Physical safeguards** refer to the actual storage of information – the location where respondents can collect and drop the form, the location of the interview (group or individual), locking the cabinets, and so on. **Technical safeguards** refer to computer passwords, data sent through email (personal or official), data encryption and coding, and so on.
   - In some instances, the researcher may not be able to provide complete anonymity and confidentiality. For example, in a focus group, the researcher cannot promise that each respondent would also respect the other's privacy. This should be noted in a consent form so that the respondents participate with a full understanding of the potential lack of privacy. Such concerns should be fully noted in the IRB proposal. For any sensitive topic, the IRB may decide against using such a method that exposes anyone to potential risk. In that case, the researcher would have to consider another method.

- While collecting visual data (still and moving images), if the subject wants to hide their face, name, and so on, the researcher should do so. It is also important to blur the names of the location or any other marker that may identify the individual's location. Extra care should be taken when such information may be in a different language as the researcher may not immediately identify it.
- In some instances, the research subject(s) may insist on sharing their information for greater visibility and need for assistance. In such a scenario, the researcher should accommodate accordingly on a case-by-case basis, but not presume the same for everyone in the setting.
5. **The benefits of the research should outweigh the risks**: As discussed in Chapter 2, one needs to examine what makes for a good research question. As research involves ethical considerations and, more often than not, presents ethical dilemmas, the researcher must provide a logical justification for undertaking any research. The IRB would evaluate whether the risks involved in the research are reasonable or excessive and approve, modify, or reject the proposal accordingly.

Along with the above-listed five ethical guidelines, there are additional guidelines and concerns that should be considered while doing social science research.

Ethics Abroad

Some ethical concerns are more pronounced when collecting data in foreign locations or cultures that one does not belong to. Researchers may be working in settings where the guidelines are either not in place or not enforced. It does not excuse the researcher's responsibility to abide by the ethical guidelines. Honesty, integrity, and authenticity are basic tenets of any scholarly work. Even when information is considered beneficial for the research project and the larger cause being investigated, the data should not come at the cost of compromising these basic values.

Helicopter researchers – Then there is the issue of helicopter researchers, whose only concern is to get data for their research without any sincere interest in examining the question, exploring the context, or, for that matter, recording data from the respondent's perspective. It is a bigger ethical concern in cross-cultural or foreign settings where many tend to approach people and settings with either some sort of exotic lens or a utilitarian view – that is, for them, the respondents' only purpose or utility is to be a part of that study.

Ethnocentrism – When doing any research, and especially when using qualitative methods, as we do not know much about the setting, topic, or people ahead of time, one of the first things is to guard against ethnocentrism. Approaching the setting and collecting data authentically from the subject's viewpoint is critical in maintaining the integrity of research. If someone has a sense of superiority about *their* understanding of the different settings, human behavior, conflict, crime, justice, or so on, they are likely to make these errors, intentionally or habitually. That is, the authentic views and experiences of the respondents may not fit the preset frameworks within which a researcher may be working. Masoga, Shokane, and Blitz (2021) note that a lot of the existing knowledge of indigenous peoples in African countries is tainted by Eurocentric perceptions, assumptions, and prejudices. However, this is not unique to non-Western settings only. Alvi (2021) examines similar issues regarding research on the experiences of indigenous peoples in Canada. There may also be almost a reductionist view of people and cultures, and even toward researchers or voices in non-Western settings or of non-Western sensibilities. It is also a disservice to the audience that relies on the researcher to collect, interpret, and share information authentically and sincerely. Despite its seriousness, it is not easy to identify ethnocentrism in one's work, especially if it fits the preset views of the reader as well as the audience. It also does not mean automatically dismissing every piece of research in or about transnational and cross-cultural settings by researchers who are not part of that setting *per se*. Identifying one's limitations and accordingly placing communities at the forefront to examine social issues and consider solutions would be a better approach.

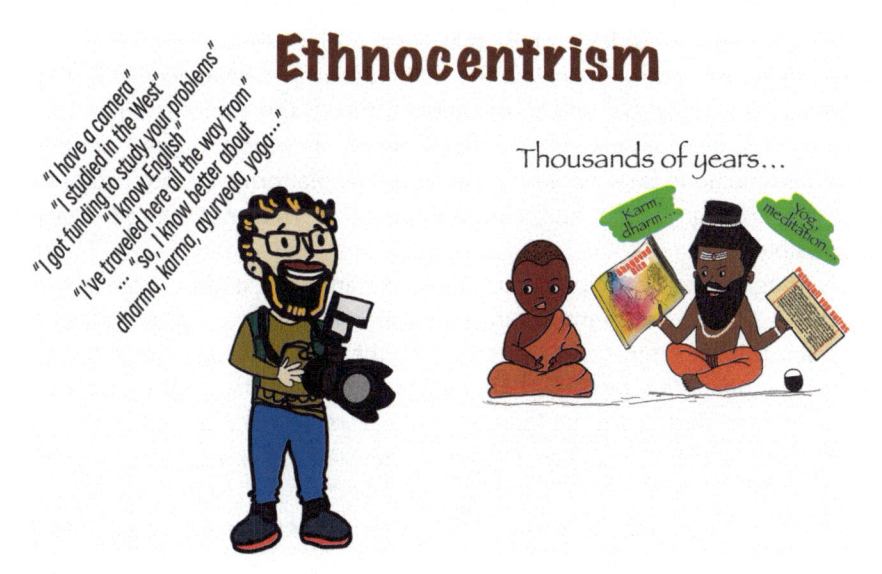

Figure 3.3 Ethnocentrism

It is best to read works by scholars from various backgrounds as it will help train your mind to be open to ideas from different perspectives, cultures, and lenses. **Reflexivity** could also create a heightened awareness for researchers as they acknowledge and realize that their personal experiences, beliefs, assumptions, and attitudes, as well as their environment, may influence their research process. Having this awareness can prepare the researcher to observe and interpret data more carefully and from the subject's perspective.

Digital Data and Ethics

According to Beneito-Montagut (2011), **netnography** can be used to study how people create online interactions and relationships. It can also give insight into the nature of interactions in the online space vis-à-vis physical space; on the one end of the spectrum, the digital space may be considered to be as real as the physical space, and on the other end, it may be divorced from reality. Through research, one can examine how people negotiate and navigate this space, how people shape this environment, and vice-versa. The researcher can either unobtrusively collect data or actively become engaged.

More often than not, netnography is a qualitative approach to media research. The creation of an "online culture" is indicative of the communities that have shared values, norms, beliefs, and ways of doing things (Wagner, 2008). It aims to examine interactions in social media space. It is a **digital ethnographic** approach to understanding communities, cultures, and communication in the digital space. It creates immense opportunities for researchers to explore topics that were earlier beyond one's reach or were high-cost. Sitting in one's office or workspace, one can access videos, photographs, podcasts, and so on, about innumerable topics from around the world. It gives an insight into people's lives in a short amount of time. Many interactions take place only due to digital platforms as they establish contact among people and communities that may not be otherwise accessible.

Netnography also helps create networks and access data even about hostile settings. For example, in September 2022, a 22-year-old Iranian woman, Mhasa Amini, was beaten up by the morality police for refusing to wear a hijab. She later died and widespread protests erupted. Despite the efforts to shut down the Internet, protestors in Iran were able to share videos about police brutality. Though far fewer, similar videos have been posted from Afghanistan. The videos and images about Uyghur Muslims in China; Yazidis in Iraq, Syria, and Turkey; Baloch people in Afghanistan and Pakistan; religious and sexual minorities in Turkey, Pakistan, Bangladesh; and so on have helped to create awareness about people that otherwise have limited means to get their information out. The racial strife and gun violence in the United States have become more widely known due to digital data shared across social media platforms. It also allows researchers to collect information on sensitive topics. However, just like any other research practice, in netnography also the data needs to be verified, overgeneralizations should be avoided, and the context must be examined. A few examples include studies on anorexia (Crowe and Watts, 2014), male bodybuilding (Smith and Stewart 2012), sex and porn on the Internet (Jacobs, 2010), and so on.

Phone cameras have revolutionized this field, where anyone can take photos and videos and share them online. In many ways, it has challenged communication hierarchies by empowering people to create and share content as per their perspectives and interests. Researchers can curate such digital data and use it for analysis. However, the informed consent of the people whose information is shared online is not always stated or clear (Lamb, 2011). It is a greater challenge in closed settings that restrict a free flow of information or where there is limited direct access. Kozinets (2015) emphasizes narrowing the research group of interest and has listed 12 steps of netnography: introspection, investigation, information, interview, inspection, interaction, immersion, indexing, interpretation, iteration, instantiation, and integration. Netnography can be an excellent tool as long as one is mindful of ethics and validity.

- The ease of access to digital data, including imagery, and the speed of sharing it raises concerns about ethics, privacy, and the dignity of the subject in question. It is a particular concern when the imagery is consumed about tragedies, crimes, victims, and so on. One needs to differentiate when imagery contributes to understanding and carries affective value, and when it is used for shock value only. Many people may not be aware of how and where their information has been shared by known and anonymous users. The researcher, therefore, needs to extend dignity to them even when there is no direct data collection by the researcher.
- Despite the fast pace of digitization around the world, there is still a digital divide. Therefore, even while curating information online, one needs to guard against errors in reasoning (Chapter 1), understand the limitations of the gatekeepers, and recognize the limited digital data available about autocratic and theocratic societies.
- A vast majority of digital information consumed around the world is in the English language. Implicitly, the researcher may have access to skewed information that would impact validity and generalization.
- The researcher also needs to recognize the lack of context, manipulation, and incorrect information. Online sources may not always provide

an avenue to verify every bit of information. Yet, many are driven by sharing information fast. Even if the correct information is corrected later on, it is unlikely to get the same traction, and the misinformation remains available.
- As long as the researcher is aware of its limitations, open-source information in the digital space can be used to examine wide-ranging topics. It is not unreasonable to expect the development of more regulations and guidelines for netnography in the coming years.

Researchers and IRBs are increasingly faced with new questions when collecting or working with digital data. Many images and information are shared online without an indication of the owner or if one consented to sharing it. Many content analysis projects focus on social media posts, online forums, group chats, and so on. The data may include text, audio, videos, and photographs. A vast majority of users do not read the terms and conditions on various apps and online forums and do not know how their information across platforms is linked and could be traced back to them or used by third parties. When using such data, the researcher should identify if they can inform the online community. Additionally, following the guidelines of confidentiality and the anonymity of research subjects, the researcher should remove all personally identifiable information. The researcher should also avoid taking large portions of textual information that can be traced back to the poster even if it has been paraphrased.

When taking information from public posts or groups, the researcher will need to cite the source as per the APA (or as required) guidelines. However, if the post is about a minor, the researcher should not use it without informed consent from the parent or guardian.

As you can probably guess, digital data and ethics is a fast-evolving field that presents new challenges every day. It perhaps deserves a book or two on itself, but for now, the above introduction to netnography and the challenges associated with it should suffice.

Funded Research

The researchers should disclose the source of their research funding. It is also important to note that not all topics get the same share of funds. Some topics are funded more easily and extensively than others. As a result, there will be more papers, books, chapters, documentaries, films, panels, and discussions on certain topics than on others. While studying any topic, one should be mindful of such limitations of published research as it creates a skewed view of the topic and gives only a partial understanding. It also creates a hierarchy of victims where one may be able to find more extensive work on one group of victims than another. Social activists, media, and lawmakers may also address only those who have been given visibility. It does not make the research invalid but just cautions researchers to be mindful of the complete picture, avoid overgeneralizing, and recognize selective observations. As a student-scholar, therefore, work with your professor to examine topics about which there may not be ample information and create original knowledge while expanding the existing knowledge base.

As we next start discussing the sampling and research methods, start to think about what ethical challenges you would face while selecting a particular method to study the research topic. You will need to address them in your research proposal. It is relatively easy to remember these guidelines, but to understand their application, it is important to select an actual topic and critically evaluate the ethical dilemmas that it may present, and how to address them. Discussing these ideas in class with your professor will bring more clarity and help you refine your research proposal before it is submitted to the Institutional Review Board or the Ethics Committee.

Further Reading

- APA Reference Examples, https://apastyle.apa.org/style-grammar-guidelines/references/examples
- Cohen, Jodi. (2019). University of Illinois at Chicago Missed Warning Signs of Research Going Awry, Letters Show. ProPublica, March 20, 2019. Retrieved from https://www.propublica.org/article/university-of-illinois-chicago-uic-research-misconduct-letters-documents
- OHRP https://www.hhs.gov/ohrp/index.html

Key Terms

Administrative safeguards
Charity patients
Chicago Baby Project
Confidentiality
Digital data
Digital ethnography
Ethnocentrism
Helicopter researchers
Informed consent
Institutional review board
Milgram experiment
Netnography
No harm to subjects
Physical safeguards
Reductionist view
Reflexivity
Research ethics
Stanford prison experiment
Tearoom trade experiment
Technical safeguards
Tuskegee experiment
Voluntary participation

Class Activity

Complete the Institutional Review Board application on a hypothetical topic. Invite a guest speaker from the Institutional Review Board and critically evaluate the topic. If it is a large class, ask students to work in groups. Guide students to pick a wide variety of topics. This will result in a richer discussion on the topic of research ethics.

Works Cited

Allen, Scott. 1994. "Free Care Came with a Price." *Boston Globe*, February 28, pp. 25–26.

Alvi, Shahid. 2021. "Social Science Research in Canada: Ethical and Methodological Issues." In Divya Sharma (ed.), *Ethics, Ethnocentrism and Social Science Research*. New York, NY: Routledge.

Beneito-Montagut, R. 2011. "Ethnography Goes Online: Towards a User-Centred Methodology to Research Interpersonal Communication on the Internet." *Qualitative Research*, Vol.11(6), pp. 716–735.

Boissoneault, Lorraine. 2017. "A Spoonful of Sugar Helps the Radioactive Oatmeal Go Down." *Smithsonian Magazine*. Retrieved from https://www.smithsonianmag.com/history/spoonful-sugar-helps-radioactive-oatmeal-go-down-180962424/

Cohen, Jodi. 2019. "University of Illinois at Chicago Missed Warning Signs of Research Going Awry, Letters Show." *ProPublica*, March 20. Retrieved from https://www.propublica.org/article/university-of-illinois-chicago-uic-research-misconduct-letters-documents

Crowe, N., and M. Watts. 2014. "'We're Just Like Gok, But in Reverse': Ana Girls – Empowerment and Resistance in Digital Communities." *International Journal of Adolescence and Youth*, Vol.21(3), pp. 1–12.

Humphreys, Laud. 1975. *The Tearoom Trade*. England edition with perspectives on ethical issues. Chicago: Aldine.

Jacobs, K. 2010. "Lizzy Kinsey and the Adult Friendfinders: An Ethnographic Study of Internet Sex and Pornographic Self-Display in Hong Kong." *Cult Health Sex*, Vol.12(6), pp. 691–703.

Kozinets, R. 2015. *Netnography: Redefined*. 2nd ed. London: SAGE Publications Ltd.

Lamb, R. 2011. "Facebook Recruitment." *Research Ethics*, Vol.7(2), pp. 72–73.

Lee, Gary. 1995. "Stillborn Babies Used in '50s Radiations Test: Energy Dept. Widens Disclosure of Experiments." *Washington Post*, May 3, p. A3.

MacPheran, Karen. 1995. "40s Ethics Policies Ignored in Human Radiation Testing." *Houston Chronicle*, January 23, p. 2A.

Masoga, Mogomme Alpheus, Allucia Lulu Shokane, and Lisa V. Blitz. 2021. "When Research Violates Local Indigenous Communities." In Divya Sharma (ed.), *Ethics, Ethnocentrism and Social Science Research*. New York, NY: Routledge.

Mintz, M., and Jerry S. Cohen. 1976. "Human Guinea Pigs." *Progressive*, Vol.40(12), pp. 32–36.

Mitford, Jessica. 1973. *Kind and Usual Punishment: The Prison Business*. New York: Knopf.

"Police Hit Back at BBC Over Racism Film." 2003. *The Guardian*, October 22. Retrieved from https://www.theguardian.com/media/2003/oct/22/bbc.race

Schneider, Keith. 1994. "Stillborns' Ashes Used in Studies of Radiation, Documents Show." *New York Times*, May 5, p. B12.

Smith, A. C. T., and B. Stewart. 2012. "Body Perceptions and Health Behaviors in an Online Bodybuilding Community." *Qualitative Health Research*, Vol.22(7), pp. 971–985.

"Standford Prison Experiment." In *Social Psychology Study*. Britannica. Retrieved from https://www.britannica.com/event/Stanford-Prison-Experiment

"The Tuskegee Timeline, The U.S. Public Health Service Syphilis Study at Tuskegee." Center for Disease Control and Prevention. Retrieved from https://www.cdc.gov/tuskegee/timeline.htm

Wagner, P. 2008. "Does Europe Have a Cultural Identity?" In H. Joas, and K. Wiegandt (eds.), *The Cultural Values of Europe* (pp. 357–368). Liverpool: Liverpool University Press.

Yemma, John. 1997. "Ex-Fernald Residents Awarded $1.85m." *Boston Globe*, December 31, pp. B1, B7.

chapter 4

Defining and Measuring Concepts

This chapter explains the process of defining abstract concepts and identifying measurable indicators for the same. It explains the importance of selecting the most suitable research method, and levels of measurement for different types of variables.

After completing this chapter, students will be able to:

- Define abstract and multidimensional concepts
- Identify dimensions, variables, and indicators
- Understand the importance of selecting the most suitable method for the research question and setting
- Understand different levels of measurement for qualitative and quantitative variables

Introduction

Words such as justice, harm, happiness, fear, adventure, poverty, struggle, prestige, bias, discrimination, coping mechanism, assimilation, alienation, and so on create a mental image in our minds about what they mean. This mental image may be based on personal or vicarious experience, including what we watch in media, read, or hear about. These concepts manifest differently for different people. Many concepts may be multidimensional or have many types and variations. Therefore, the first step is to define a concept. For example, fear of crime may manifest differently for people living in the same neighborhood. One person may stop going out after it gets dark, another may stop children from playing outside, and another may decide to move out of the area altogether.

Figure 4.1 Concept – Fear of Crime

Kaplan (1964) defined concept as a construct, and that applies to many issues in social sciences. Conceptualization, therefore, is an important step before measurement. Think of a concept as a rough, abstract, or open-to-interpretation idea that you will refine to make it measurable. It helps to explain as to what your work focuses on, how your work interprets a certain concept, or what aspect of a particular concept your work measures. Similarly, while it is easy to ask if a person is stressed or not, it is better to next explore how it manifests and impacts a person's life. The researcher does not need to study every aspect of every concept but needs to a) clearly define what is being studied, and b) select a research tool that is best suited to study it.

When dealing with various types and dimensions of a concept, the researchers must also specify which aspect or dimension they are examining. For example, victims of white-collar crimes may be impacted financially, emotionally, psychologically, socially, and so on. Domestic violence may include physical, emotional, psychological, or financial harm. Depending on what aspect or type of victimization the researchers are planning to study, they need to select indicators of that aspect or dimension. The researcher, therefore, needs to make the concept measurable. This is a natural process of research and begins once the researcher has decided what to study. As we consider how to study something, we start the measurement process. This may be refined further during data collection and data analysis as well. For example, while evaluating the effectiveness of drug laws, we will need to figure out what indicates or reflects *effectiveness* – incarceration

defining and measuring concepts

rate, recidivism rates, treatment and rehabilitation behind bars or in the community, and so on.

The Chicago (Ilinois) Alternative Policing Strategy, commonly known as CAPS, is a community-policing approach that involves five steps: "identifying and prioritizing problems, 2) analyzing problems, 3) strategizing designs to deal with problems, 4) implementing a plan, and 5) evaluating effectiveness" ("Program Profile," 2013, para.5). The CAPS program started in 1993 in 25 police districts in Chicago. It was aimed at crime control and crime prevention and for either objective, police have to rely on community support. It is somewhat easier to have successful community policing strategies in relatively stable (residential and economic stability) and safer neighborhoods. The Chicago Police Department, however, identified five vastly diverse districts with varying crime problems. These included Englewood, Marquette, Austin, Morgan Park, and Rogers Park. Each district had a Community Advisory Community that worked with the community members to identify and prioritize problems in the area. The direct communication made community members feel that they were stakeholders and had a say in the matter ("The Chicago Alternative."). The problems identified by the community members included graffiti, trash-strewn lots and sidewalks, gang violence, drug dealing, assault, and robbery, among others. The interim report published in 1995 noted that "An analysis of reported crime figures and survey reports of victimization and neighborhood problems found a significant decrease in perceived crime problems in all five prototype areas. Optimism about the police increased significantly in four prototype areas" ("Community Policing in," 1995). According to the interim report, these problems declined significantly in Englewood and Austin ("Community Policing in," 1995, p.5).

Many problems that reflect **physical incivilities** often impact **social cohesion** and reduce natural **social surveillance** and a sense of a safe community. Concepts such as safety, social cohesion, trust, and so on could mean different things for different people, depending on their circumstances, life experiences, location, and so on. **Exploratory research** discussed in Chapter 1 would be a good starting point to study these ideas, which are not very precisely defined for everyone.

Programs such as **Weed and Seed** also support these findings as restructuring neighborhoods sends a message that people living there care about the area, property, and people, and it acts as a deterrent for potential criminals.

The report ("Community Policing in," 1995) also notes that the supervisors with a year's CAPS experience were more optimistic about the community-policing approach. The residents also showed involvement, took ownership, and made it easier to implement changes. Stronger leadership helped shape the agenda and the police helped to implement solutions

Figure 4.2 Physical Incivilities

("Community Policing in," 1995, pp. 6–7). Hence, while measuring the impact, the researcher can, and perhaps should, evaluate both quantitative and qualitative data. It is not always about numbers only! In a particular jurisdiction, a police officer may not receive any complaints about domestic violence from one community. The researcher or the police department will need to examine this. It could be that there is no incidence of domestic violence in that community, or that it is not being reported. Lack of reporting would further warrant examining the reasons for non-reporting – cultural reasons, familial reasons, a lack of trust in the police, the fear of stigma, or anything else. It is also possible that certain crimes may show an increase after community outreach. However, this is not always negative and may reflect an increase in crime reporting as residents start trusting the police more. Therefore, effectiveness is not measured only by looking at increasing or decreasing numbers on a certain scale – it is more interpretive.

As we examine concepts, we start reaching from abstract to specifics. In sum, the researcher deals with the questions – what indicates X, and how to measure it? The researchers may collect data themselves (primary data) or use data that others have collected (secondary), and, as noted earlier, this can be qualitative or quantitative.

It is possible for the researcher to not find any data about certain issues or jurisdictions. The absence of crime data does not mean an absence of crime. The Uniform Crime Reports (UCRs) in the United States did not start to collect data on bias crimes until the mid-1990s. The data collection on white-collar crimes also gained momentum after the 1990s. Even then, the sentences for white-collar and corporate crimes were less harsh than street crimes, and the victims were often overlooked. In many of the introductory criminal justice textbooks before the mid-2000s, white-collar crimes were listed as victimless crimes which is factually incorrect.

Levels of Measurement

The four levels of measurement for variables in social science research are nominal, ordinal, interval, and ratio. Nominal and ordinal levels are qualitative or categorical, while interval and ratio are considered quantitative, numerical, or continuous variables.

Nominal level – These variables do not have any precise mathematical interpretation or meaning and include, for example, race, gender, blood type, location, marital status, eye color, religion, and so on. The researcher can code the categories as 1, 2, 3, or 4, but these numbers do not carry any weight or hierarchy – they are just labels. The values of a variable can be placed in separate categories but there is no natural order or mathematical sequence. The categories or values of the variable are mutually exclusive.

For data analysis, the **frequency distribution** is a good way to organize data that can be further reflected through graphs such as **bar charts**. For a nominal variable, the researcher can only measure **mode** – the most common category or value of a variable.

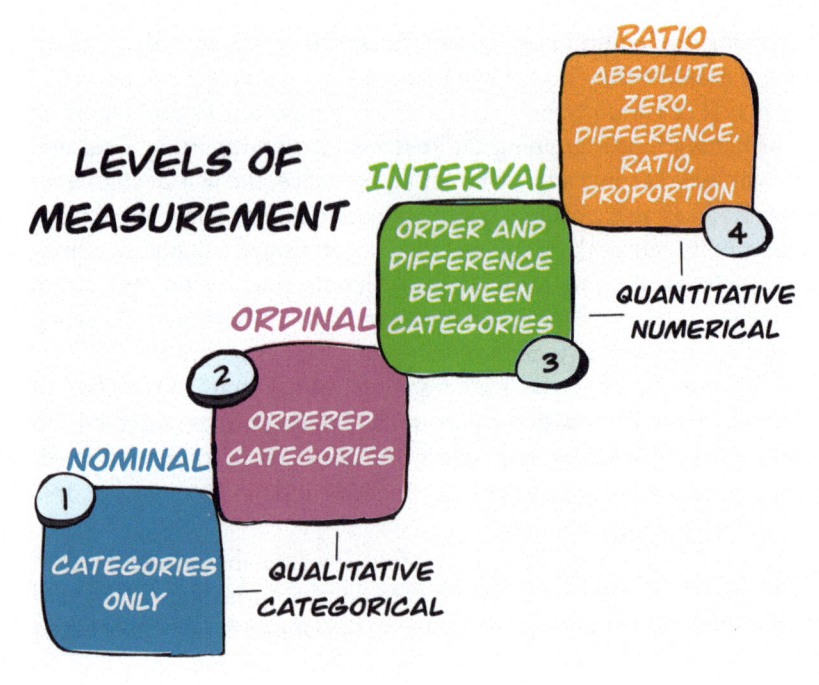

Figure 4.3 Levels of Measurement

Bar chart – This denotes a categorical variable where there is no overlap and continuity between the values reflected through separate bins or bars.

Ordinal level – These variables can be placed in an order, but the difference in the values or categories is not mathematically precise or quantifiable. For example, the researcher may ask a question about trust in lawmakers, and use index questions as follows:

Response Scale: Strongly Agree (SA), Agree (A), Neutral/No opinion (N), Disagree (D), Strongly Disagree (SD)

Statements/Questions	Circle One Response
Do you believe that your vote makes a difference?	SA, A, N, D, SD
Do you believe that lawmakers have an interest in solving people's problems?	SA, A, N, D, SD
Do you believe that lawmakers are less interested in maintaining power than solving people's problems?	SA, A, N, D, SD
Do you believe that corrupt lawmakers are held accountable?	SA, A, N, D, SD

The responses will show an order in terms of lower and higher levels of agreement, but the difference between the values cannot be calculated. The option 'strongly agree' reflects a stronger agreement than 'agree' or 'disagree', but the difference between these categories cannot be measured.

Nominal and Ordinal Levels of Measurement

Nominal	Would you say that you are happy with the new ice cream machine at work?	a. Yes b. No	Non-ranked categories
Ordinal	How would you rate your happiness about the new ice cream machine at work?	a. High b. Normal c. Low d. Extremely Low	Ranked categories

Similarly, if the researcher asks about income levels by using a scale of low, middle, and high as opposed to precise numbers, it would be considered an ordinal variable as it can be ranked in order, but there are no precise numbers. That is, the difference between low to middle and middle to high is not exact or consistent.

> **Helpful Hint:** If the researcher measures income in exact numbers such as $40,000 per year, $50,000 per year, and so on, it will become a ratio variable.

defining and measuring concepts

Ordinal Level
Pepper Hotness Test

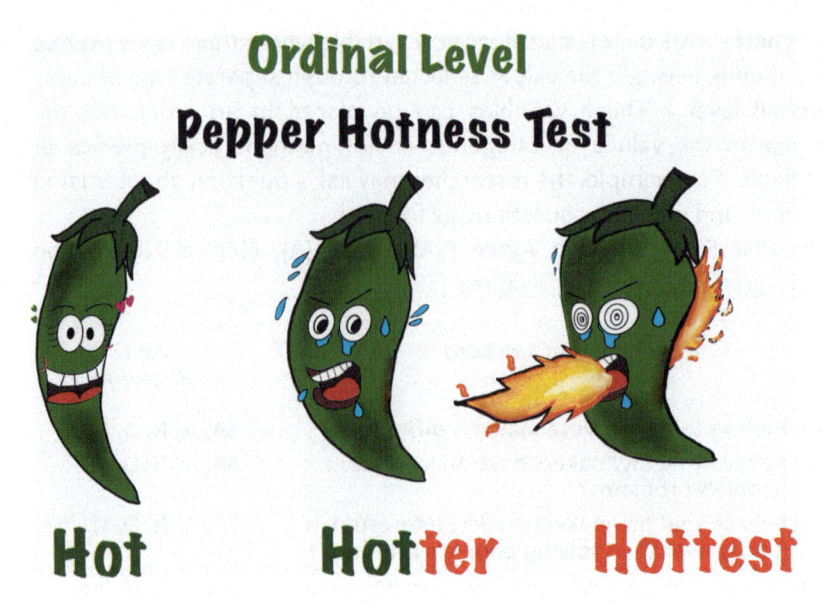

Hot **Hotter** **Hottest**

Figure 4.4 Ordinal Level – Pepper Hotness Test

For an ordinal variable, the researcher can measure the **mode, median,** and **interquartile range**.

Median – This is the middle value or 50th percentile for a dataset. It divides the values in half with 50 percent of values greater than the median and 50 percent placed lower than the median.

Interquartile range – When the data set or all the values of the variable are divided into four equal parts, the second and third quartiles are the interquartile range.

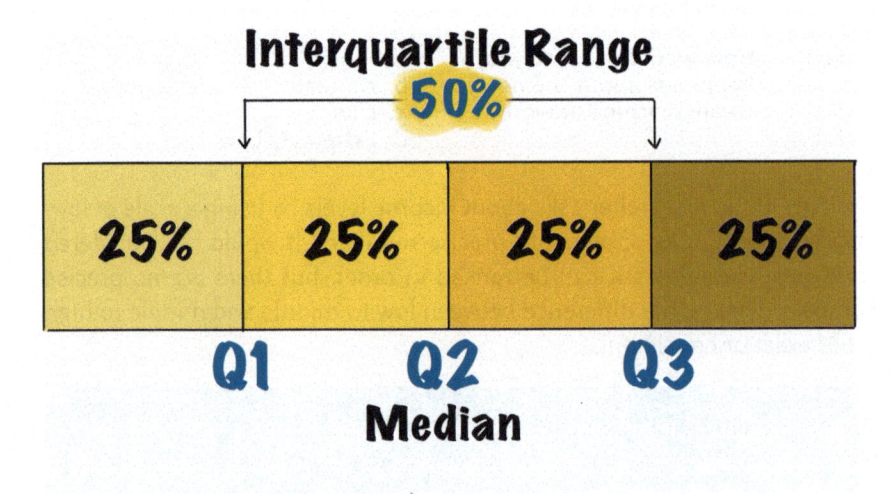

Interquartile Range
50%

25%	25%	25%	25%
	Q1	Q2	Q3

Median

Figure 4.5 Interquartile Range

defining and measuring concepts

Interval level – These variables have finite numbers or values, but the zero is not fixed. The most common example used to explain it is temperature. The temperature of 20 degrees Celsius is not twice that of 10 degrees Celsius as there is no fixed zero. Similarly, a temperature of zero degrees Celsius does not mean a lack of temperature.

> **Helpful Hint:** If the researcher is measuring temperature in Kelvin instead of Celsius or Fahrenheit, then it will become a ratio variable.

Using the same example of trust in lawmakers, the researcher can use a numerical scale.

Response Scale: The responses range from 1 to 5, where 5 indicates the most trust and 1 indicates the least trust.

Statements/Questions	Circle One Response
Do you believe that your vote makes a difference?	1, 2, 3, 4, 5
Do you believe that lawmakers have an interest in solving people's problems?	1, 2, 3, 4, 5
Do you believe that lawmakers are less interested in maintaining power than solving people's problems?	1, 2, 3, 4, 5
Do you believe that corrupt lawmakers are held accountable?	1, 2, 3, 4, 5

If Respondent A selects all 5s (total 20) and Respondent B selects all 1s (total 4), the researcher can identify who has more or less trust and also by how many points. However, it does not mean that Respondent A has 5 times more trust in the lawmakers than Respondent B.

Ratio level – These variables are mathematically the most precise as there is an absolute zero, and there is a quantifiable difference between values of a variable. For example, zero candy in the bag means a lack of candy. Like ordinal scales, the researcher can rank values; like interval scales, the researcher can measure the difference between values, and because of an absolute zero, the researcher can also multiply and divide, or calculate ratios. If Bag A contains 10 candies and Bag B contains 20 candies, one can calculate that Bag B has more candies, it has 10 more candies than Bag A, and it has twice the candies as Bag A. Income, weight, speed, height, and so on are some of the examples of ratio variables.

Along with the **mode, median,** and **interquartile range**, for interval and ratio variables, the researcher can also measure **mean, range, variance,** and **standard deviation**.

defining and measuring concepts

Mean – Arithmetic mean is the average of the set of values. It is the sum of all values divided by the number of values.

Range – This is the difference between the highest and the lowest values in a distribution.

Variance – This is a measure of the dispersion of all data points in a data set. It is the averaged squared deviation from the mean and shows how the data points are spread or deviate from the mean.

Standard Deviation – This is also a measure of the dispersion of data. It is a square root of the variance. In a **normal distribution**, 68 percent of data points would fall within +/- one standard deviation of the mean; 95 percent of data points would fall within +/- two standard deviations of the mean; and 99 percent of data points would fall within +/- three standard deviations of the mean.

The **normal distribution** is also called a **bell curve** or a **sampling distribution**. The actual data distribution may not look like the normal distribution and may be skewed. More extreme dispersion of higher or lower values or concentration of values on one or the other end would impact the shape of the curve. It does not mean that the researcher cannot use that data – it only means that the researcher needs to assess how much of the data falls within what standard deviation. For example, a local police department may be developing a new community-based program. It collects data from the residents about the program's favorability or lack thereof. The data may show that only 30 percent of data points fall within +/- one standard deviation of the mean as opposed to the 68 percent in the normal distribution. The data may be skewed at one end of the curve which may reflect a great deal of support for the program. If it is concentrated at the other end, it may show a lot of opposition to the program. It is also possible to have data on both extremes away from the mean and this would reflect a greater divide among the people about the program.

It is important to know the variation or distribution of data to understand outliers as well as a wider gap in responses or data. For example, two pizza stores have 10 employees each that earn hourly wages. Store A pays 5 of them $14 per hour and 5 of them $18 per hour. Store B pays 5 of its employees $10 per hour and 5 employees $22 per hour. The average pay is $16 per hour in both stores, but the distribution of hourly wages is much different.

Store A	Store B
5 × 14 = 70, 5 × 18 = 90 70 + 90 = 160 160/10 = $16	5 × 10 = 50, 5 × 22 = 110 50 + 110 = 160 160/10 = $16

While planning for research, it is important to know the levels at which the variables would be measured. You would want to know if the study would produce only qualitative information that is mostly measured at the nominal level, or if are there ways to get mathematically more precise data for analysis. It would also help to plan coding methods ahead of time. Researchers would always try to keep analyzing if there are variables that can be measured at a higher level – moving from nominal to ratio. These decisions would influence the collection, description, analysis, and interpretation of data.

> **Helpful Hint:** In Chapter 1, we discussed different types of measurement validity and reliability. It would be useful to have another look at them before moving on, as you start examining if your research proposal includes abstract or exact concepts, and what methods would be best to study them.

Further Reading

Chicago Alternative Policing Strategy, https://nationalgangcenter.ojp.gov/spt/Programs/48

Key Terms

Bar chart
Bell curve
Chicago Alternative Policing Strategy (CAPS)
Community policing
Concept
Exploratory research
Frequency distribution
Interquartile range
Interval level
Likert scale
Measurement validity
Median
Mode
Nominal level
Normal distribution
Ordinal level
Outlier
Physical incivilities
Primary data
Range
Ratio level
Secondary data
Social cohesion
Social surveillance
Standard deviation
Uniform crime reports
Variance

Class Activity

Select any two or three concepts. Divide the class into groups of three or four students. Assign topics to each group ensuring that at least two groups get the same topic. Each group should identify which aspect(s) or dimension(s) of the topic they would like to study. They should also identify

defining and measuring concepts

relevant indicators for each aspect or dimension of interest. As each group makes their presentation, engage in a class discussion on which level it would be measured and if it is possible to measure it on a mathematically more precise level – why, or why not?

Works Cited

Kaplan, Abraham. 1964. *The Conduct of Inquiry.* San Francisco, CA: Chandler.

"Program Profile: Chicago Alternative Policing Strategies (CAPS)." 2013. National Institute of Justice, Crime Solutions. Retrieved from https://crimesolutions.ojp.gov/ratedprograms/299

"The Chicago Alternative Policing Strategy (CAPS)." 1993. Fact Sheet, City of Chicago, Department of Police. Retrieved from https://popcenter.asu.edu/sites/default/files/library/unpublished/OrganizationalPlans/36_(CAPS).pdf

"Community Policing in Chicago, Year Two: An Interim Report." 1995. U.S. Department of Justice, Office of Justice Programs. Retrieved from https://www.ojp.gov/ncjrs/virtual-library/abstracts/community-policing-chicago-year-two-interim-report

chapter 5

Sampling

This chapter explains the significance, purpose, and methods of taking a sample from a population or a setting that the researcher wants to study. It begins with discussing the basic steps and issues to consider before deciding on which sampling method to use. The chapter walks the reader through the process of drawing samples using probability methods of simple, systematic, stratified, and cluster sampling. Among the non-probability sampling methods, the chapter explains the significance and process of availability, quota, purposive, snowball, and theoretical sampling methods. The reader will not only learn the steps involved in using these sampling methods but also when and why to use which method. The chapter concludes with a note on sampling error and the need to keep doing research.

After this chapter, students will be able to understand and explain:

- The purpose and process of taking a sample
- Meaning and types of probability sampling methods
- Meaning and types of non-probability sampling methods
- Generalizability and sampling error

Introduction

We are inundated with information and opinions on practically every topic of politics, crime, justice, culture, media, economics, and so on. Some voices are louder and more *visible* than others. In making policy decisions, laws, or programs, or addressing any social issues, we have to figure out if the people that we are listening to – and influencing or making policies for – represent the **population** that will be impacted by those decisions. For example, to get a

DOI: 10.4324/9781003314738-6

STOP sign installed at the intersection near my house, it is easy for me to ask my neighbors for their opinion as I know them and we have often discussed it. But does that adequately represent the neighborhood? Not quite, as except my neighbors, I do not know what other residents would think of the proposal to get a STOP sign installed. Also, most of them are away from the intersection while my neighbor and I are closer to it. As the decision would impact the whole neighborhood – residents and commuters – I must try to get a **sample** that represents the neighborhood.

In the same vein, the researcher collecting data cannot presume what the respondents in the setting may think about the topic based on personal anecdotes of a few; they have to take a sample that adequately represents the population (Philliber, Schwab, and Sloss, 1980). While taking a sample, one must also consider issues of **generalizability** while guarding against **overgeneralization**.

In social sciences, there is no perfect sample; there will always be errors or gaps. The goal is to identify, acknowledge, and minimize those errors, and of course, keep researching as society (including my neighborhood) evolves.

Sampling

Figure 5.1 Sampling

Sample for Blood Work

Figure 5.2 Sample for Blood Work

Generalization or generalizability is the ability to take a sample from a population, study it, and then apply the findings to the population from where it was taken. Come to think of it, many of us have taken or given a few samples. Sometimes it is possible to conduct a census as well.

Census

That was sweet!

Ate the whole bunch.

Figure 5.3 Census

sampling

However, more often than not, it is not possible to study the entire population (Hagan, 2012) as the researcher may have limited resources – time, money, and research staff, the population may be too large, or it may just not be possible because of the nature of the research question and method. Even for smaller populations including relatively homogenous ones, sometimes it may not be feasible to conduct a census.

That is why it is important to know when it is useful to take a sample and which sampling method is the best in a given setting.

Figure 5.4 Census not Possible and Census not Needed

Sample Planning

There is no default good or bad sampling method *per se*; its utility – that is, its *goodness* – depends on the nature of the research question, population, or setting from which you are planning to take a sample, and your access to that population, setting, or respondents. Before discussing the types of sampling methods, one needs to tackle the question of where and how to start. So, let us look at the basic steps involved in sample planning.

Figure 5.5 Where to Start

- The first step is to define the population. **Population** refers to a whole set of people, groups, settings, or other entities to which the research findings would be applied. The researcher must clearly define the population; it cannot be vague. If it is vague, the sample will be vague as well. If the definition of the population is ambiguous, there will be errors of reasoning and poor generalizability. As a criminologist, sociologist, or criminal justice practitioner, you need to provide a very specific definition because you need to take a sample from the population that you say that you are studying, and then apply findings to that population only.

- It does not matter if it is a small population or a large population. What matters is a) to clearly state what population you want to study; and b) to take a sample from that population only. The size of the population or the subsequent sample has little to do with whether your study is good or bad. It could be the homicide rate around the world, or it could be female students taking a research methods course in social sciences at your university in the current semester. What is important is that *you* should know what the population is that you are studying and take a sample from that population only. Therefore, if the population is 'female students taking a research methods course in social sciences at your university in the current semester', then you need to have *only* 'female students taking a research methods course in social sciences at your university in the current semester' in your sample.
- A **sample** is a section or part of a population that the researcher is studying. There is no perfect sample size. In large and diverse settings, one may need to draw a large sample, while in small homogeneous groups, even a smaller sample may be fine. The sample quality is also determined by how many variables or their values a researcher is interested in studying. For example, it is easy to draw a sample of students in my research methods course, but if I am also interested in the variables of race and sex, the sample would require more planning and effort.
- The second step is to examine if there is a sampling frame. The **sampling frame** refers to the list of all entities in the population. If the 'criminal justice students taking the research methods course with me this semester' is the population, then their roster or list of names would be the sampling frame. Here is a simple rule to remember: If you have a sampling frame, then you can use either probability or non-probability method to draw a sample, but if you do not have a sampling frame, you can only use the non-probability method of sampling. Let me keep the mystery for now as this will become clear as we go over different types of probability and non-probability methods of drawing a sample from a population.
- The third step in sample planning is to understand and explore population diversity. It is critical to select a sampling procedure that would best represent it.
  - This does not mean that you have to study every diverse element in the population or get everyone's opinion on every topic. However, if you are going to generalize the findings to the whole of a population that happens to be quite diverse, then you need to know what groups may be overrepresented and underrepresented. That is when you will need to ensure that the sample represents the diverse population or

the variables of interest. For example, if I live in a city that has four different ethnic groups and I say that my findings apply to the city and ethnicity is a variable of interest in my study, then I must a) know the diversity by ethnic groups, and b) include members of all ethnic groups in my sample.

At times, it is easy to miss smaller groups, and therefore, confuse *majority opinion* with *public opinion*. It is also possible that though there are four different ethnic groups in my city, I am interested in studying the opinions of one ethnic group only. In that case, I need to define the population not as 'city' but as only that ethnic group in the city. That is why a clear and specific definition of the population is an important starting point.

Here is another scenario to consider. You may be working as a police officer or a social worker in a diverse setting and proactively trying to identify at-risk populations for domestic violence. When you look at the existing data, you may see that some communities or subgroups have a higher incidence of domestic violence than others. It right away tells you what groups to focus on. However, you may also be interested in knowing more about the subgroups that have lower incidence – is there genuinely low domestic violence or is it not reported due to various familial, religious, cultural, or economic factors? Therefore, while conducting research, it is important to consider what may not be obvious or convenient; build on the existing information, but also look to explore further and create new knowledge.

The fourth step is to evaluate the **generalizability** of your sample. That is, even before you collect data, you should be able to assess whether your study would have high or low generalizability. This may be further affected by low response rate, partial sample, length of the study, research method, and so on. Based on the research question, population, nature of the setting, and potential access to respondents, you can have a reasonable idea of whether your sample would adequately represent the population or not. It again goes back to step one – what population you are studying. For example, if you were to collect data from the full-time faculty at a university or all the counselors working with schools in the city, it is possible to know the size of the population, have a sampling frame, know how diverse it is in terms of sex, race, or any other variable of interest, and draw a subsequent sample. However, if you were to collect data from drug dealers in the city, it is not like there is a list of how many of them exist in the city, where they are located, and so on. Without the sampling frame, and without knowing the size and type of the population, you cannot claim generalizability.

In one of my research projects, I collected data from the people involved in informal banking systems or those involved in a parallel or informal economy. The sample had no generalizability as I collected information from whomsoever I could find and was willing to talk to me.

It is a reality in many conflict settings as well where researchers may be trying to collect data from victims of civil war, traffickers, informal and illegal economies, and so on. It is also true for much simpler topics where the researcher may want to collect data about the new traffic lights from pedestrians crossing a busy intersection between 1:00 pm and 2:00 pm on a particular day. It is valuable information, but the sample does not represent the population. And that is okay! What is not okay is when a researcher tries to make their study more than what it is. If the sample does not represent the population, but we claim that it does – that is not okay – it will result in everything from stereotypes to bad policies. Therefore, understand the population, the limitations of accessing the setting, and the sample generalizability.

Remember, it is easier to access certain populations than others. For example, employees at the local Department of Motor Vehicles, adjunct faculty in the sociology department, shoppers at a mall near you, and so on are easy to locate and add to a sample. However, certain populations such as victims of abuse, drug dealers, online bullies, and so on are more difficult to find. Similarly, for some research questions, you will have a higher response rate and more reliable data as compared to others. Asking respondents in the sample about their favorite store to shop at would get a higher response rate as compared to asking respondents if they shoplift! The focus of the study and research question, therefore, would also impact the sample and research method. All these factors impact the sample quality and generalizability. Remember, many researchers do not try to establish **cross-population generalizability** as there is always sampling error even in sampling generalizability. It is more challenging to generalize findings to a population from which you did not even take a direct sample.

Studies that have weak or no generalizability also offer valuable insights. Do not get bogged down by it, but it is important to recognize the limitations of the sample ahead of time to avoid force-fitting conclusions or overgeneralizing the findings. *Ceteris paribus*, non-probability methods have lower or no generalizability, but in certain populations, these are the only methods that one can use to get a sample.

The fifth step is to consider a **census**, that is, instead of taking a sample, consider if you can include everyone in the population in your study. Generally, this is not possible, but if you can conduct a census, then you do not have to bother about sampling error or generalizability. However, as explained earlier in the chapter, due to the limited resources, that is, time, money, and people (research personnel), most researchers and professionals cannot conduct a census.

Though there are exceptions, a larger sample would usually have a smaller sampling error. However, as noted earlier, in relatively homogenous groups, even a smaller sample may be fine.

> **Helpful Hint:** To use this material in the best way possible, as you read about sampling methods, keep your proposed research topic in mind. This will help you to understand which sampling method would be most suitable for your research proposal, and why. For example, if there is a sampling frame for the population in your study, you can certainly select a probability method. You will also need to remember if you need specific groups or subgroups in your sample, and therefore, select a method accordingly. It will help you to understand the usefulness of each sampling method in relation to your research topic.

Probability and Non-Probability Methods

Before collecting data, it is important to decide what the best sampling method is in relation to the setting and the population, and one's access to it. The two broad categories are probability sampling methods and non-probability sampling methods. Though their meaning and purpose will become clearer when we discuss the types of sampling methods, for starters, probability methods allow the researcher to ensure that every element or respondent in the population has an equal and unbiased chance of getting selected in the sample. These methods are generally preferred and, if taken properly, they can represent the entire population (Champion, 1993; Senese, 1997). Generally speaking, it is easy to do so if there is a sampling frame. Contrary to this, in non-probability methods, the researcher cannot ensure the same. For example, when I was collecting data from brokers involved in informal banking systems, it was not like I could get a list of all the brokers. As pointed out earlier, without knowing the various elements of the population or having the sampling frame, the sample that I got was whomever I could find and whoever was willing to talk to me. Therefore, I relied on a non-probability method of taking a sample as there was no sampling frame.

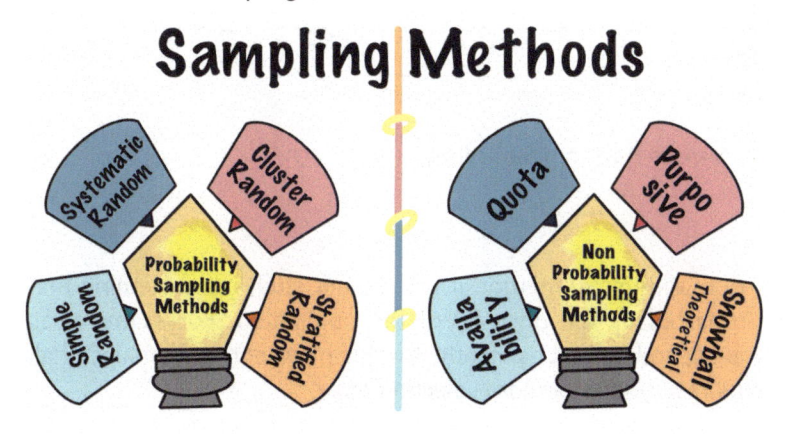

Figure 5.6 Sampling Methods

Probability Sampling Methods

In this section, I will explain four types of probability sampling methods: simple random, systematic random, cluster, and stratified random. In all these methods, each respondent or element should be selected into the sample based on equal and unbiased chance. Chance does not mean haphazard. It means that the researcher has to ensure that the selection is based on chance and chance alone.

Simple random sampling: The preconditions for choosing this sampling method are a clearly defined population and a sampling frame, that is, the list of everyone in the population from which you plan to take a sample. For example, if I want to take a sample of ten students in my research methods class, I already have a sampling frame (roster) for that population (students in my research methods class). I could put everyone's names in a hat and randomly pick ten names. If the population is large, I can use the Random Digit Dialing system to select a random sample.

Figure 5.7 Simple Random Sampling

It is an easy and useful method if you are *not* studying something that could be impacted by the diversity of the population. For example, as everything is dependent on chance, the sample may contain all males or all females, thus resulting in random **selection error**.

RANDOM SELECTION ERROR

Figure 5.8 Random Selection Error

However, as long as sex (or any other variable) is not important to the study, this sampling method should be fine. It also means that if you are interested in having certain variables (sex, race) or values of a variable (male, female; White, African-American, and so on) represented in your sample, you should not use this method. Similarly, if you had a bag of different brands of tennis balls and randomly picked five, it is possible to get the same brand. As long as the brand is not relevant to your study, you can use this method as it is simple and easy and adequate for your study. In short, know what you are looking for in relation to your research study, and then select the method accordingly.

Systematic random sampling: Just as in simple random sampling, the preconditions for choosing this sampling method are a clearly defined population and a sampling frame. In the sampling frame, the first element is selected randomly, and then every *n*th element is selected until you get the desired sample size. The *n*th element is selected based on a **sampling interval**. To calculate the sampling interval, divide the sampling frame by sample size. For example, if there are 3,200 full-time students in my school and I want a sample of 64, by dividing the sampling frame (3,200) by the sample size (64), I get a sampling interval of 50. To draw a sample, I will select the first respondent randomly and then every 50th respondent to get the eventual sample of 64.

Compared to the simple random sample, this ensures getting a sample from a cross-section of the population, but it may still have the problem of **periodicity** or recurrence. That is, every 50th respondent that I selected in the sample may be male. Again, if there are certain variables or values of a variable that must be included in the sample, this may not be the best method, or at least one must be aware of potential over- and underrepresentation. Essentially, just be mindful of the errors and limitations of each sampling method and guard against them.

Remember, these tools or methods are only as intelligent as the person using them! So, pay attention and be mindful of what you are doing and why – just as when you follow the GPS for driving directions, you also watch out for pedestrians, dogs, deer, or potential errors in the directions.

Figure 5.9 GPS

Cluster sampling: This is most useful when dealing with a very large population across a large geographical area, for example, the population of the United states (US). Yes, technically, you may get a sampling frame, but it is going to be very, very tedious. Instead of wasting time on creating a sampling frame for such a large population, it is easier to identify clusters, groups, or blocks such as regions. Let us say that you divide the US population into four regions; each region would include a list of states in that region. Next, you can draw two states from each region. To maintain randomness or equal chance, remember to use a simple random method (if the lists are longer, use the systematic random sampling method). You will keep identifying clusters or groups and drawing the next set until you reach a sample. For example, if you want to collect data from criminology majors in 4-year degree programs across the US, it is challenging to get a list of all students in such programs from across the country. However, once you have narrowed down the US population to the cluster of academic institutions that offer '4-year degree programs in criminology,' you can easily draw the final list of institutions, create sampling frame/s of actual students in the criminology programs in those institutions, and take a sample that represents the US population.

Cluster sampling is a multi-stage sampling method. The two crucial things to remember are a) finding clusters or blocks, and b) ensuring randomness or equal and unbiased chance at every stage.

Stratified random sampling: Just as in the previously explained methods, in stratified random sampling the preconditions are a clearly defined population and a sampling frame. This is the best method to use while studying a diverse population and for adequately representing that diversity in the sample. It requires dividing the population into multiple strata or sampling frames as per the characteristics of interest and then drawing the eventual sample while taking respondents from each separate sampling frame. Once again, to ensure randomness or equal chance within each stratum, remember to use the simple random or systematic random sampling method to select respondents from each stratum or sampling frame. For example, if there is a population of 10,000 people and I want to take a sample of 100 people, including 50 men and 50 women, the simple and systematic random sampling methods could result in the over- and under-representation of men or women. To ensure that I get 50 of each in my sample, I will create two separate sampling frames – one will contain the list of all men and the other will contain the list of all women. I will then randomly select 50 respondents from each list. I can do this for multiple variables as well. For instance, if I also want to ensure certain racial groups in the sample, I can create strata not just by sex but also by race – White men, African-American women, and so on – and then draw the sample. This is an extremely useful sampling method if one is drawing a sample from a diverse population and is interested in getting different elements represented in the sample.

Stratified Random Sampling

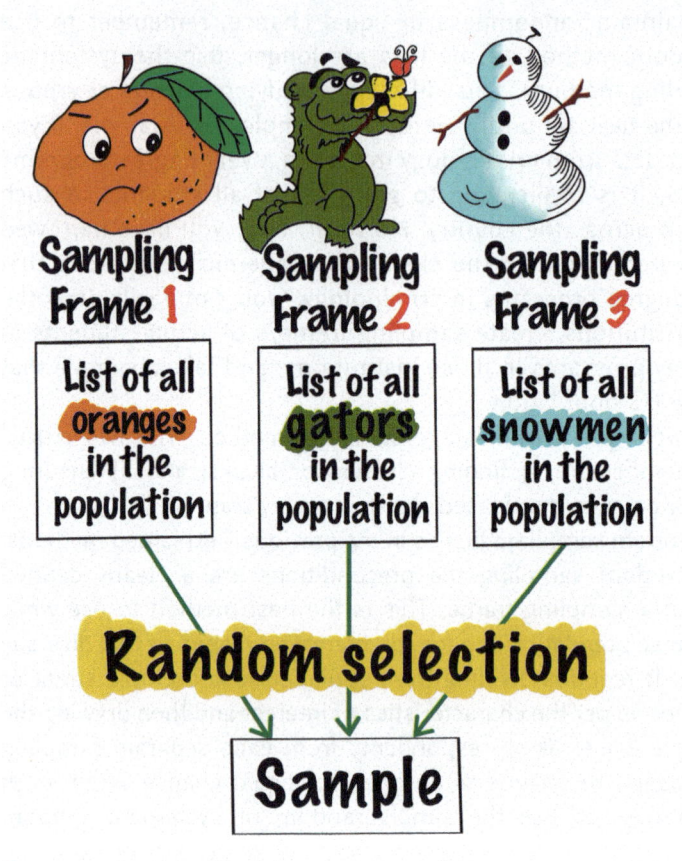

Figure 5.10 Stratified Random Sampling

Similarly, let us say in a population of 1,000 people, 60 percent are teachers, 15 percent are doctors, 5 percent are engineers, and 20 percent are plumbers. While taking a sample of 100 and only focusing on the occupation for now, if the sample consists of 60 teachers, 15 doctors, 5 engineers, and 20 plumbers – the same as their proportion in the population – there is an issue of over- and under-representation. To give equal representation to smaller or underrepresented groups, and to counter the redundancy of overrepresented groups, it may be better to give equal proportion to each group irrespective of their proportion in the population – 25 each. No matter what, remember that there will always be criticism and limitations. For example, in the first instance, one large group (teachers) will dominate the sample and the eventual data, while in the second scenario, the three smaller groups may collectively dominate the views. If you are studying a topic where occupation may affect people's opinions, you need to identify these gaps and limitations. Many researchers would draw multiple samples and study them to minimize possible errors.

As explained in Chapter 1, being a social scientist, criminal justice professional, social worker, lawmaker, journalist, and so on, you must guard against the everyday errors in reasoning at every step of the research (primary and secondary), as they crop up quite often, and it is important to remain aware of these issues even when taking a sample.

Non-probability Sampling Methods

This section will explain five types of non-probability sampling methods: availability or convenience, quota, judgment or purposive, snowball, and theoretical. These methods are used when there is no sampling frame or the researcher does not want to use a sampling frame.

Figure 5.11 Non-probability Sampling Methods

In the **availability or convenience** method, as the name suggests, respondents are selected based on their availability and willingness to participate in the study. It is a useful method to get a general sample where you are not interested in any particular variables. It may be as simple as standing in a parking lot to ask people about parking issues and stop collecting data as soon as you reach the desired sample size. It may take 2 hours or it may take 2 days!

Talking of time, in some instances, this may set the sample size. For example, during a 1-hour TV show, you may see media personnel standing outside a TV studio, stopping and asking people their opinions about the weather, filing tax returns, holiday shopping, a gator spotted at the mall, and so on. Whatever sample they get during that one hour, that is it. As you can probably tell, this will not be a representative sample and, therefore, if you use this method, the report should indicate the lack of generalizability. Far too many people – lawmakers and academics included – increasingly form opinions based on what is trending on social media, a documentary that they watched, or a news show, while ignoring the inadequacy of such a sample or larger population. It is one thing to have uninformed opinions, but it is dangerous to make policies based on the same.

Availability Sampling

Figure 5.12 Availability Sampling

It does not mean that this sampling method is useless. Consider the population of victims in an active conflict zone; there is no sampling frame, you do not have unlimited time, and yet you want to get information. So, you talk to whomever you can safely locate and get the information. In such settings, you often cannot set a sample size either. That means, while presenting data or writing a report, you must know the limitations of your study and not overgeneralize the findings to the whole setting, culture, and so on. Feel free to consider other scenarios where availability may be a useful sampling method.

If you need to ensure that certain variables or values of a variable must be included in the sample, but you do not have a sampling frame or do not want to use one, you can use the **quota sampling method**. Here you would set up quotas within your sample – that is, in the sample, there must be at least 5 males and 5 females, or at least 5 Asian students, or at least 5 Asian faculty, and so on. This resembles availability sampling as you may simply stop and ask people to participate in your study, but the difference is that you must remain mindful of the quota.

For example, one of my students collected data about parking woes on campus and used this method to draw a sample. He was able to set quotas for faculty and staff, and another quota for students divided into commuters and residents. He spent about 2 hours each on 2 different days and got the sample that he was looking for. As you will note, this will also have little to no generalizability as it does not take into consideration the whole population and there is no equal chance given to all the elements in the population – whoever is available and is willing to talk before you reach the quota ends up in the sample.

Purposive or judgment sampling is used when the researcher can identify the people in the population who would have the relevant information about the topic of study and purposively selects them in the sample. Their position in the population may give them access to the information that the researcher is looking for. In terms of preconditions for using this method, the researcher would need to know whom to contact for specific information and must have access to them. For example, you may not need to take a sample of all faculty to study their concerns; you can just talk to faculty union leaders. Similarly, you may not need or get access to criminally insane patients, but you can collect data from mental health professionals and social workers working with them.

Purposive Sampling

Figure 5.13 Purposive Sampling

It is possible to have sampling frames in these examples, but either you choose to not use them or you realize that this approach will not be as useful due to the sensitive nature of the topic, saves you time, and so on, and thus, it is best to use purposive sampling.

In some settings, the **snowball sampling** method may be the most effective technique (Atkinson and Flint, 2001). In this approach, the researcher identifies one or two members of the population who would have information about the topic of study. That respondent will then refer the researcher to other potential respondents, and so on. There may be some dead ends, but generally, it makes life a bit easier, as the researcher is approaching the subjects with someone's reference, thus making it a bit less difficult to gain trust.

Figure 5.14 Snowball Sampling

In this method, the sample is 'constructed' over time. This is also called **respondent-driven sampling**. You may also have to identify gatekeepers and see if they can point you in the right direction to get started. For example, when I collected data from brokers involved in the informal banking systems, there was no sampling frame or list of all such brokers. I approached a special investigator at the Central Bureau of Investigations in Delhi, India. He shared extensive information and case files, and guided me to the general locations where I could find informal bankers – **Hawala** brokers

(Sharma, 2008). It was difficult to find the first respondent, but once I did that, it was relatively easy to build the rest of the sample. However, it was difficult to set a sample size as there were a few dead ends – respondents that I could not locate or who were not willing to talk to me. The only thing that I could control was the time spent in the field and the sample constructed during that time. Depending on the topic and the setting, sometimes researchers may be able to get a large sample, while at times, it may not yield the desired results. This could happen due to non-response about sensitive topics as well as the unwillingness of the gatekeepers to share information about respondents.

If you plan to use snowball sampling in your study, if possible, collect the data until it reaches the **saturation point** (this would also depend on the research method that you have selected). As you do not have a sampling frame, you do not know the length and breadth of the population or types of respondents, therefore, you would want to get some repetitive information. This helps identify commonalities and patterns and also somewhat verifies information given by others. However, if you stop getting any new information, it means that the sample has reached its saturation point. This method has been used relatively successfully for many sensitive settings and topics (Biernacki and Waldorf, 1981) as well including in research on illegal drug users (Avico, Kaplan, Korczak, and Van Meter, 1988).

Lastly, in **theoretical sampling**, one follows the same steps as snowball sampling except that the researcher modifies sample traits as they find new information. For example, while collecting data from informal bankers, when I came across a female banker if I were using theoretical sampling, I would then actively look for more females involved in the informal banking system. It helps to get a more diverse sample that is modified based on the information that one encounters in the field. For the record, in my study, I was using snowball sampling method and did not need to modify the sample traits.

Remember, there is never 100 percent generalizability. No matter how careful you are, there will always be some **sampling error**. Since the sample will never fully and precisely represent the population, there will be errors, and we can only estimate the degree of generalizability and try to keep the errors at the minimum possible. This has to be kept in mind while analyzing data and writing reports. That is, one may have drawn the best possible sample, but if there is a low response rate across the sample or subset of a sample (it is possible to get a higher response from one group and lower from another) or if the researcher only met male drug offenders (or any other variable), it would impact the overall generalizability. Research tools and techniques aid in all aspects of studying complex phenomena, but they do not replace the researcher's analytical skills and critical thinking. Therefore, be aware of what you are studying, why, and how.

In summation, to get a good sample, always define the population. There must be clarity of rationale for using a particular sampling method. Understand generalizability issues ahead of time, as these are directly related to the representativeness of the sample, and be mindful of the issue of non-response and skewed response.

Generally, no research is good forever as human social sensibilities evolve and there are demographic, legal, and cultural changes. Therefore, it is important to keep re-testing and reevaluating old policies and ideas to see if they are still valid and also develop new thinking, policies, and programs. It is always extremely useful to do research before implementing any policies, laws, or programs. Think of it like this: If your understanding of policing or any aspect of the criminal justice system and American society is based on your understanding of the material in the 1970s or 1980s, and you have not conducted any research or even educated yourself on current issues and current research studies, or if you formulate opinions about people, cultures, institutions, and systems based on the day's trend on social media, you would not do a good job of teaching that material, making effective policies, or training future practitioners, scholars, and leaders.

As noted earlier, in any study, there can also be the problem of non-response, which also results in sampling error. Some of the respondents or elements may be consistently missed in the sample.

Figure 5.15 I Never Get Picked in Any Sample!

Despite having the best possible sample, you may have people who, for example, in an experiment, may drop out of it, refuse to complete a survey, and so on. You may run into similar issues while using qualitative methods as well. From any population, it is possible to draw many samples using different permutations and combinations, and each sample may show some differences in the findings. Therefore, be humble about gaining knowledge. A scholar has an unending hunger for learning and knowledge, and also the core humility of knowing that the learning can never be complete, or that one can never learn everything at all times. As a social scientist, when dealing with human life and experience, you must keep an open mind to always learn more, and recognize that learning is not automatic – it requires consistent effort.

Key Terms

- Availability or convenience sampling
- Census
- Cluster sampling
- Cross-population generalizability
- Generalizability
- Hawala brokers
- Non-probability sampling
- Overgeneralization
- Periodicity
- Population
- Probability sampling
- Purposive or judgment sampling
- Quota sampling
- Random Selection Error
- Sample
- Sampling error
- Sampling frame
- Sampling interval
- Saturation point
- Simple random sampling
- Snowball sampling
- Stratified random sampling
- Systematic random sampling
- Theoretical sampling

Class Activity

Using various sampling methods, the instructor can take multiple samples of students in the classroom and see the difference in their composition. To make it more fun, select a topic on which students can give opinions. Let us say that you want to get their opinion on their favorite professor (don't take the findings personally!) or something less controversial. Set aside different boxes or small containers for each sample. Ask each sample to put their opinions on a piece of paper and drop them in the box for their sample type. In the end, study the difference of opinions (data) based on different types of samples drawn from the same population.

If your students have a sweet tooth, try this M&M sampling method: https://www.apa.org/ed/precollege/topss/lessons/tasty-sampler.pdf

Works Cited

Atkinson, R., and J. Flint. 2001. *Accessing Hidden and Hard-to-Reach Populations: Snowball Research Strategies* (Social Research Update No. 33). Guildford: Department of Sociology, University of Surrey.

Avico, U., C. Kaplan, D. Korczak, and K. Van Meter. 1988. *Cocaine Epidemiology in Three European Community Cities: A Pilot Study Using a Snowball Sampling Methodology*. Brussels: European Communities Health Directorate.

Biernacki, P., and D. Waldorf. 1981. "Snowball Sampling: Problems and Techniques of Chain Referral Sampling." *Sociological Methods & Research*, Vol.10, pp. 141–163.

Champion, D. J. 1993. *Research Methods for Criminal Justice and Criminology*. Englewood Cliff, NJ: Regents/Prentice Hall.

Hagan, F. E. 2012. *Essentials of Research Methods in Criminal Justice and Criminology*. 3rd ed. Upper Saddle River, NJ: Pearson.

Philliber, S. G., M. R. Schwab, and S. G. Sloss.1980. *Social Research: Guides to a Decision-Making Process*. Itasca, IL: F.E. Peacock.

Senese, J. D. 1997. *Applied Research Methods in Criminal Justice*. Chicago, IL: Nelson-Hall.

Sharma, D. 2008. "Research Ethics and Sensitive Behaviors: Underground Economy." In Donna M. Mertens and Pauline Ginsberg (eds.), *Handbook of Social Research Ethics*. Thousand Oaks, CA: Sage.

chapter 6

Collecting Primary Data
Survey Research Methods

This chapter explains the quantitative research method of designing and using surveys. It explains different types of survey research methods, the preconditions or settings where they can be used, and the strengths and limitations of each type of survey. It also explains the key considerations while developing survey questions. The chapter explains survey research methods with reference to validity, generalizability, and ethics.

After this chapter, students will be able to understand and explain:

- Uses of survey research
- Types of survey research
- Validity and generalizability in survey research
- Ethical considerations in survey research

Introduction

We have data all around us – newspapers, social media, blogs, posters, films, and so on. Then there are books, journal articles, agency reports, conference papers, databases, and so on. This is information that others have collected, collated, and shared. Though many researchers use the existing data – secondary data – to examine various research questions, you can also collect data yourself after getting all the required approvals to do so by the Institutional Review Board or Ethics Committee (IRB/EC).

DOI: 10.4324/9781003314738-7

You were briefly introduced to quantitative and qualitative methods in Chapter 2. Surveys and experiments are quantitative research methods, and this chapter explains the uses and types of survey methods and issues of validity, generalizability, and ethics while using one or the other type of survey. Most of you probably have been part of survey research. For example, you may get an email or text for feedback after interacting with customer service. Many of you may have completed student opinion surveys or teaching evaluations at the end of the semester. Some of you may have answered a few questions by phone or email. Some of the surveys may have involved several questions, while some may have consisted of only one question. Surveys are extremely flexible and can be used for a wide variety of topics. They represent probably the most commonly used research method in criminal justice, sociology, marketing, political science, media studies, retail, restaurants, and so on. You will not select a particular research method because it sounds fun or easy, but only if it best suits your research question and sample. In Chapter 1, we discussed measurement validity – that is, is the method or tool of data collection best suited for the study, and does it measure what it is designed or expected to measure? You can decide if it is the most suitable method based on the nature of the study as well as access to and location of the sample. Before moving on, let's have a look at a few types of surveys.

National Crime Victimization Survey

Survey research can be used to study a wide range of topics across social sciences. Students of criminology in the United States would be most familiar with the National Crime Victimization Survey (NCVS), which currently includes a sample of about 150,000 households (interviewed). This is a longitudinal survey in which data is collected every 6 months for 3 years from each member of the household 12 years and older. The survey focuses on "nonfatal personal crimes (i.e., rape or sexual assault, robbery, aggravated and simple assault, and personal larceny) and household property crimes (i.e., burglary/trespassing, motor vehicle theft, and other types of theft) both reported and not reported to the police" ("National Crime Victimization"). Some of the key features of this survey are to find out "whether the crime was reported to police, reasons the crime was or was not reported, and victim experiences with the criminal justice system" ("National Crime Victimization").

> National Crime Victimization Survey: https://bjs.ojp.gov/data-collection/ncvs
>
> Sample size and response rates: https://bjs.ojp.gov/content/pub/sheets/samplesize.xls

BOX 6.1 – National Crime Victimization Survey (NCVS) Methodology

"The Bureau of Justice Statistics' National Crime Victimization Survey (NCVS) is an annual data collection carried out by the U.S. Census Bureau. The NCVS is a self-reported survey that is administered annually from January 1 to December 31. Annual NCVS estimates are based on the number and characteristics of crimes respondents experienced during the prior 6 months, not including the month in which they were interviewed. Therefore, the 2021 survey covers crimes experienced from July 1, 2020 to November 30, 2021, and March 15, 2021 is the middle of the reference period. Crimes are classified by the year of the survey and not by the year of the crime.

Survey respondents provide information about themselves (e.g., age, sex, race and Hispanic origin, marital status, education level, and income) and whether they experienced a victimization. The NCVS collects information for each victimization incident about the offender (e.g., age, race and Hispanic origin, sex, and victim-offender relationship), characteristics of the crime (e.g., time and place of occurrence, use of weapons, nature of injury, and economic consequences), whether the crime was reported to police, reasons the crime was or was not reported, and victim experiences with the criminal justice system.

The NCVS is administered to persons age 12 or older from a nationally representative sample of households in the United States. The NCVS defines a household as a group of persons who all reside at a sampled address. Persons are considered household members when the sampled address is their usual place of residence at the time of the interview and when they have no usual place of residence elsewhere. Once selected, households remain in the sample for 3½ years, and eligible persons in these households are interviewed every 6 months, either in person or over the phone, for a total of seven interviews.

First interviews are typically conducted in person with subsequent interviews conducted either in person or by phone. New households rotate into the sample on an ongoing basis to replace outgoing households that have been in the sample for the 3½-year period. The sample includes persons living in group quarters (e.g., dormitories, rooming houses, and religious group dwellings) and excludes persons living on military bases and in institutional settings (e.g., correctional or hospital facilities) and persons who are homeless" ("National Crime Victimization," BJS).

Feel free to explore the basic screen questionnaire and the NCVS survey in class and engage in a discussion about it with your professor and classmates.

> NCVS Basic Screen Questionnaire: https://bjs.ojp.gov/content/pub/pdf/ncvs22_bsq.pdf
> NCVS Crime Incident Report Survey: https://bjs.ojp.gov/content/pub/pdf/ncvs22_cir.pdf

Monitoring The Future Survey

Another commonly known survey in the United States is the Monitoring the Future (MTF) survey. "Since 1975 the MTF survey has measured drug and alcohol use and related attitudes among adolescent students nationwide. A nationally representative sample of survey participants report their drug use behaviors across three time periods: lifetime, past year, and past month" ("Monitoring the Future").

Monitoring the Future: https://nida.nih.gov/research-topics/trends-statistics/monitoring-future

Surveys can be used to get a snapshot of the population, study trends, causes, attitudes, and so on. These are helpful tools for policymakers, criminologists, sociologists, social workers, economists, and criminal justice practitioners alike. They can contain **open-ended questions**, **closed-ended questions**, or both. In an open-ended question, the respondents can give any response, while in a closed-ended question, the respondent is required to pick a response from the options listed by the researcher. This can be completed in person (individual or group), online, over the phone, and so on. The researcher decides on the type of survey based on the research question and the sample. In survey research, a **questionnaire** refers to the survey that the respondents complete themselves, while a **schedule** or interview schedule refers to the survey that the researcher completes for the respondent by asking questions. While it may take more time to complete a questionnaire, it gives more privacy to the respondent to answer or skip any questions. The schedule assists in clarifying any confusion about an item on the question but also creates potential ethical dilemmas and **reactive effect** – change caused by the researcher's presence. This chapter will explain the most commonly used types of surveys, issues to consider while developing survey questions, and the topics of ethics and generalizability for each type of survey.

Types of Surveys

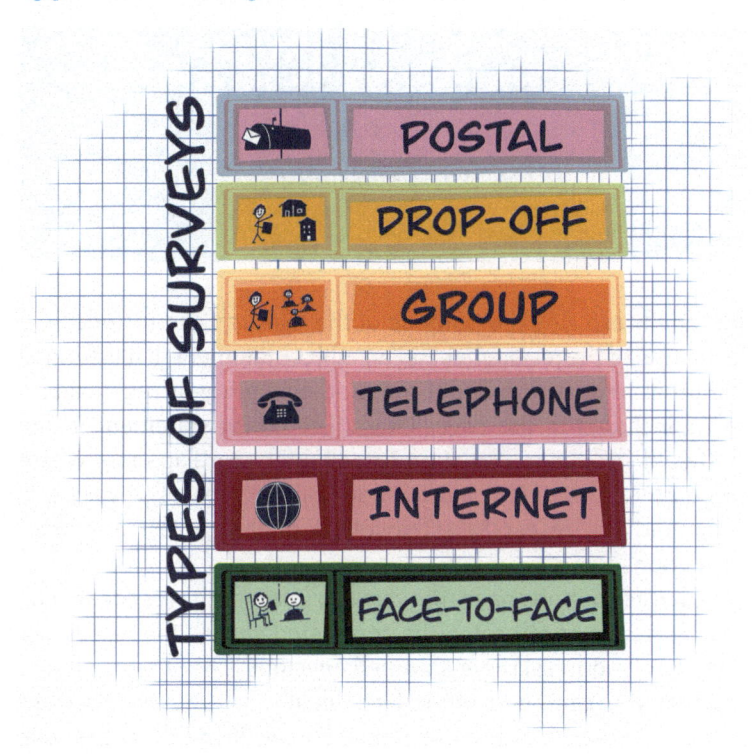

Figure 6.1 Types of Surveys

> **Helpful Hint:** For your research proposal, if you have settled on the survey research method, it can be helpful to read about different types of surveys while keeping your research topic and setting in mind. This will help you to understand the usefulness of each survey method in relation to your research topic. Doing so will help you to achieve measurement validity.

Postal surveys: This type of survey is delivered to the targeted sample by post. The respondent is requested to complete the survey by a set date and mail it back.

> **Issues to consider:** Postal surveys are particularly useful when the sample is spread over a larger geographical location and it is not easy to contact people in person or by phone. The researcher must set aside enough time for mailing surveys, sending reminders, and receiving the completed surveys. Postal surveys allow for very large samples and can

> be sent to thousands of people, but they tend to have a lower response rate. Compared to some of the other research methods, it is relatively less strenuous for the respondent to use postal surveys as they are free to not complete it, not mail it back, or skip any questions that they do not want to answer. The ease of *not* participating may also lower the response rate. To increase the response rate, include a cover letter and, if possible, incentives.

A **cover letter** briefly explains the purpose of the research and includes the contact information of the researcher and an ethics statement. If it is funded research, then that information about the funding agency or organization should also be included in the cover letter. The **ethics statement** in the cover letter should include information on voluntary participation, where and how the data is to be kept and for how long, issues of privacy and confidentiality, and the researcher(s) involved in the project and their contact information.

Incentives such as coupons or a raffle can also increase the response rate. To minimize the hassle of returning the completed survey, the researcher should include a self-addressed pre-stamped envelope. The surveys should be coded so that you can send reminders. Ideally, a reminder postcard should be sent 2–3 weeks after the initial mail survey. If you do not receive a completed survey even after a month or so and want to follow up, then include a new copy of the survey as the respondent most likely has not kept the initial mailed survey.

The response rate would vary by time, topic, and sample, but when done right, many postal surveys can have upward of a 70 percent response rate. A larger response rate improves **generalizability**.

Some of the surveys returned to the researcher may be incomplete. If a certain question is unanswered on several surveys, the researcher may need to evaluate it in terms of the language of the question, limited response options if it is a closed-ended question, lack of clarity, factors associated with social desirability, and so on. The researcher can make note of these issues for future researchers as well, and use the category of non-response in the data analysis for that question or item.

Door-to-door or drop-off surveys: These surveys are delivered to the respondents at the target location. The respondent can either complete the survey while the researcher waits, or the researcher can ask questions and note down answers for the respondents. The completed survey can also be collected in a matter of a few hours or a day or so. This approach combines the advantages of postal and group surveys. It has the convenience and privacy of a postal survey (if the respondent fills it in) but removes the impersonal nature by placing the respondent and researcher face-to-face which, depending on the topic, may improve the response rate or, to the contrary, can present ethical dilemmas.

> **Issues to consider:** Though usually door-to-door surveys are used in smaller geographic locations, they can also be used to collect data from isolated populations who may not participate or be reachable through other methods of post, phone, and email. It is best to either complete the survey right away or collect the completed survey in a relatively short amount of time. The cover letter and consent form should also be included. If the researcher does not want to include a separate consent form, an ethics statement addressing consent can also be included in the cover letter. The researcher can answer any queries about the research project and ethics in person. The response rate for door-to-door surveys is generally quite high, however, the sample size may not be as large as phone or postal surveys.

The researcher must be aware of the potential for coercion in door-to-door surveys as the respondent may feel compelled to answer questions due to the researcher's presence. The respondent may also feel uneasy about any personal questions. The ethics statement should explain that the respondent can quit participating at any time without explanation or skip any questions. Some of these issues can be addressed by requesting the respondent to complete the survey on their own rather than the researcher asking questions.

In one of my undergraduate research methods courses, my students and I worked with city officials in Rome, New York. We were asked to evaluate the **Weed and Seed** program. After getting the research proposal approved by the Institutional Review Board, we collected data using door-to-door surveys and focus groups. For door-to-door surveys, I visited the area with a local police officer, who advised me to not knock on certain doors due to various reasons such as parole, probation, mental health, and so on. The officer also helped to narrow down the neighborhoods and streets that were directly targeted by the Weed and Seed program. It was also helpful to know the linguistic diversity of the neighborhood to consider whether we needed surveys in different languages or not.

Group surveys: A group survey is completed by respondents assembled in a group. The response rate is usually very high in group surveys as the sample is in a controlled setting.

Issues to consider: Group dynamics and power hierarchy are the main considerations in group surveys. A respondent may feel compelled to complete a survey due to the presence of others in the group setting or the presence of the researcher, thus compromising voluntary participation. Additionally, the researcher must recognize the power equations in a setting. For example, it is not the best tactic to ask employees to complete a survey about work conditions in the presence of the employer. Similarly, asking a prison guard to distribute surveys to the prison population would be a clear violation of ethics. The researcher must consider using neutral parties to distribute and collect surveys. The IRB may reject a research proposal if there is a conflict of interest or power dynamics that may cause coercion.

In the United States, most colleges and universities use teaching evaluation or student opinion surveys to collect feedback about the course and the instructor. The instructor designates a student from the class to distribute, collect, and deliver the completed surveys to the division or department office secretary or any third-party location. The instructor receives the completed survey the following semester.

Telephone surveys: Researchers collect data over the phone and record the respondents' answers. This is a very commonly used method, particularly in settings where a vast majority of households have access to telephones (landline or mobile). It is less expensive than mail and even door-to-door surveys while allowing for large sample sizes. It poses a minimum risk to the researcher.

Issues to consider: Telephone surveys are convenient, save time, and help researchers to gather data from a large sample. However, some populations would be excluded from this approach, such as homeless people. "Studies prior to the pandemic on [the] feasibility of using mobile phones as a means of administering surveys or delivering care found homelessness is associated with lower survey completion and non-reporting" (Thomas et al., 2022). Traditionally, studies have collected data from homeless people using shelters and soup kitchens (Brousse et al., 2001), however, a crisis such as a pandemic presented a new hurdle in providing medical assistance through digital means, and it was challenging to serve certain populations through such means.

According to the United States Health Department, by May 2017, more than 90 percent of all households in the United States had telephones: 50.8 percent wireless only, 39.8 percent wireless and landline, 6.5 percent landline only, and 3.2 percent were phone-free. This makes it relatively easy to reach large sections of the population by phone. Random digit dialing can be used to select and dial numbers. It "is a method of probability sampling that provides a sample of households, families, or persons through a random selection of their telephone numbers" (Wolter, Chowdhury, and Kelly, 2009).

While using telephone surveys, the researcher needs to take into account that due to a high incidence of telemarketing, robocalls, and spam calls, many phone users are unlikely to answer unknown phone numbers or will block them. Training is also critical in picking a time that is convenient for the respondent. For example, the response rate would be affected if people are in their offices, busy with household work, traveling, driving, and so on. Just as in a cover letter, it is best to introduce oneself, briefly explain the purpose of the study, voluntary participation, and so on in the first phone call, and to ask for the best time for the survey.

Figure 6.2   Phone Surveys

collecting primary data

The initial call would also help the researcher to assess the linguistic needs of the respondent. Politeness and professionalism go a long way in collecting data in any research, and it is equally critical when using a phone survey as it is very easy for respondents to disconnect the phone call. The researcher should also inform the respondent about the approximate time that the survey may take.

As the researcher punches in the responses in a computer program, they can easily see how many respondents they have contacted and how many completed the survey, and even glance at the basic information based on sex, age, location, and so on to assess how the sample is being constructed. Computer programs can also use skip patterns or sequences that would

Skip Pattern

7. Have you read Chapter 6 on survey research methods?
a) Yes
b) No

If <u>yes</u>, continue to the question number 8.
If <u>no</u>, skip to the question number 11.

Without a skip pattern...

8. Which type of survey would you like to use for your research topic?
_____
_____

How would I know? I just answered that I haven't read it yet!

9. Which types of survey methods present most ethical dilemmas?
_____
_____

10. Which types of survey methods have a higher generalizability than door-to-door survey?
_____
_____

11. Do you feel that you had adequate time to prepare for the upcoming exam?
a) Yes
b) No

Figure 6.3 Skip Pattern

help the researcher to skip questions that may not be relevant to some of the respondents. For example, the study may be about job satisfaction, work conditions, commute to the office, and so on. Before getting to these questions, the researcher would ask if the respondent is employed or not. If the response is 'no', then the researcher does not need to ask job-related questions. The skip pattern in the computer would automatically skip these questions and get to the next question relevant to the respondent.

Skip patterns are useful in all types of surveys – computer or phone-based as well as paper and in-person (group and individual). Despite the issue of non-response and blocked calls, phone surveys allow for a large sample size, and thus they increase generalizability.

Text surveys: Mobile phones have also facilitated the use of surveys by text message. These are generally very short surveys that are used for quick feedback. In the United States, pharmacies, doctors, retail stores, phone and Internet providers, postal services, and so on often send a quick text message to the user for immediate feedback on the service provided. The questions are usually very simple and require a response by text message in the form of a rating (such as 1 to 5), or a *yes* or *no* response. This is a quick way to receive feedback from the target sample in a short amount of time.

> **Issues to consider:** In smaller settings, if someone has had a poor experience, let's say, with a medical facility that they are likely to visit again, it creates a dilemma for them over whether to give honest feedback due to health-related vulnerabilities. There is also a concern about a lack of privacy and confidentiality that would impact the response rate. Respondents are less likely to face such dilemmas while giving feedback in larger settings, let's say, about phone service, shopping experience, dining, and so on. Across the board, a better response rate can be achieved through text surveys of the questions that are closed-ended and short.

Internet surveys or email and web surveys: The terms **email surveys** and **web surveys** are often used interchangeably, and that is fine. However, some may differentiate between the two based on whether:

- The survey is delivered as an attached file that the respondents complete and return to the researcher (email survey), or
- The survey is delivered as a link that the respondent clicks on. This opens an online survey in a new window that the respondent completes and submits (web/online survey).

Figure 6.4 You've Got Mail!

> **Issues to Consider:** As many respondents may open emails on their phones, the surveys (email and web) need to be compatible with Android and iOS platforms. If the survey is sent as an attachment, it is best to not do so in the initial email. Due to the increased rates of spam and scams, many users are unlikely to click on unknown emails with attachments. Therefore, it is best to introduce oneself in the initial email by typing information in the main body of the email itself – think of it as a cover letter. It should contain information about the research and funding agency and the contact information of the researcher. It should inform the respondent about the next email that would contain attachments – survey, ethics statement, and consent form. The same can be done for the web surveys as well.

When using any e-surveys (email or web), it is also important to make note of the **digital divide** – inequalities between demographics or regions in access to digital tools of communication and information. Some respondents may not have access to fast Internet at all or may be able to access it only in school, at work, or in a public library. If the attached file is too large or the link to the online survey takes too long to load (heavy on images, font type, or special effects), the respondent may not keep trying to access it.

Despite the issue of non-response, email and web surveys allow for large sample sizes, have a low cost, and pose relatively fewer ethical dilemmas than in-person surveys as the respondents can easily ignore or even block the sender. Internet or computer surveys are also commonly used in public places, driving license offices, and so on, where the respondent can sit and take an online survey in a computerized kiosk. In smaller settings, clearly mentioning that the results would be anonymous and cannot be traced back to individual respondents would increase the response rate.

Face-to-face surveys: These surveys include one-on-one face-to-face interaction between the researcher and the respondent. Multiple researchers may be required to facilitate collecting data from a larger sample. Researchers would need to coordinate efforts to minimize gaps due to the different styles and personalities of researchers.

> **Issues to Consider:** Due to face-to-face interaction, in-person surveys generally yield a high response rate. They also allow the researcher to ask complex questions, answer any questions that the respondent may have, and provide more clarity. Due to face-to-face interaction, the researcher would need to take into account the physical and social circumstances of the interview. The respondent would need to be comfortable in the setting where the survey is being conducted. If the respondent is required to reach a certain location, the researcher would need to arrange travel expenses. If the researcher is meeting respondents in locations of their choice, then travel and time considerations also have to be made. This is a more time-consuming and expensive type of survey, but depending on the topic of research, it may be the best option. For example, while collecting data about victimization, stress, rehabilitation, community corrections, and so on, one may be better off reaching respondents where they feel most secure and comfortable in participating in the study.

In-person surveys are also used to examine attitudes and perceptions about any topic, screen candidates for recruiting, measure the impact of a training course, the usefulness of new employee orientation, and so on. For such topics, one may locate respondents in a group setting, such as an office place, but collect data one-on-one.

With increased connectivity online, face-to-face surveys may also be carried out through a video chat. This would have benefits in terms of the respondent staying in their comfort zone, ease of refusing to participate, and reduced cost, but it would limit the ability of the researcher to observe the respondent's body language.

> **Helpful Hint:** In qualitative methods, we will discuss the research method of intensive interviews. Unlike in-person surveys, intensive interviews are relatively unstructured.

The in-person surveys can be structured, semi-structured, or even unstructured. In the in-person surveys, the researcher knows enough about the research topic and has decided on the types of questions to ask. The in-person surveys allow for more open-ended questions, and though it is not an absolute rule, it is suggested that the researcher avoid using a very long interview schedule. Though the survey research method is preferred to get quantitative data, open-format questions – across types of surveys – can also help to get qualitative data on items that need deeper insight.

These are some of the commonly used surveys and the basic issues to consider while selecting one or the other type of survey. The usefulness of the survey depends on its measurement validity – that is, whether the researcher has selected the best method for the research topic, and whether that method measures what the researcher aims to measure. While designing surveys and analyzing data, it is important to keep in mind the sampling method and sampling size, as both impact generalizability. This does not mean that one cannot or should not use non-probability sampling methods or have smaller samples as they have weak generalizability. It only implies that the researcher needs to be mindful of it and not force-fit conclusions. Though we have discussed the importance of consent forms in surveys, many researchers do not include a separate consent form and may simply include a paragraph at the top of the survey or in the cover letter (if applicable) that informs the respondents about their voluntary participation, confidentiality, and so on. Making a brief but sincere altruistic appeal while using any type of survey can also improve the response rate.

Questions – Format and Considerations

Closed-ended or closed-format questions are also called **forced-choice** or **fixed-choice** questions. These are the questions where the respondent has to select from one of the response options given by the researcher. Such questions can be used when the researcher can reasonably anticipate the possible responses or wants to limit answers to a few preset responses. For example, many factors may motivate a person to climb Mount Everest, however, the researcher may narrow it down to three or four choices. Closed-ended questions produce easily quantifiable data. Here are a few examples of closed-ended questions:

- **Dichotomous** or two-point questions include yes or no.
- **Multiple-choice** questions include numerous response options.
- A **Likert-type scale** question can be used to measure attitudes, beliefs, or opinions. This type of question provides a range of options on a scale indicating responses from one end to the other. For example, a question about the quality of yogurt may contain responses from *extremely agree* to *extremely disagree* while also providing a neutral option. Some researchers may decide to exclude the neutral option as they want the respondent to think about the issue at hand instead of picking the 'middle option'.
- **Semantic scale** questions can also be used to measure attitudes, opinions, and so on. They may seem similar to a Likert-type scale, but the slight difference is that they may not contain a scale that shows a gradual increase or decrease in agreeability or likeability, and so on. Instead, they may only contain contrary response options at the opposing ends while only including the numerical scale between the extreme options. The following example should clarify the difference between the Likert and Semantic scales.

Likert-type Scale

The new yogurt place is amazing.

Strongly Agree	Agree	No opinion	Disagree	Strongly Disagree

Semantic Scale

The new yogurt place is ...

1	2	3	4	5
Terrible				Great

- The Likert-type scale and semantic scale are also used in Index questions.

Open-ended or **open-format questions** do not contain any predefined answers or response options, and the respondent can give their own answers. Using this approach also means that the answers could vary from a few words to a paragraph, depending on how much space the researcher has provided for the answer. These questions produce qualitative data. They are very useful in providing the respondent's perspective. Instead of giving the response options, the researcher may simply ask the respondents what they think about the new yogurt place. A survey can contain both open-ended and closed-ended questions. The researcher must have an in-depth understanding of the setting or the topic when designing the closed-ended questions. If their understanding is limited or they are exploring subjective attitudes and meanings, it is better to include open-ended questions. Open-ended questions reduce or eliminate the researcher's preset notion about the topic and allow respondents to frame answers as they want. One of the major drawbacks of open-ended questions is the difficulty in quantifying information or identifying common themes and patterns, as each respondent may give a different answer, making it difficult to extract insight from unstructured responses. Open-ended questions also take more time to answer and may potentially include more non-response. However, that can be somewhat addressed by keeping the survey short. Closed-ended and open-ended questions can also be combined to examine the same question.

Closed-ended

How likely are you to recommend the new yogurt place to your family and friends?

1	2	3	4	5	6	7	8	9	10
Very Unlikely									Very Likely

Open-ended

What is the main reason for your score on the previous question?

> **Helpful Hint:** Even when using mostly closed-ended questions, it is useful to include an open-ended question at the end, asking respondents if they would like to add anything that the survey did not ask about the topic.

While using closed-ended questions, the researcher should also take into account the issue of **floaters** – respondents who may not know about the topic – and therefore, the researcher should give the option of 'Don't know'. The researcher should also include the option of 'Undecided' to cater to **fence-sitters** – respondents who may know about the topic, but have not made up their minds one way or the other or may be neutral about it.

While writing any questions, the researcher should also guard against bias or leading language as well as vagueness. Here are a few examples.

How many hours do you spend studying for the research methods course every week?

a. A lot less than average
b. Somewhat less than average
c. Average
d. Somewhat more than average
e. A lot more than average

In the above question, the word *average* may mean different things to different respondents. Therefore, for such a question, it is better to use an actual number of hours to study responses.

Don't you think that it's high time for people to stand up against bias in the mainstream news media?

a. Yes
b. No
c. Maybe
d. No opinion

In the above question, though the response options are relatively exhaustive, the language of the question itself reflects the researcher's bias. It can be rephrased – '*Do you agree that there is bias in the mainstream new media?*' – while keeping the same response options. It can also be rephrased in another way: '*What is your view on the bias in the mainstream news media?*' If rephrased as the latter option, the responses would need to be modified as well.

While writing closed-ended questions, the researcher should also guard against double-barreled and double-negative questions. **Double-barreled questions** ask the respondent two questions in one, which may confuse the respondent. For example, the question '*How much do you enjoy reading about survey research methods and collecting primary data?*' contains two questions. There will not be any problem if it is an open-ended question as the respondent can write whether they like reading about survey research or not and whether they enjoy collecting primary data or not. However, it would create confusion or produce unreliable data as a closed-ended question, as the respondent may enjoy reading about the survey research methods but not enjoy doing actual data collection.

Double-negative questions contain two negative words that can create confusion or mislead. For example, the question '*Do you disagree that there should not be any questions from this chapter on the exam?*' would create confusion as a closed-ended question as it contains two negatives. Here are a few more examples of these errors.

Double-barreled Questions

Do you think that cars are now more or less safer than in the 1950s?
a. Yes
b. No
c. Don't know
d. No opinion

In the above question, it would be unclear what the respondents feel if they select any of the response options because both more or less are included in the question.

Do you think that there should be a tax credit given to single people and there should be a tax increase on married people?
a. Yes
b. No
c. Don't know
d. No opinion

In the above question, one may agree with the tax credit for single people but not with the tax increase for married people, and vice-versa. Even if the respondent selects an answer, the researcher would not be able to figure out what part of the question the respondent has answered. In both such examples, the researcher can fix the error while maintaining the same question format (closed-ended) by creating two separate questions, each having a set of response options.

Double-negative Question

Do you disagree that there should not be a tax increase on single people?
a. Yes
b. No
c. Don't know
d. No opinion

In the above question, the response options are exhaustive, but the question itself is confusing. Double negative is fine in Math but not in English! For example, saying, '*I won't buy you no yogurt*' creates a double-negative. For best practice, it is suggested to not include any negatives.

Double-negative

Figure 6.5 Double-negative

Peterson (2000) suggests a simple acronym, BRUSO which helps to remember the qualities of a good question. BRUSO stands for brief, relevant, unambiguous, specific, and objective. The researcher does not need to ask basic demographic questions such as age, sex, education level, marital status, race, and so on if the study does not require it. As noted at the start of the chapter, surveys may contain one question or over 100 questions. If asking one question serves the purpose, then just ask one question. The respondent is taking time out to complete the survey. It is imperative to make it as clear, purposeful, and well-organized as possible. The researcher would also need to consider if the respondent has the necessary information needed to answer the question. For example, *'three-strikes and you're out'* may bring to mind baseball. However, it is also a commonly used phrase that refers to a mandatory prison term after a third felony or generally refers to the habitual or persistent offender laws. Specifically, this phrase refers to the mandatory sentences for repeat violent and serious felons (third felony) in California. Similarly, as a student or scholar of criminal justice in the United States, one may be aware of Jessica's Law and may be able to answer questions about it. However, to minimize the hassle for the respondents, it is advised to include a brief description of the topic at the top of the survey, unless the purpose of the study is to measure the awareness level about the topic itself.

While creating closed-ended questions, the researcher needs to ensure that the response options are **exhaustive** and **mutually exclusive**. Exhaustive

collecting primary data

response options refer to covering all the potential responses to a question. However, this does not mean that one needs to create tens of response categories.

For example, when asking a question about the number of times the respondent ate pizza last month, the options can be:

a. 0
b. 1–4
c. 5–8
d. 9–12
e. 13 or more

The above options cover all possible responses. However, if the options of 0 and 13 or more were not included, the list would not be exhaustive. The response options are also mutually exclusive as one response appears in one category only.

The following set of response options shows the error where responses are not mutually exclusive.

a. 0–4
b. 4–8
c. 8–12
d. 12 or more

In the above example, if several respondents ate four pizzas in a month, they may pick option a or option b, and so on. When asking questions about qualitative variables such as race, religion, ethnicity, marital status, and so on, it is relatively easy to create mutually exclusive categories. However, the researcher can also use the option of 'other' or 'other (please specify)' to reduce the number of options while ensuring that all potential responses can be recorded.

In almost all surveys, the researcher needs to account for non-response and incomplete items that would impact generalizability depending on the type of survey, setting, and so on. This should be kept in mind while analyzing data and drawing conclusions. If the sample size is large, it is the best practice to run a **pilot survey**. Asking a smaller subset of the sample to complete the survey would help to identify whether the respondents are reluctant to answer any questions, do not understand a particular question, feel that response options do not include what they want to say, feel embarrassed to answer certain questions, and so on. Converse and Presser (1986) suggest using a participatory pilot survey in which the respondents are told ahead of time that they are part of a pilot survey. The researcher can engage in a discussion with the respondents (in a group or individually, depending on the type of method for the study) in the subset and identify and address these issues. The pilot survey helps to test the correctness and reliability of the survey. If needed, the researcher can even change the type of survey method due to logistical and technical issues identified in a pilot survey. Identifying all potential errors and limitations before collecting data helps to improve the quality of research.

Researchers do not need to reinvent the wheel! That is, many people have conducted several surveys on many topics. It is suggested that

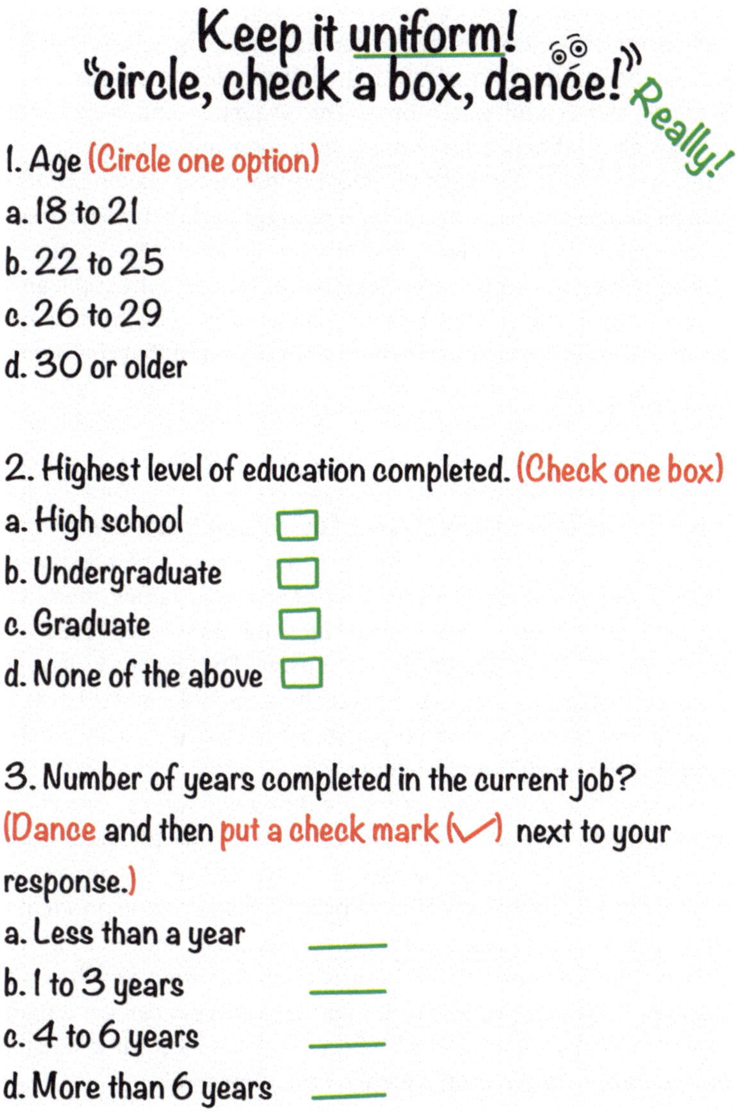

Keep it uniform!
"circle, check a box, dance!" *Really!*

1. Age (Circle one option)
a. 18 to 21
b. 22 to 25
c. 26 to 29
d. 30 or older

2. Highest level of education completed. (Check one box)
a. High school ☐
b. Undergraduate ☐
c. Graduate ☐
d. None of the above ☐

3. Number of years completed in the current job? (Dance and then put a check mark (✓) next to your response.)
a. Less than a year ____
b. 1 to 3 years ____
c. 4 to 6 years ____
d. More than 6 years ____

Figure 6.6 Uniform Style in Survey

researchers examine the instruments that others have used. It would help to gain insight into what errors to avoid, how to phrase certain questions, how to organize the material for readability, and so on. Just because there are different types of question formats, it does not mean that the researcher should include all types of questions. If it is sufficient to only use questions with a Likert-type scale, then that is fine. If the respondent is answering questions by selecting from predefined response options, the researcher should make them uniform. The cleaner the questionnaire looks, the easier it will be to complete it.

While creating questions, the researcher should keep in mind the research topic and attributes that need to be measured and only ask questions relevant to it. Gathering data on items that are not relevant to the study would only create clutter and waste time. The sequence and placement of questions can also influence responses. In a long questionnaire, it is that suggested researchers start with the most important questions. If the questionnaire includes sensitive questions, it is suggested that researchers ask a few warm-up or less sensitive questions before gradually getting to more sensitive questions. It would also help to contextualize the topic and prepare the respondent about what type of questions may be coming up next. For the postal survey or questionnaire, it is suggested that the open-ended questions be placed at the end of the survey. Using filter questions and skip patterns and creating categories or sections improve readability.

Once I participated in a study on diversity at my workplace. It included the same questions for different criteria. For example, it asked if the respondent knew anyone of a different race, if the respondent knew anyone of a different race in a professional setting, if the respondent socialized with anyone of a different race, if the respondent had a family member of a different race, and so on. It then asked the same questions based on immigration status, religion, disability, and so on. The survey was very well organized and each section was marked by a variable on which the questions were being asked. A poorly organized survey could easily create an impression that the questions were repetitive.

Always remember that the respondents are doing you a favor by taking time out to participate in your study. Therefore, ask only the necessary questions, be polite and sensitive, be alert to whether the respondent is uncomfortable or feeling under any kind of duress, thank the respondents for their time, and so on. Some researchers also share the findings of the research with the respondents or inform them of where and how to access it. Systematically planned and well-organized surveys can get a high response on wide-ranging topics and are effectively used by criminologists, sociologists, lawmakers, and criminal justice practitioners alike.

Further Reading

NCVS Basic Screen Questionnaire: https://bjs.ojp.gov/content/pub/pdf/ncvs22_bsq.pdf

Key Terms

Closed-ended question
Cover letter
Dichotomous questions
Digital divide
Double-barreled questions
Double-negative questions
Drop-off survey
Email surveys
Ethics statement
Exhaustive responses
Face-to-face surveys
Fence-sitters
Floaters
Generalizability
Group survey
Likert-type scale
Monitoring The Future survey
Multiple-choice questions
Mutually exclusive responses
National Crime Victimization Survey
Open-ended questions
Pilot survey
Postal surveys
Questionnaire
Schedule
Semantic scale
Telephone survey
Text surveys
Web surveys
Weed and Seed program

Class Activity

Divide the class into groups of three or four students. Pick a topic from current events and ask each group to develop a questionnaire on the same topic. If it is a larger class, you can select two or three topics from current events and assign them to groups while ensuring that at least two groups are assigned the same topic. The questionnaire could contain ten questions (eight closed-ended, and two open-ended). Engage in a class discussion as each group shares its questions and the rationale behind them.

Works Cited

Brousse, Cécile, Bernadette Guiot de la Rochère, and Emmanuel Massé. 2001. "The French Survey of Homeless People Using Shelters and Soup Kitchens." *Proceedings of Statistics Canada's Symposium 2001. Achieving Data Quality in a Statistical Agency: A Methodological Perspective.* Retrieved from https://www150.statcan.gc.ca/n1/en/pub/11-522-x/2001001/session13/6272-eng.pdf?st=o8WbiLaC

Converse, Jean M., and Stanley Presser. 1986. *Survey Questions: Handcrafting the Standardized Questionnaire.* Thousand Oaks, CA: Sage Publications Inc.

"Methodology. National Crime Victimization Survey." Retrieved from https://bjs.ojp.gov/data-collection/ncvs#18s6hz

"National Crime Victimization Survey." Retrieved from https://bjs.ojp.gov/data-collection/ncvs#methodology-0

Peterson, R. A. 2000. *Constructing Effective Questionnaires.* Thousand Oaks, CA: Sage.

Thomas, Tina, Namrata Walia, Landon Presnall, Jasper Shei, and Hamilton Jane Elizabeth. 2022. "Feasibility of Cell Phone Surveys in People with Mental Illness Experiencing Homelessness During COVID-19." *Journal of Digital Psychiatry*, Vol. 1(1), Article 2. Retrieved from https://digitalcommons.library.tmc.edu/jdigipsych/vol1/iss1/2

Wolter, Kirk, Sadeq Chowdhury, and Jenny Kelly. 2009. Chapter 7 "Design, Conduct, and Analysis of Random-Digit Dialing Surveys." In *Handbook of Statistics*, Vol.29(Part A), pp. 125–154. Retrieved from https://www.sciencedirect.com/science/article/abs/pii/S0169716108000072

chapter 7

Collecting Primary Data
Experiment Research Methods

This chapter explains the quantitative research method of designing and using experiments. It explains classical and quasi-experiments, the potential preconditions or settings where they could be used, and the strengths and limitations of each experimental design. The chapter explains criteria for causal explanation, and experimental research methods with reference to validity, generalizability, and ethics.

After this chapter, students will be able to understand and explain

- Why experimental research
- Types of experiments
- Validity and generalizability in experimental research
- Ethical considerations in experimental research

Introduction

Many topics in social sciences are better examined by placing people in life-like situations and studying how they act, react, or interact. Experiments help to explain and predict behaviors as influenced by situational factors, external stimuli, group dynamics, and so on. By identifying the cause(s), researchers can have confidence in predicting the outcome. Experiments can be used to study a wide range of behaviors, including prejudice, anger, coping mechanisms, social skills, online behavior, the abuse of power, the impact of counseling, new training program, and so on. Practically every topic in social sciences can be examined using experimental research design. On some topics, it is relatively easy to ask questions, for some topics, however, people may not be able to predict even their own behavior. For example, asking about the impact of distracted driving may not get you very reliable information, but placing research subjects in a computer-simulated environment and measuring their responses would help to understand it better.

Figure 7.1 Nothing Can Distract me!

BOX 7.1 – Experiment on Distracted Driving

"The present study examined the behavior of teens and young adults operating a driving simulator while engaged in various distractions (i.e., cell phone, texting, and undistracted) and driving conditions (i.e., free flow, stable flow, and oversaturation). Seventy five participants

16-25 years of age (split into 2 groups: novice drivers and young adults) drove a STISIM simulator three times, each time with one of three randomly presented distractions. Each drive was designed to represent daytime scenery on a 4 lane divided roadway and included three equal roadway portions representing Levels of Service (LOS) A, C, and E as defined in the 2000 Highway Capacity Manual. Participants also completed questionnaires documenting demographics and driving history. Both safety and traffic flow related driving outcomes were considered. A Repeated Measures Multivariate Analysis of Variance was employed to analyze continuous outcome variables and a Generalized Estimate Equation (GEE) Poisson model was used to analyze count variables. Results revealed that, in general more lane deviations and crashes occurred during texting. Distraction (in most cases, text messaging) had a significantly negative impact on traffic flow, such that participants exhibited greater fluctuation in speed, changed lanes significantly fewer times, and took longer to complete the scenario. In turn, more simulated vehicles passed the participant drivers while they were texting or talking on a cell phone than while undistracted. The results indicate that distracted driving, particularly texting, may lead to reduced safety and traffic flow, thus having a negative impact on traffic operations. No significant differences were detected between age groups, suggesting that all drivers, regardless of age, may drive in a manner that impacts safety and traffic flow negatively when distracted" (Stavrinos et al., 2013).

BOX 7.2 – Computational Simulation of Visual Distraction Effects on Car Drivers' Situation Awareness

"This paper presents a computational modeling approach for negative effects simulation of visual distraction while driving a car. In order to investigate these effects, an experiment was firstly implemented on a driving simulator. Twenty participants were invited to perform a car following task in different driving conditions (12 driving scenarios), with or without a secondary task of visual distraction. Empirical data collected through this experiment show that visual distraction negatively impacts the driving performance at both perceptive and behavioral levels, and then increase the risk having a crash. Beyond these effects on the observable performance, the aim of this study is also to investigate and simulate such distractive effects on mental models of the road environment. Indeed, drivers's decisions and behaviors are based on a temporal-spatial mental model, corresponding to the driver's situational awareness (SA). This mental representation must be permanently updated by perceptive information extracted in the road scene to be efficient. In case of visual distraction requiring off-road scanning, mental model updating is un-perfectly done and driver's actions are thus based on a mental representation that can dramatically differ of the situational reality, in case of a critical change in the traffic conditions (e.g. sudden braking in the lead car). From these empirical results, a computational model (named COSMODRIVE for COgnitive Simulation MOdel of the DRIVEr) was implemented for simulating visual distraction effects and human errors risks at perceptive (visual scanning changes) cognitive (erroneous Situational Awareness) and behavioral levels (late reaction time and crash risk increasing)" (Bellet et al., 2012).

Asking people if they have any bias or if that bias plays a role in their professional decision-making may not get reliable data, but placing them in experiments may give more reliable insight.

BOX 7.3 – The Consequences of Race for Police Officers' Responses to Criminal Suspects

"The program presented participants with digital color photographs of nine Black and nine White college-age males selected from a set of pictures matched for attractiveness (Malpass, Lavigueur, and Weldon, 1973). A picture of a gun or a neutral object (e.g., wallet, cell phone), formatted to be equivalent in size and background, was superimposed on each of the faces. The gun or other object was positioned with the face still visible, but the location varied so that participants could not predict where the object would appear. Two stimuli were created for each face, one with a gun and one with a neutral object. On each trial, the computer program randomly selected one of the pictures and displayed it on the screen. So that the program would be challenging, the picture randomly appeared toward the top, middle, or bottom of the screen and toward the right, center, or left of the screen. Each picture appeared on screen until the participant responded or until the 630-ms time limit elapsed. When a participant did not make a correct decision (i.e., hit the wrong key or exceeded the time limit), an error message

> appeared on screen for a full second. Each participant completed 20 practice trials and 160 test trials" (Plant and Peruche, 2005, p. 181).

Most people would not be able to predict exactly how they would behave if placed in situations that involve abuse of power, following seemingly biased orders, being faced with bullying, getting agitated while waiting for a real person to answer a customer service call, and so on. This may be studied by placing people in experimental research and the findings can be used for better training, behavioral management, and service.

The Minneapolis Domestic Violence Experiment (MDVE)

The Minneapolis Police Department and the Police Foundation carried out an experiment on police response in domestic violence cases. The experiment was carried out in 1981–1982 and its findings were published in 1984. The experiment involved testing three responses in domestic violence calls – making an arrest, counseling, and advising both parties and separating them for a few hours. These were cases of minor assault. The arrest was found to be the most effective as it produced the lowest recidivism.

BOX 7.4 – The MDVE Methodology

"How the Experiment Was Designed

The design of the experiment called for a lottery selection, which ensured that there would be no difference among the three groups of suspects receiving the different police responses (Cook and Campbell, 1979). The lottery determined which of the three responses police officers would use on each suspect in a domestic assault case. According to the lottery, a suspect would be arrested, or sent from the scene of the assault for eight hours, or given some form of advice, which could include mediation at an officer's discretion. In the language of the experiment, these responses were called the arrest, send, and advise treatments. The design called for a six-month follow-up period to measure the frequency and seriousness of any future domestic violence in all cases in which the police intervened.

The design applied only to simple (misdemeanor) domestic assaults, where both the suspect and the victim were present when the police arrived. Thus, the experiment included only those cases in which police were empowered, but not required, to make arrests under a recently liberalized Minnesota state law.

The police officer must have probable cause to believe that a cohabitant or spouse has assaulted the victim within the past four hours. Police need not have witnessed the assault. Cases of life-threatening or severe injury, usually labeled as a felony (aggravated assault), were excluded from the design.

The design called for each officer to carry a pad of report forms, color coded for the three different police responses. Each time the officers encountered a situation that fit the experiment's criteria, they were to take whatever action was indicated by the report form on the top of the pad. The forms were numbered and arranged for each officer in an order determined by the lottery. The consistency of the lottery assignment was to be monitored by research staff observers riding on patrol for a sample of evenings. After a police action was taken at the scene of a domestic violence incident, the officer was to fill out a brief report and give it to the research staff for follow-up. As a further check on the lottery process, the staff logged in the reports in the order in which they were received and made sure that the sequence corresponded to the original assignment of responses.

Anticipating something of the background of victims in the experiment, a predominantly minority, female research staff was employed to contact the victims for a detailed, face-to-face interview, to be followed by telephone follow-up interviews every two weeks for 24 weeks. The interviews were designed primarily to measure the frequency and seriousness of victimizations caused by a suspect after police intervention. The research staff also collected criminal justice reports that mentioned suspects' names during the six-month follow-up period" (Sherman and Berk, 1984, pp. 2–3).

A Class Divided Experiment, 1970

The 1970 documentary *Eye of the Storm* chronicles Jane Elliot's experiment on racism, bias, and discrimination involving students in her third-grade classroom. The PBS Frontline documentary *A Class Divided* involves a reunion of those students and gives an overview of the experiment and its long-lasting impact.

After the assassination of Dr. Martin Luther King, Jr. in 1968, Jane Elliot decided that she wanted to teach children about the gravity of racism and prejudice. She divided the class according to students' eye color – blue and brown. On the first day, blue-eyed kids received preferential treatment, such as 5 extra minutes on the playground and sitting at the front of the class. They were also told not to talk to brown-eyed kids. The brown-eyed kids had to wear collars. The next day, she reversed the situation, and brown-eyed kids received preferential treatment. During the experiment, kids also started to associate positive or negative behavior with eye color. She gave the kids a test; while kids who faced discrimination scored lower on the test, results showed that the group that received preferential treatment did better on the test. In a matter of a couple of days, she created a microcosm of society and showed how easy it was to manipulate people and create an 'us versus them' environment.

The same experiment was repeated with correctional officers in Iowa, and incredibly, the results were not too different. The respondents, in this case, correctional officers, became agitated and frustrated with the biased treatment based on eye color. If this can happen in a very short amount of time in a controlled experiment, it gives powerful insights into the real-life impact of bias, prejudice, and discrimination.

Zimbardo's Experiment on Vandalism, 1969

Phil Zimbardo carried out an experiment on visible indicators of social disorder inviting criminal activity. It was designed on the premise that early

Figure 7.2 False Correlation

signs of disorder, when left unattended, may invite more serious criminal activity. Zimbardo left one car in a poor, crime-ridden neighborhood in New York City and another car in a relatively affluent neighborhood in Palo Alto, California. The car in New York City was vandalized and passersby stripped it for parts within 10 minutes or so. The car in Palo Alto was left untouched for more than a week. Zimbardo then smashed its windows, and it quickly met the same fate as the car in New York City. Zimbardo argued that it proved the argument that when neglected, or when there are early signs of disorder, property and places invite further crime. The experiment served as one of the basis for Kelling and Wilson's Broken Windows Theory. The theory argued that instead of focusing on major crimes, police departments could reduce serious crime by addressing early signs of disorder, including loitering, graffiti, prostitution, and drug use.

An American TV show, *What Would You Do*, is a rudimentary but effective example of social experiments. https://abcnews.go.com/WhatWouldYouDo.

Figure 7.3 What Would You Do?

Many social experiments are available on YouTube as well. The 2014 Domestic Abuse in the Lift Experiment by STHLM Panda in Sweden created quite a furor. In this experiment, the content creators placed cameras in a lift. The team members played an abusive boyfriend and his victim. The 'domestic abuse' was clearly visible. Out of 53 people who got in the lift, only one woman said that she was going to call the police if the abuser put her hands on her (victim) again. The 'abusive boyfriend' commented that he was prepared to take a hit from the bigger guys, but was disappointed to see them walk out without any intervention.

In Chapter 3, the Milgram Experiment and the Standford Prison Experiment also show the significance of experimental research in social sciences as well as the potential for ethical violations. Compared to surveys, experiments face more methodological challenges and ethical dilemmas. Experiments, like any other research, should never be conducted without proper training and supervision and the requisite approvals.

Conditions of Causality

Causal explanations can be nomothetic, idiographic, or a combination of the two. The **nomothetic** causal explanation is concerned with providing a general explanation or more broad causal statements; for example, examining if 'violence in media results in violence among children' is a general causal statement or a nomothetic approach. While establishing a nomothetic explanation, the researcher is more concerned about identifying common trends and patterns, general traits and causes, and large-scale social patterns.

Figure 7.4   Causal Explanations

The **idiographic** causal explanation is concerned with a narrower subject of study. It focuses on an individual or an individual or unique event. For example, in July 2012, James Holmes went to the midnight screening of Christopher Nolan's *The Dark Knight Rises*, threw gas canisters in the audience, and opened fire. In the horrific mass shooting, he killed 12 people and injured 70. It led to immense speculation as to whether he was inspired by the Batman character and comic books. In another example, in Britain, the 1991 horror film *Child's Play 3* was cited in the brutal murder of Suzanne Capper. When examining such cases, using the idiographic approach means that the researcher would only focus on the above-stated mass shooting and examine cause and effect. This approach does not extend the generalization beyond the **case study** or event in question. Researchers may also combine the two approaches. For example, one may examine the Bernie Madoff scandal to study how he was able to run the **Ponzi scheme** for such a long time (idiographic). The researcher may examine other such schemes and identify common motivations, reasons why someone may fall victim to these schemes, lapses in the investigation, and so on, that may be common across all examples under examination (nomothetic). Similarly, on a class test, a professor may examine why one student did poorly (idiographic) or examine if several students struggled on a particular question (nomothetic).

> **Helpful Hint:** In social sciences, you are unlikely to find absolute causal connections. Instead, the focus is on identifying strong and weak correlates.

A **causal model** involves creating and examining if-then or hypothetical scenarios. It proposes a relationship between independent and dependent variables. It may contain multiple independent and dependent variables as well. Think of variables as nodes and the relationships between them as links. Any causal model must meet the basic conditions of causality – causal association, time order, and irrefutability.

Causal Association

To establish a causal association, the researcher must be able to prove an association between variables; the independent variable and the dependent variable must change together. The experiment should show that a change in X (the independent variable or the cause) is associated with a change in Y (the dependent variable or the outcome). However, empiricism alone is not enough to prove causality. To have a stronger explanation, there must also be a **theory of causality** – knowledge of relevant causes. For example, many argue about the correlation between climate change and terrorism, while ignoring more direct and better proven political and ideological correlates or causes of terrorism.

The causal association can be positive or negative. The **negative association** is also called an inverse relation or inverse association. Variables are said to have a **positive relationship** or association when variation on both nodes is in the same direction. For example, more economic strain results in more crime, or fewer people drinking and driving results in fewer motor vehicular accidents. The negative relation denotes that the nodes or variables are changing in opposite directions. For example, an increase in crime results in a lowering of social cohesion, or an increase in educational and rehabilitation programs behind bars results in reducing recidivism rates.

Time Order

The researcher must be able to establish which variables are independent and which are dependent. The change in the dependent variable must occur *after* the change in the independent variable and must be related to it.

Figure 7.5 Time Order

Irrefutability

An irrefutable relationship between variables means that the correlation is genuine or not false. The researcher needs to establish that there is no extraneous, extra, or third variable. An **extraneous** or third variable may be influencing the independent, dependent, or both variables. If the researcher fails to identify the extraneous variable, the causal association would be considered false or refutable.

Additionally, the researcher can also define the **causal framework** within which causal association exists. It helps establish the specific situation or case to which that causal explanation applies. It particularly helps if the researcher is aiming to prove or seeking an idiographic explanation. For example, many kids may watch violent shows on television, but a vast majority of them would not commit crimes. While addressing a particular case where a kid is supposed to have been influenced by violent shows, it would be beneficial to establish a framework – that is, the said explanation of cause and effect applies only to that particular case or event.

> **Helpful Hint:** Though conducting an experiment may seem like a really cool idea, remember that *ceteris paribus*, experiments present more ethical dilemmas than most of the surveys. If you are developing a research proposal for the first time, it might be better to select a survey method in your proposed research work. However, feel free to examine the possibility of carrying out an experiment. As you read about the types of experiments, work with your professor to see if your research topic may benefit from it, and consider the issues surrounding ethics and sample generalizability.

Types of Experiments

Depending on the research question and sample, the researcher can use one of the following experiments. There are several other types of experiments in social sciences, but for this course, the following should suffice. Experiments are generally classified into classical and quasi-experiments based on their components.

Classical Experiment

A classical experiment has three components:

a. **Groups:** This allows comparing the impact of treatment on a group or research subjects with a group that does not receive a treatment or receives a different treatment. For example, in an experiment about the impact of a rehabilitation program, the research subjects that go through the actual rehabilitation program would be the **treatment group**. The research subjects that do not go through any program would be the **control group**. The comparison may also be made against a group that goes through a different program than the one being evaluated. In a classical experiment, there must be a treatment and at least one comparison or control group. Some experiments may include all three groups.

b. **Random assignment to groups:** The research subjects in a sample must be randomly assigned to the groups in the experiment. For example, if the researcher has proposed the hypothesis that exposure to violence in media results in higher aggression among children, the researcher may be tempted to place aggressive research subjects in a treatment group as it is more likely to prove the hypothesis. The random assignment would control such researcher's bias. However, it may still create random selection error. That is, even if the researcher is flipping a coin to randomly assign subjects to one or the other group, those with higher levels of aggression may still end up in one or the other group. In that case, the pretesting can help identify such errors and the groups can be randomly reconstituted.

c. **Pretesting and post-testing**: The research subjects should undergo an assessment before they receive the treatment. For example, an organization may have new compliance training for employees to avoid information leaking, improve workplace safety, and maintain corporate responsibility. Through vignettes or a similar measure, their decision-making and approach must be assessed before they undergo compliance training. After the training, there should be another assessment – this is called post-testing. The difference between the two assessments would show the impact of the training (treatment/intervention).

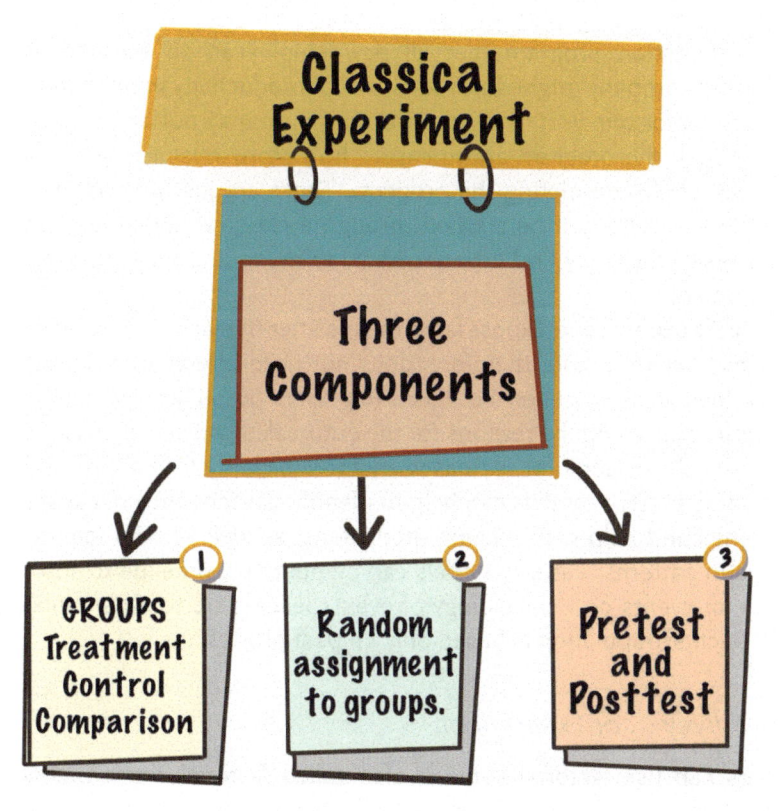

Figure 7.6 Classical Experiment

Quasi-experiments

There are research topics and samples in which the researcher may not see the classical experiment as the most appropriate choice and may use a quasi-experiment. The two most commonly used quasi-experiments in criminal justice and sociology are non-randomized groups designs and time series designs.

Non-randomized groups design: In a study, the researcher may not want to randomly assign research subjects to groups. For example, we have discussed the experiment based on eye color where kids with a particular eye color received preferential treatment. If the kids were assigned randomly to groups, it would not have been possible to carry out the experiment as it was predicated on the fact that groups be divided by particular eye color. Therefore, if random assignment is not possible, or it is considered unnecessary for the experiment, the researcher can use the non-randomized groups design. This would have the other two elements – groups and pre- and post-testing.

Time series experiment: The researcher may not find it necessary to divide the sample into groups. That automatically removes the need for random assignment to groups as well. For example, there may be a new employee orientation program that all new employees go through. A manufacturing company might study its workers' productivity in relation to work conditions for one year. A deaddiction program may put all research subjects through the program and measure how many relapsed within a year of successfully completing the program. These are just a handful of examples. Such topics can be studied through a classical experiment as well, but a researcher may find it unnecessary to do so and may choose a quasi-experiment.

Expost facto experiment: Expost facto means after the fact. It starts after the event has occurred and, therefore, does not need intervention by the researcher. Instead, it examines the causes to present possible explanations – for example, examining the reasons for the outbreak of a disease, reasons for a plane crash, reasons for increased motor-vehicle theft in a city, and so on. Creating pattern models can help to identify the sequence of causes and outcomes and help with making predictions, as well as help identify any change in patterns. Pattern models can be built as a timeline to show a sequence of events or a chronology of events leading up to a particular outcome. Such extrapolation is based only on past projections.

Factorial Survey ... or Experiment

Researchers can use factorial surveys, also called factorial experimental design, to study a wide range of hypothetical situations by asking research subjects what they would do in a certain situation. The researcher can test several causal explanations involving multiple independent and dependent variables. This helps to identify how variables or factors interact with each other. A simple factorial table below shows four possible conditions. A lot more complex interactions can be examined through factorial tables and vignettes. In a **between-subjects factorial design**, each research subject would be tested in only one condition. That is, each subject can be tested for either eating pizza for lunch or dinner *or* not eating pizza for lunch or dinner. The **within-subjects** is a more complex design and allows the manipulation of independent variables within subjects. That is, all respondents can be tested for eating pizza *and* not eating pizza for lunch and dinner.

Factorial designs allow for a larger sample size than many traditional classical and quasi-experiments, thus improving generalizability. They are more efficient in evaluating multiple interventions. While testing hypothetical situations, factorial designs also allow for examining independent variables that are not manipulated. For example, the researcher may measure *happiness levels* (high and low) in relation to respondents' *willingness to volunteer in a community garden* (dependent variable). In this example, the researcher is not manipulating the independent variable (happiness levels).

Factorial Designs

		Eating Pizza	
		Yes	**No**
Time of the day	**Lunch**		
	Dinner		

Figure 7.7 Factorial Designs

Factorial designs raise a concern about causal conditions as there could be other factors that might be at play that the researcher did not recognize, as there is no active manipulation of the independent variable; there is a lack of control over the causal conditions of the experiment. Therefore, as noted earlier, empiricism alone cannot establish causality, and the researcher must have a knowledge of relevant causes. It all goes back to selecting the best possible method – including the type of experiment – based on the research question, number of variables, sample, setting, and so on. As an aside, this is the kind of example that is considered non-experimental, and this is why factorial designs are also called factorial surveys and not just factorial experiments.

Validity and Generalizability in Experiments

Experiments have strong **causal validity** as at every stage they focus on conditions of causality. Researchers not only try to identify correlations among variables but also actively guard against false correlations.

Compared to surveys, experiments have limited **generalizability**, mainly due to the smaller sample size. Though researchers try their best to take the most representative sample, experiments have low generalizability. The findings based on experiments have resulted in many policies in different locations; it is best to keep examining the issues with more current experiments. Some researchers may draw multiple samples from the population and conduct several experiments as they combine to give them a larger sample and thus more confidence in their findings.

Generalizability may suffer in **field experiments** more than in lab experiments as it is more challenging to control conditions in a field experiment. For example, though the Minneapolis Domestic Violence Experiment is a very well-designed experiment on paper, there were some challenges in carrying it out. Sherman and Berk (1984) note that several police officers in the experiment did not follow all the requirements as many forgot to carry their report pads, did not understand the rules of experiments in certain complex situations that they encountered, and used their judgment to exclude certain cases, resulting in random selection error. The experiment also suffered as many of the victims could not be located either for the initial or the follow-up interviews. According to Sherman and Berk (1984), many victims left town, refused to participate, or moved elsewhere. **Subject fatigue** is a real concern in field experiments. Out of the 330 (few repeat victims counted twice) cases, only 205 victims could be located and interviewed. Sherman and Berk (1984) also wondered if deterrence was created due to the interviewer or reactive effect as the victims were interviewed over a six-month follow-up. "It is possible that the interviewers created a "surveillance" effect that deterred suspects. Whether the same effects would be found without the interviews is still an open question" (Sherman and Berk, 198, p.8).

If the research subjects start modifying their behavior because of being in the experiment rather than because of the actual intervention, the researcher cannot learn the impact of the intervention. The researcher may fail to identify that the behavioral change is independent of the intervention or treatment.

- **Placebo:** In a clinical trial, a sugar pill is used to see if the research subjects feel better despite using a nonactive treatment. This helps researchers to examine if the actual treatment has any impact or not. In an experiment, an error may occur if research subjects modify their behavior because they *feel* that they are getting the treatment and not *because* of the actual treatment, *and the researcher fails to recognize it.*
- **Contamination:** The research subjects in the comparison or control group may become aware of the experiment group and realize that they are being treated differently. Even if they do not know the nature of treatment or intervention, this realization may cause them to change their behavior – positive or negative – independent of the experiment.
  - Contamination may also result in the *Hawthorne effect*. In the 1920s, the National Research Council researchers studied the impact of work conditions on productivity levels. The expectation was that the poor lighting would lower productivity levels. However, it did not significantly impact the productivity levels as the research subjects had become aware of being observed or being part of a study. As a result, the actual impact of the intervention or treatment (poor work conditions) could not be measured.
  - As an aside, Levitt and List (2009) argue that the Hawthorne effect is overstated, and productivity did not jump whenever lighting was dimmed; instead, the output is higher during *any* experimental manipulations.
- **Sample attrition:** In field experiments, just as in the Minneapolis Domestic Violence Experiment, certain elements of a sample may stop participating or move away. It is also possible to lose specific values in a sample. For example, the sample may have 20 men and 20 women, and after 6 months, 16 out of 20 women may stop participating. This changes the composition of the sample and would severely impact generalizability. If sex is an important factor in the study, it would impact the validity as well.

Ethical Considerations in Experiments

In Chapter 3, we discussed several ethical considerations when collecting or dealing with data on research subjects. Among quantitative methods, experimental research presents more ethical dilemmas than most survey methods.

- **Voluntary participation, informed consent, and no deception:** In experiments, the research subjects may participate voluntarily and sign an informed consent; however, deception may be part of the research design itself. For example, in many experiments, research subjects are placed in a simulated environment or make-believe situation to measure their behavior. In the Milgram experiment, the research subjects genuinely believed that they were giving electric shocks to the person in the other room. It was not true. The machine that the research subjects were using to 'administer the electric shocks' was phony. Milgram argued that the deception was necessary to measure how many research subjects would administer electric shocks. That was the aim of the experiment – to measure to what extreme people might go when given orders by someone in a position of authority. The experiment, as explained in Chapter 3, was heavily criticized.

- Many experiments on discrimination, stress, bias, aggression, coping mechanisms, online conduct, and so on may involve some degree of deception, as revealing the expected outcome or what the experiment is expected to achieve may defeat the purpose of the experiment. The Institutional Review Board or the Ethics Committee (IRB/EC) will closely examine any proposals that present such a scenario. The proposal may also be reviewed in terms of the methodology itself. That is, is there another way to study the same research question? The researcher has to make a clear, convincing, and logical case for using experimental research that may involve deception.

- Many experiments regarding voluntary participation and informed consent are also criticized. For example, researchers may put together a lab experiment with computers in a few different rooms. The research subjects may engage with each other online in that controlled environment. However, neither researchers nor research subjects may be able to anticipate every aspect of the actions and reactions of the users. This often happens due to situational factors and group dynamics, and researchers hope to study them. Researchers expect what is likely to happen, but they cannot predict human behavior with absolute certainty. It is also possible for the respondents to get caught up in the moment and 'forget' about the voluntary nature of participation. In the Standford Prison Experiment, one of the research subjects noted after the experiment that he forgot that he could have just walked out of the experiment as it started to take a toll on him. This is why it is critical for researchers to closely monitor the experiment and be prepared to intervene when needed, particularly if it begins to harm research subjects.

- **Disclose identity:** In many experiments, the researcher may also have to hide their own true identity in order to reduce the reactive effect or due to the element of deception being part of the experiment. Again, these are challenging arguments, and such proposals would need to be closely and critically evaluated by the IRB/EC.

- **No harm to subjects:** Researchers using experiments also face the constant dilemma of potential harm to subjects. As discussed in Chapter 3, in the Standford Prison Experiment, Phil Zimbardo (researcher) got so involved in the experiment that he did not notice the psychological and emotional toll that it was taking on the research subjects. Though we have discussed experiments that caused visible harm, for researchers, it is critical to be mindful of emotional and psychological harm as well. Many topics in social sciences – using any method for that matter, not just experiments – may cause stress. It may be the purpose of the study to examine how research subjects behave when placed in stressful situations, but these are extremely challenging research designs and would need thorough vetting by the IRB/EC as well as by the researchers while carrying out the experiment.

- **The benefits of research should outweigh the risks:** Other than the overall benefits of research, experiments that involve comparison groups face another dilemma: that the study only benefits some of the research subjects. For example, if the study is on a 9-month deaddiction program and involves an experiment and control group, the research subjects in the experiment or treatment group would receive the actual treatment while the ones in the control group will not. Even though the research subjects would have signed the consent form and may be aware of the fact that the study may involve deception, it could be a tough call for the IRB/EC and the researcher to let research subjects believe that they are going to benefit from the study only for them to find out after 9 months that they were in the control group; though they followed every guideline and did exactly as they were told, they did not receive any benefit due to the nature of the experiment. For example, it may be the nature of the study to compare groups and thus assess the validity of the deaddiction program. However, it cannot be ignored that the study inherently potentially benefits only some of the research subjects though it may have a positive outcome for the larger population in general. This dilemma of selective or **unequal benefits** could be avoided by choosing a quasi-experiment design of the time series experiment. Many researchers may also make the actual treatment available to the subjects placed in the control or comparison groups after the experiment is completed.

Debriefing: This is an important additional guideline for experimental research. It occurs after the experiment is complete. The researcher would engage with the research subjects – in a group or individually – and debrief them about the nature and purpose of the experiment, the points of deception, and stressors; and also identify if the research subjects may need additional information or assistance of any kind. It gives the research subjects an opportunity to ask questions and get clarity on any aspect of the experiment that they were part of.

Generally speaking, it may be more challenging to use experiments than most of the surveys. However, their utility cannot be ignored as they allow researchers to create near-natural scenarios and study behaviors in as normal a setting as possible. Such findings about human behavior can help to shape many policies and programs. Experiments can not only explain correlations of the events that have occurred in the past but can also help to make predictions.

Further Reading

- A Class Divided Experiment, 1970, https://www.pbs.org/wgbh/frontline/documentary/class-divided/
- Bernie Madoff's Ponzi Scheme, https://www.pbs.org/wgbh/frontline/documentary/madoff/
- Minneapolis Domestic Violence Experiment, 1984, https://www.policinginstitute.org/wp-content/uploads/2015/07/Sherman-et-al.-1984-The-Minneapolis-Domestic-Violence-Experiment.pdf

Key Terms

Between-subjects factorial design
Case study
Causal association
Causal framework
Causal validity
Classical experiments
Comparison group
Contamination
Control group
Debriefing
Dependent variable
Experiment/treatment group
Expost facto experiment
Extraneous variable
Factorial survey
Field experiments
Generalizability
Hawthorne effect
Idiographic explanation
Independent variable
Informed consent
Irrefutability
Negative association
Nomothetic explanation
Non-randomized groups design
Placebo
Ponzi scheme
Positive association
Post-testing
Pretesting
Quasi experiments
Random assignment
Sample attrition
Subject fatigue
Theory of causality
Time order
Time series experiment
Unequal benefits in experiments
Voluntary participation
Within-subjects factorial design

Class Activity

The professor should select two or three experiments. Divide the class into groups and ask students to examine the experiments in terms of their design and ethical considerations. After the initial examination, ask groups to exchange their designs and reevaluate them. Based on the discussion, select the design that presented the *least* ethical dilemmas, and work with students to redesign it for further discussion.

Works Cited

Bellet, Thierry, Jean-Charles Bornard, Pierre Mayenobe, Jean-Christophe Paris, Dominique Gruyer, et al. 2012. "Computational Simulation of Visual Distraction Effects on Car Drivers' Situation Awareness." *ICCM 2012*, April. Berlin. HAL Id: hal-01674303. Retrieved from https://hal.science/hal-01674303/document

Cook, Thomas D., and Donald T. Campbell. 1979. *Quasi-Experimentation: Design and Analysis Issues for Field Settings*. Chicago: Rand McNally.

Levitt, Steven D., and John A. List. 2009. "Was There Really a Hawthorne Effect at the Hawthorne Plant? An Analysis of the Original Illumination Experiments. National Bureau of Economic Research, Massachusetts." NBER Working Paper Series. Retrieved from https://www.nber.org/system/files/working_papers/w15016/w15016.pdf

Malpass, R.S., H. Lavigueur, and D. E. Weldon. 1973. "Verbal and Visual Training in Face Recognition." *Perception & Psychophysics*, Vol.14(2), pp. 285–292.

Plant, Ashby E., and B. Michelle Peruche. 2005. "The Consequences of Race for Police Officers' Responses to Criminal Suspects." *Psychological Science*, Vol.16(3), pp. 180–183. Retrieved from https://www.jstor.org/stable/40064198

Sherman, L., and R. Berk. 1984. *The Minneapolis Domestic Violence Experiment*. Washington, DC: National Policing Institute, The Police Foundation. https://www.policinginstitute.org/publication/the-minneapolis-domestic-violence-experiment/

Stavrinos, Despina, Jennifer L. Jones, Annie A. Garner, Russell Griffin, Crystal A. Franklin, David Ball, Sharon C. Welburn, Karlene K. Ball, Virginia P. Sisiopiku, and Philip R. Fine. 2013. "Impact of Distracted Driving on Safety and Traffic Flow." *Accident Analysis and Prevention*. http://doi.org/10.1016/j.aap.2013.02.003. Retrieved from https://pubmed.ncbi.nlm.nih.gov/23465745/

chapter 8

Collecting Primary Data – Qualitative Methods
Focus Groups, Observation, Intensive Interviews

This chapter explains the qualitative research methods of designing and using focus groups, observation, and intensive interviews. It explains different qualitative methods, the preconditions or settings where they could be used, and the strengths and limitations of each method. The chapter explains issues of validity, generalizability, and ethics in relation to each qualitative method. It concludes with a quick note on qualitative research and digital data, particularly focusing on visual digital data.

After this chapter, students will be able to understand and explain:

- Why do qualitative research
- Types of qualitative methods
- Validity and generalizability in qualitative research
- Ethical considerations in qualitative research
- Qualitative research and visual digital data

Introduction

Qualitative research is rooted in and oriented to social contexts. It extensively pursues **exploratory** research but is used with the same effectiveness to carry out other types of research, including **descriptive, evaluative**, and **explanatory**. Qualitative methods make tremendous space for personal or subjective experiences and interconnections to examine current and previously unexplored topics, settings, and subjects. In Chapter 2, we discussed the research process including the **inductive approach**. Many topics of interest may not have been examined in detail previously, or researchers may be interested in examining a new dimension about which they do not have enough information to begin with. That is where qualitative research methods can be very helpful, as qualitative methods effectively employ an inductive approach.

The inductive approach begins with data collection where one does not have a precise **hypothesis** to test as there is not much prior information available about the topic. It begins with collecting data, followed by examining the data to identify any patterns or themes, and possibly developing a **grounded theory** from that data. It allows for building a knowledge base from the evidence that is collected. In the inductive approach, the researchers must have a willingness to learn as they do not know much about the setting or the people. It may also be more challenging to identify a reliable source of information as one has a limited foundation to build on.

> **Helpful Hint:** None of the approaches or methods are perfect. Any research method is as good as the people involved in using it, and the first step is to evaluate if it best serves the research topic and the setting. (*Did I mention this already? Yes, it is worth repeating!*).

This chapter gives an overview of three qualitative methods – focus groups, observation, and intensive interviews.

Focus Groups

A **focus group** is classified as a qualitative research method, and in this guide, we will examine it as a tool to get qualitative data. In a focus group, the researcher moderates a discussion with several participants. The participants share their thoughts on the topic, and the researcher guides them to stay on topic. In one of my undergraduate research methods courses, students evaluated the **Weed and Seed** program in Rome, New York. Along with using a door-to-door survey, they also used a focus group.

The discussion started with a general opinion about the program and its impact on the residents, and then gradually went on to discuss its impact on local businesses, its impact on children and outdoor activities, its impact on community and police relations, and so on. In a focus group, the researcher wants participants to speak freely but also to keep them on topic. Focus groups are used in many fields such as communication and media studies, marketing, sociology, criminal justice, political science, food industry, healthcare research, and so on. Think of it as a group discussion with guidance from the researcher.

- Focus groups are used to study attitudes, feelings, beliefs, experiences, and perceptions within a group. Some experiences may be unique to individuals and start a wider discussion, while some experiences may be common across the sample.
- Researchers should be aware of any **conflict of interest** or power dynamics among participants. For example, if you are collecting data about community policing and police and public relations, it may be better to have one group with residents only and another one with police officers only; a third one, if possible, could include select members from both police and public as long as the participants are comfortable.

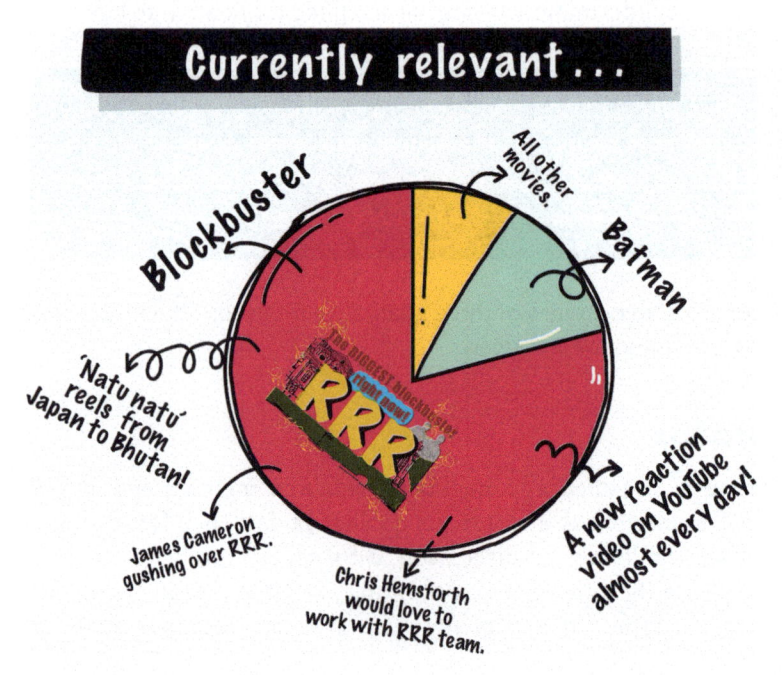

Figure 8.1   RRR

- Focus groups can also be used to study topics that are of immediate or even limited relevance. For example, there may be a major criminal case or a movie that creates a public interest, or the issue could be the deteriorating water quality for the past decade in a specific setting. More often than not, focus groups are a good method to understand people's opinions about an issue while it is still topical.
- For many issues in social sciences, focus groups can be used to gain a preliminary understanding of the research topic. They can help to bridge scientific research and local knowledge (Cornwall and Jewkes, 1995).

Process: Based on the research topic, the researcher would identify the potential participants, assess the need for a facilitator or assistant, and examine any need for an expert on language or culture. The researcher will develop a list of questions that serve as a guide for the participants. This helps the researcher to remain mindful of the issues to discuss and not lose track of time and topic. The researcher will identify any conflict of interest and be mindful of potential hesitation of participants to speak in group settings, their comfort level, any concerns about confidentiality and anonymity and potential risk, the possibility of embarrassment, and so on. Identifying participants before submitting the proposal to the Institutional Review Board (IRB) greatly reduces ethical dilemmas. Depending on the topic, participants can be identified after the IRB approval as well while following the IRB guidelines.

While selecting a venue, the researcher needs to assess how the participants may be traveling or from what locations. For many topics, there may be more than one moderator (Krueger and Casey, 2000). Their roles and functions within the focus group must be clearly defined to avoid confusion. The researcher also needs to plan ahead of time the seating arrangement, name tags (whether actual names, pseudonyms, or numbers), food or light refreshments (taking food allergies into account), and incentives, and also do a full tech-check (recording device, batteries, chargers, data cards). In the case of hand-written notes, the researcher will need to arrange for the notetakers, assign them specific tasks, and arrange for the writing material.

The researcher will need to get a sample that is relevant to the research topic. For example, if you are interested in studying how happy do the parents feel about the new skating park built in the neighborhood, you need to ensure that you have parents in the sample. If you are examining what were the deciding factors for participants to vote for one or the other political party in the last election, you will need to ensure that you have a sample of people who actually voted in the last election. Therefore, as

Figure 8.2 Incentives

noted earlier, the researcher would need to do some homework about the potential respondents and select them as needed.

Sample size: I have seen focus groups ranging in size from 3 participants to almost 35! It depends on the topic and the setting. Ideally, 8–14 participants should be enough for a focus group. A very small group may not give you enough insights, and a much larger group may be difficult to manage. You can also choose to keep a part of the discussion, ideally at the start, more structured. That is, initially, ask each member their opinion on a topic, and then guide them into a discussion.

Before engaging the participants in a discussion, the researcher should establish the ground rules about mutual respect and the use of pseudonyms or numbers (discussed ahead of time if not using actual names). The participants should be informed that they can speak as much or as little as they want to. The researcher should not ask leading questions, should intervene only when needed, should pay attention to verbal and nonverbal cues during the discussion, and should cover all pre-selected questions while keeping enough room for participants to elaborate and discuss. At the end of the discussion, the researcher should conclude and thank each participant for their time.

With advances in online communication, there have also been online focus groups. These can be quite flexible and dynamic and involve people from a wider geographical location. For some participants, the online environment may create a better sense of security and control over their participation, while for others, the impersonal nature of online interaction may act as a barrier. You will also need to keep in mind the **digital divide**, the lack of opportunity to observe body language, and the potential compromise in observing the group dynamic by not having everyone in the same room. To understand the difference between the two settings, think of a class dynamic while taking an online course vis-à-vis an in-person course.

The researcher must know the topic, have a clear idea of what kind of questions must be asked during the discussion, and maintain radical neutrality.

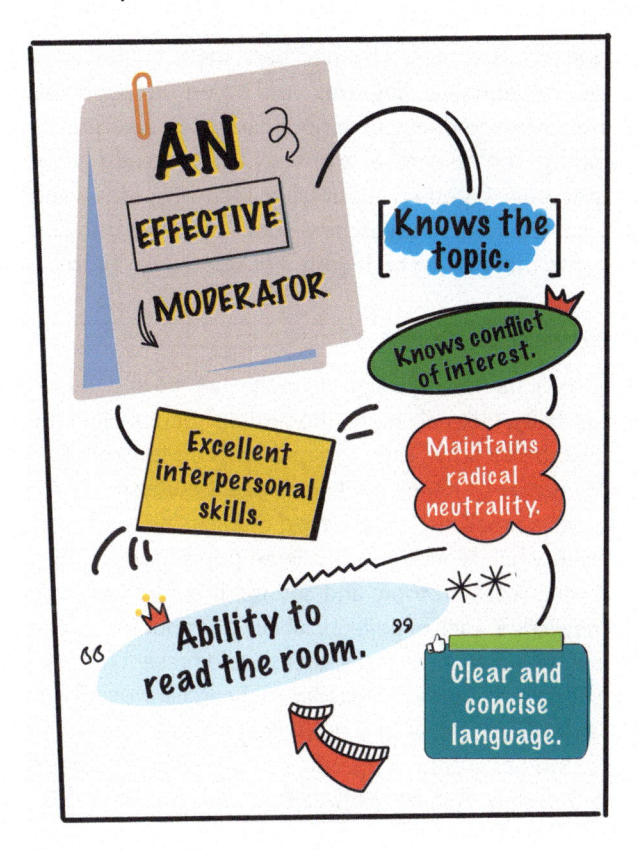

Figure 8.3   Effective Moderator

Notetaking in focus groups can be tedious especially if recording devices – audio or video – are not allowed. In that case, having multiple notetakers may be better. The participants can also be assigned numbers such as 1, 2, 3, 4, and so on as this will allow note-takers to be more precise in their note-taking. For example, women in a focus group may have different opinions than men. During data analysis, the researcher should be able to identify this through notes – the opinions of women vis-à-vis men. The

qualitative research methods   165 use of recording devices has made data collection and analysis a much smoother process.

Analyzing data: Data collected from a focus group can be coded by creating categories. As it is qualitative data, you may *not* know ahead of time how many or what categories are needed. You can create as many categories as needed during data description and organization. At the preliminary stage of data analysis, it is best to describe data in detail and not skip anything. You can also do coding by identifying keywords. For example, when discussing community policing, you may have a list that contains keywords such as fear, trust, bridge, stakeholder, care, and so on. As you start reading data and categories, you will begin to see if there are some common ideas or perceptions shared by members, identify what were unique experiences, create **relationship diagrams**, and so on. Relationship diagrams describe the interconnectedness of various factors in a setting or event. After the initial coding, the researcher can start the focused coding by collapsing certain categories together, identifying recurring ideas and common patterns, and so on. Many researchers identify any significant quotes from the participants that can be highlighted or quoted verbatim.

Focus Groups – Generalizability

One of the major limitations of using a focus group is the sample size, which results in a lack of **generalizability**. Not only might the sample not represent the population, but it could also be so small that it may be difficult to generalize the findings. A few exceptions may be if the population itself is quite small – for example, people living across a small stretch of a road that gets flooded every time it rains. However, even when working with a large population, as long as the focus group serves the research topic and setting, it is fine to use it, especially to gain initial knowledge. Lack of generalizability does not mean that the data has no value. It just means that the researcher should present findings in their limited context and not overgeneralize. Many researchers use focus groups to get a preliminary understanding or a quick snapshot of the setting. This can help develop case studies – study a specific setting, event, or context and the findings apply to that only. A **case study** can be about an individual, event, organization, group, family, and so on – it must be understood within that context, setting, or framework only (Tight, 2017).

Focus Groups – Ethics

Among ethical considerations, researchers using focus groups should pay very close attention in particular to no harm to subjects, voluntary participation, and anonymity and confidentiality. While planning to constitute a focus group, the researcher would be mindful of power dynamics and potential conflicts of interest among participants.

Figure 8.4 Conflict of Interest

For example, asking employees to talk about problems with the senior management in a focus group that also includes members of senior management is not likely to result in valid data. Power dynamics as well as group dynamics may also raise concerns about **voluntary participation, anonymity**, and **confidentiality**. The face-to-face interaction among participants will automatically bring these considerations to the fore. Therefore, the IRB would evaluate the proposal to use a focus group as a tool for the data collection on these ethical grounds. The researcher would need to consider how to best constitute a focus group or if it may be useful to have more than one focus group.

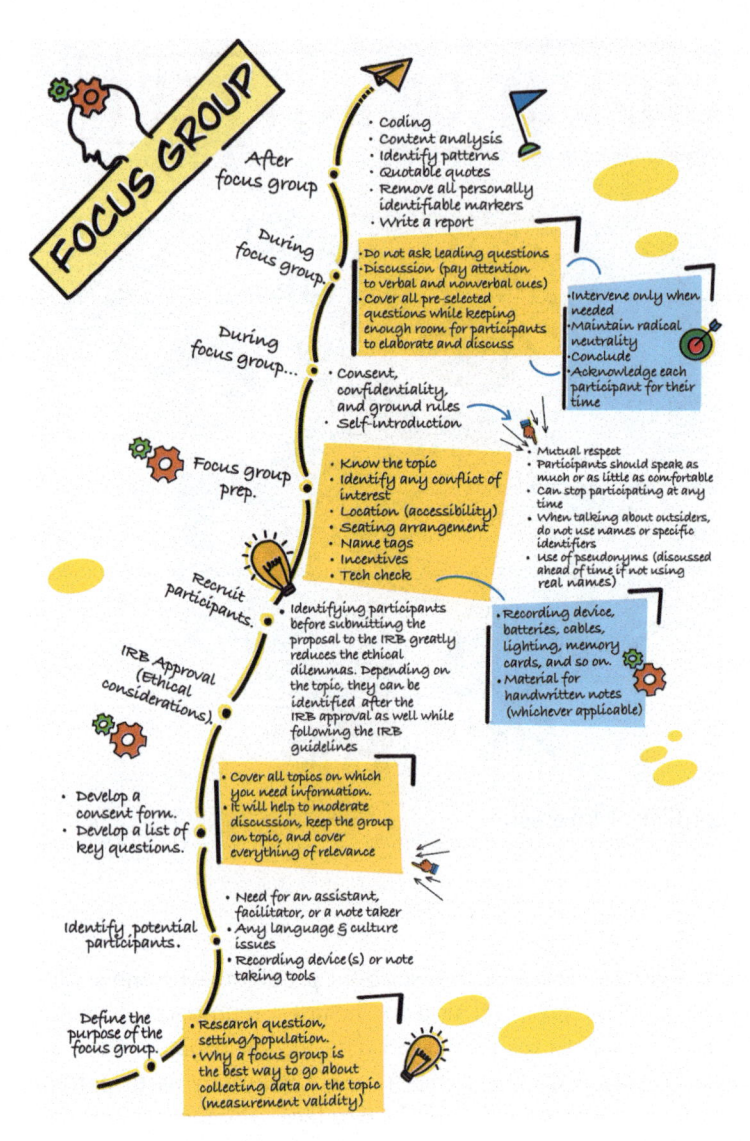

Figure 8.5 Focus Groups

Planning for Observation and Intensive Interviews

The following are the basic steps involved in planning **observation** and **intensive interviews**. Depending on the research method and the question, some steps may need more critical planning and evaluation than others. As you read about covert and overt observations and intensive interviews, examine each of the following steps.

Research topic and question → the group or setting → training and preparation (language, culture, customs, tech needs, notetaking, etc.)

168 qualitative research methods

methodological considerations (sampling method, type of observation, intensive interview) → ethical considerations → expectations about generalizability → gaining access → establishing a rapport → making observations/conducting interviews (data collection) → exiting the setting → analyzing and organizing data → writing a report and presenting findings.

Observation

Observation is another widely used qualitative method. It allows direct understanding and examination of settings and behaviors. Field observation allows for a better understanding of research subjects in their natural social settings instead of observations made in a lab or controlled setting. It allows researchers to observe behaviors and situations that cannot be replicated in an artificial setting.

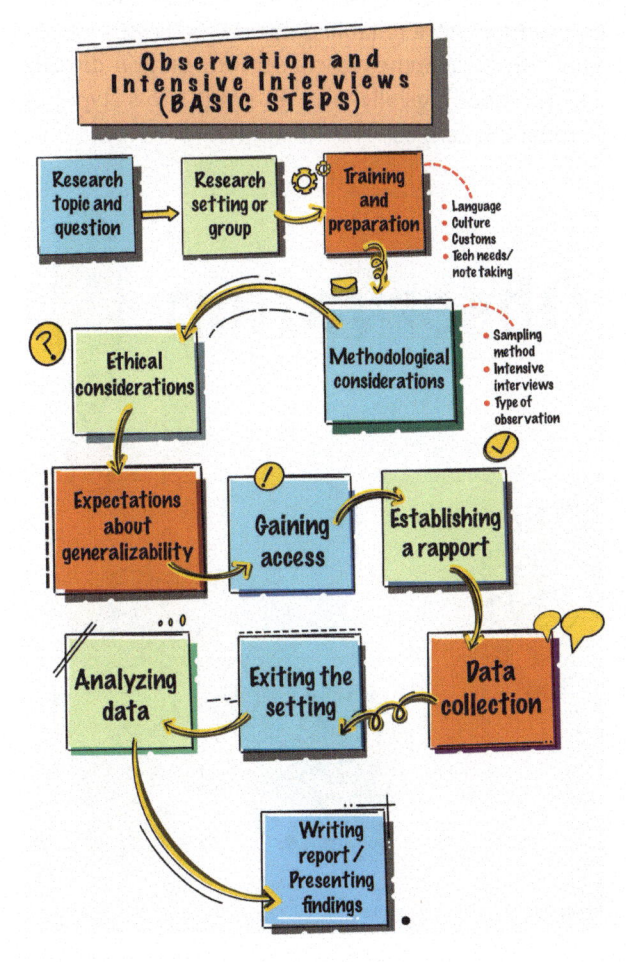

Figure 8.6 Observation and Intensive Interviews – Basic Steps

Types of Observation

Observation can be covert or overt. In **covert observation**, also called **covert participation**, subjects do not know that they are being observed. The researcher immerses in the setting and observes and interacts with people without revealing his or her actual identity or the purpose of the research. In using this type of observation, gaining access to the setting is extremely challenging as it is predicated on the ability of the researcher to come across as a member of the setting. This would be impacted by language, appearance, mannerisms, cultural understanding, and so on.

For many topics, research subjects may report more positively about their own behavior. For example, self-report surveys may suffer from bias. In experiments, the subjects may not be able to assess their abilities accurately. Similarly, in observation, research subjects may modify their behavior as they become aware of being observed. In such situations, covert observation would produce more reliable data.

Covert observation allows the researcher to collect information directly without any filters, but, methodologically and ethically, this type of observation presents the most challenges.

Figure 8.7   Covert Observation

- **Deception:** The inherent deception involved in covert observation compromises the ethical guidelines of voluntary participation. People in the setting do not know that they are being observed and that their behavior is being documented for research purposes.
- **Maintaining cover, risk, and harm:** In covert observation, maintaining cover is central to the success of data collection. However, there is a real risk of facing a dilemma that involves blowing one's cover or involves a serious risk to the researcher, research subject, or both. Both choices are bad, and in such a scenario, it is best to exit the setting. Therefore, while planning to carry out covert observation, the exit plan and conditions must be fully discussed and evaluated by the researchers and the IRB or ethics committee ahead of time.
- **Objectivity:** As the researcher spends a longer time making covert observations, there is a real concern about losing objectivity. This may result in some questionable conduct being overlooked or even justified. It is a worrisome concern in some quarters of the news media and academia where some may confuse an explanation of criminal behavior with its rationalization. Researchers may over-identify with the research subject or their views and lose objectivity. The longer the time spent in making covert observations, the higher the risk of the researcher becoming involved in the day-to-day lives of the research subjects. This is bound to pose a challenge in terms of maintaining appropriate boundaries.
  - One suggestion for researchers is to maintain contact with someone outside the setting familiar with their work. This would help to keep things in perspective.
- **Notetaking:** During covert observations, it is not possible for the researcher to just take out a notepad or a recorder and start jotting down information. The researcher will have to find a time and location to document information. The longer it takes to do so, the more memory gaps, and thus gaps in data will result.

The very reason for using a qualitative method is the lack of enough information about the subject, topic, or setting that would have allowed one to test hypotheses. It also implies that there is a greater potential for facing unanticipated events when using qualitative methods. Though the researcher may not have enough information about the research topic, still, getting as much training about the setting, language, or customs will help gain access and trust, build a rapport, navigate the setting, and exit without getting in trouble or causing harm.

In **overt observation/overt participation**, the subjects know that they are being observed.

- The researchers can make observations while also asking questions and can document information without any fear; the participants can also share some information off the record, thus allowing for the voluntary sharing of information in ways they feel comfortable with.
- The researchers face lower risk as people in the setting know who they are and do not assume a threat from an outsider or a stranger.
- When comfortable, the participants can let the researcher shadow them as they go through their routine activities.
- While making observations, the researcher is free to ask questions, learn, and become familiar with the setting and people, but should not fake familiarity.
- The researcher must use the commonsense approach to starting, engaging in, and concluding sensitive conversations.
- Understanding local language and social customs would be useful in gaining trust and carrying on conversations. It also makes a strong case for collaborating with local researchers and experts.

Despite many advantages, this type of observation has the limitation of **reactive effect** due to which participants act in a certain way as they know that they are being observed. Additionally, as people know of the presence and role of the researcher, they may share some of the information only with others in the setting and not with an outsider (researcher).

Figure 8.8 Reactive Effect

Some researchers also combine the two types of observation. In such a scenario, a few members of the setting would know the identity of the researcher, but others would not. It allows the researcher to gain access a bit more easily with the help of those who know the researcher. It has benefits of both covert and overt observation, and also challenges and limitations of both. It is a difficult balancing act and not recommended for long-term field research. It would also be challenging to remember who in the setting are aware of the researcher's identity and who are completely in the dark.

Data analysis in observation: Just as in focus groups, after data collection, the researcher must describe everything in detail. The preliminary description of data should not filter anything out. This is followed by coding, finding any common themes or observations across research subjects, identifying unique experiences, making relationship diagrams, and so on. It is always a good idea to identify any gaps in data. Researchers using qualitative methods should also attempt to inductively develop a theoretical framework that can be examined by studies in the future – a **grounded theory** – a theory grounded in the evidence collected and analyzed in the study.

A Quick Word on Technology

Murphy's Law

'Everything that can go wrong, will go wrong'

Technological advances have made it easy to record data. However, there may still be additional challenges in field research. While doing field research, many researchers may not have easy access to charge phones, recording devices, data cards, and so on. These issues must also be planned for ahead of time.

BOX 8.1 – Murphy's Law

After collecting data from Hindu refugees in the field in Kali Beri, Jodhpur, Rajasthan, India, I had almost a day to spare. The next day, I was flying back to my hometown (in India) and then returning home to the United States. I had taken immense care to carry extra battery packs and chargers as I knew that it may not be possible to charge the camera and recorder while in the field. As I had completed data collection, one of the volunteers suggested visiting the famous Mehrangarh Fort. I visited the fort and a couple of other places. At some point, the data card in the camera stopped working. Presuming that it was full, I changed it and continued with the trip. When I returned to the hotel in the evening, I tried to copy the card's contents onto a laptop. To my utter panic, the card was unreadable. It was the same card that I had used to record interviews and take pictures. It was a rudimentary mistake – I should not have used the same data card. There was no way that I would ask the respondents to narrate their painful narratives of forced and violent displacement again. After I reached my hometown and dealt with a few novices, I was finally able to find a reliable company that worked out of somewhere near Delhi. All the videos were lost, but almost 140 photographs were retrieved. What saved the project was that for every interview, I also used a digital audio recorder. Since that experience, I constantly back up data and use separate data card(s) for research activities. Nowadays, one can automatically back up data onto a 'cloud' or online storage. It would need to be noted in the IRB proposal as to where the data would be stored, for how long, and who would have access to it. It is important to have multiple plans when doing field research. In some cases, you may only have one shot at data collection, and in many cases, it would be unethical and unprofessional to ask research subjects to go through the process again.

Anonymity and confidentiality: At a conference, I once saw a video about a research subject involved in the informal banking system. The researcher had blurred the subject's face but did not blur the name of the shop behind the research subject. Anyone who knew the local language could read exactly where the shop was that this person operated the informal money transfer business from. Chapter 3 highlights the ethical issues surrounding the use of digital data. The same care should be taken while making presentations at conferences, seminars, or any other setting.

BOX 8.2 – Study on Women in Outlaw Motorcycle Gangs

In their study on women in outlaw motorcycle gangs, Hopper and Moore (1990) gathered data through interviews and participant observation over 17 years. They also interviewed and received data through correspondence from male and female motorcycles in state and federal prisons. Their analysis is based on the data collected from bikers in Mississippi, Tennessee, Louisiana, and Arkansas. Hopper and Moore estimate the sample to be in the hundreds, but note that it was not possible to give the exact number (sample size) of bikers due to the length of the time and the informal nature of interactions. The bikers did not allow notetaking or the use of any recording device. They also would not fill in any questionnaires. The researchers were clear in the purpose of their study – to learn about outlaw motorcycle clubs as social organizations. During these interactions, the study notes, the researchers at times were conflicted. At times they admired the sense of freedom, fearlessness, and commitment that the women bikers had, and at times they were made uncomfortable by some of their actions. The researchers, however, did not voice their opinions as that would have compromised the study or even put them at risk. They note that even seemingly insignificant uninvited comments could cause a problem. Though there have been several studies on men in outlaw motorcycle gangs, there has been limited work on women in motorcycle gangs. During data collection, the researchers found women to be more reluctant to talk to outsiders, especially in the presence of men. It took them a longer time to establish a rapport with women. The researchers had to ask questions and make observations, but not come across as too inquisitive. In the last few years of their fieldwork, the researchers noted that some of the bikers whom they had known for years, had become suspicious of them (Hopper and Moore, 1990).

Intensive Interviews

The third qualitative method is **intensive interviewing**. The researcher has the topic and a general understanding of what to ask. This is considered a semi-structured tool as the questions are open-ended and flow from the conversations. Even if the researcher asks similar questions on the topic, each respondent may give different answers, making for varied conversations. There is no set rule about the length of an intensive interview. Some interviews may last for 30–40 minutes, while others may last for hours. In some instances, the researcher may continue to engage with the same respondent for multiple hours each day for several days. It depends on the topic, research subject, and setting. Due to the length of the intensive interviewing, researchers take extra care in selecting the location that the respondent is most comfortable with. The researcher should be prepared to spend time taking part in routine activities or having conversations other than the main topic. Any method that involves direct interaction requires researchers to be well-trained in the art of communication and intentional listening and to have a willingness to learn. The researcher should also be able to observe body language and assess if the respondent is getting uncomfortable. The researcher should be attentive to the respondent's needs, concerns, and fears and listen and interact with compassion (Tillmann-Healy, 2003).

Ethical considerations: The length and nature of intensive interviews raise several ethical considerations. During an interview, the research subject may get emotional or feel distressed (Peled and Leichtentritt, 2002; Clarke, 2006) while sharing experiences of victimization, fear, bias, and so on. Research in the fields of medicine, social work, bereavement, and nursing can provide great insights for researchers in criminal justice, criminology, and sociology. Along with assessing any potential **harm to subjects**, it also requires a closer examination of **voluntary participation** and **informed consent** (Sinding and Aronson, 2003). Some respondents may, out of emotion, end up sharing more information than they had intended to share. The researcher would need to consider when to stop the interview and also provide information for counseling. The latter may not be available in every setting, and the role of the researcher in identifying when the respondent is feeling distressed and how to gradually close the interview becomes even more vital.

In intensive interviewing, emotions may impact the researchers as well, and they should guard against over-involvement. Though it may be more obvious to those who have a background and training in social work, psychiatry, or medicine, researchers from other backgrounds should also get adequate training to identify the risk of over-identification and over-involvement during data collection. Emotions are not divorced from research, and qualitative research, in particular, considers this. However, the research process should be carried out objectively and scientifically. When collecting data from vulnerable populations, power and access are of great importance (Cohn and Lyons, 2003). That is why researchers should disclose their professional background and affiliation to the respondents right at the start (Richards and Schwartz, 2002). However, in some settings, it may continue to gnaw at your mind. For example, in my study on Hindu refugees seeking resettlement and citizenship in India, while I stated my background and professional affiliation right at the start, all through collecting data I repeatedly emphasized that I had no power or influence to change their conditions. Despite stressing this multiple times, and though respondents expressed that they were glad that someone wanted to talk about what they have been facing, I at times wondered if everyone understood what it meant to be part of an academic research project.

Data analysis: The first step in data analysis in intensive interviewing is to transcribe all the information in complete detail without overlooking anything. Many field interviews may also require translation. In intensive interviews, the inductive approach commonly allows for thematic content analysis and narrative analysis. These are useful approaches in studies involving grounded theories.

- In **thematic content analysis**, the researcher focuses mainly on identifying and categorizing common themes and patterns. The

researcher will go through the transcripts and create categories and codes for common themes followed by analysis.
- In **narrative analysis**, the researcher focuses on individual stories and highlights the key points. This allows them to understand and present the construct from the individual respondent's perspective. It advances and frames the understanding of people's experiences with reference to space and time.

Researchers will often combine the two types of analysis by finding commonalities while highlighting or spotlighting individual quotes, incidents, and so on.

Generalizability: Similar to other qualitative methods, intensive interviews also lack generalizability or have limited generalizability. With thematic content analysis, the researcher aims to find experiences that are common across the board, and thus gain some generalizability of select factors. However, more often than not, qualitative methods, including intensive interviews, reveal individual experiences that are of immense value. After all, you are not going to say that a victim's account is not worthy enough of research and analysis as 'it is just one victim!' As long as the researcher is not force-fitting conclusions, it is an adequate method to understand and share individual narratives and personal experiences.

Figure 8.9   No Generalizability

qualitative research methods

In social sciences and humanities, researchers often argue about the significance of qualitative versus quantitative approaches. However, the utility of any research and sampling method is determined by the question at hand – as long as it helps to examine it, it is a good research method. Generalizability in both qualitative and quantitative research methods is also impacted by the sample size and sampling method. There is no perfect method that fits all types of research. The researcher needs to be aware of the limitations of the research and sampling methods and note the same in the report writing.

Qualitative research has greatly benefited from software programs such as nVivo, Atlas.ti, and HyperRESEARCH.

- HyperRESEARCH - https://www.researchware.com/products/hyperresearch.html
- nVivo - https://lumivero.com/products/nvivo/nvivo-product-tour/
- Atlas.ti - https://atlasti.com/

Qualitative Research – Visual Digital Data

Digital or online data is used in many disciplines across qualitative and quantitative research methods. This section highlights a few key issues to consider while using qualitative research methods. **Structured digital data** can be in the form of numbers organized into tables, graphs, charts, and so on. In qualitative research, **unstructured digital data** such as images, audio, and videos require additional attention.

Across many disciplines, including sociology, criminal justice, political science, mass communication, and so on, information is shared through visual imagery such as photographs, documentaries, and video clips. Almost all social space today is saturated with visual imagery. A large amount of this data is disseminated and curated digitally across news, social media, and entertainment platforms. Many narratives and perceptions are built around it. Cell phones with cameras mean that almost everyone can create or contribute to social narratives. Therefore, researchers in social sciences and humanities need to be trained in **visual fieldwork** and recognize that just taking a picture or making a video is not research. It is similar to starting with an opinion. One has to be trained in the research concepts to logically and authentically place and explain those pictures, photo essays, or videos with reference to the discipline that it applies to. **Concerned criminology** (Voorde, 2017) has been highlighting wide-ranging topics including selective coverage of socially constructed crises – *constructed* here does not mean fake, but how the crisis is presented. The researcher thus needs to recognize the limitations of unstructured digital data.

- **Representing versus Re-presenting** ("Visual Criminology," 2014): Along with framed or cropped pictures, researchers using digital data will deal with false images or video clips as well as subjective interpretations. We often look at an image and build a story around it. Many such images are printed on posters, t-shirts, mugs, and stickers. We assign positive and negative values to the subject in the image. This construction of meaning leads to the **normative argument** ("Visual Criminology," 2014); that is, we make a judgment about the person, group, situation, and so on without always knowing the context or even checking the facts. It is important, therefore, to "take a step back from theorizing *about* images" and consider the construction of meaning ("Visual Criminology," 2014).
- **Impact:** While doing research using visual data, researchers must avoid bias and cynicism, guard against the voyeurism of crime imagery, and not limit their understanding only to violent or offensive images. Instead, the researcher must be concerned about the larger impact of that moment that has been captured. Media uses images of women, children, and even animals and cartoons to get attention and reaction – these are all visual means of communication aimed at creating an impact. On the other hand, making 'fun' or 'cute' cartoons about violence and criminals glosses over or downplays the actual criminality. Researchers need to be mindful of this to avoid stereotyping, illogical reasoning, and overgeneralizations while ensuring that the authentic meaning is conveyed.
- **Phenomenology:** Images can also reflect phenomenology – the science of experience. Owing to subjective experiences and preset notions, people looking at the same image or video may interpret it differently. Images, after all, are presenting or showcasing a certain point of view. These are qualitative pieces of information that tend to set an agenda from social media to news media and academic research and from scholarship to politics. Therefore, it is better to treat visual data available online as a starting point for further investigation of any topic and not always complete or an end in itself.
- **Repeat images or over-representation:** Repeat images or over-representation of one or the other group in news about crime as well as research about crime begins to shape perceptions about the whole group or class of people (Leverentz, 2012). In visual criminology, there is a concept called **cognitive maps** – people begin to see their groups in the way the media portrays them (Leverentz, 2012). Leverentz (2012) argues that this begins to shape people's behavior within their groups, and collectively images of typical offenders are created and shared in media and media studies. By the same argument, some groups are overlooked as victims while some are overlooked as perpetrators, and that too distorts reality through omission. It does not mean that the researcher cannot focus on a specific aspect of the issue and generate or analyze imagery only on that

topic. Instead, it warrants that the researchers be clear about the limited focus and generalizability, if any, of their work just as they would do while using any other research method and data.

You may have heard the phrase 'a picture is worth a thousand words.' That is what media is tapping into – using a lot of images – and many researchers are doing the same. Come to think of it, it is interesting how much we communicate using emojis these days.

Figure 8.10 Emojis

While using images – still or moving – researchers should use the same care to guard against errors in reasoning as explained in Chapter 1 – **overgeneralization, hypothesis myopia, confirmation bias, illogical reasoning, neophobia**, and so on. It is important to remember these issues as we increasingly use data available in the online space.

> **Helpful Hint:** Unstructured data such as photos and videos are quite powerful ways to create and shape narratives. Not surprisingly, a 10-second video clip may generate more curiosity or have a more affective impact than a long research paper, but the researcher should know the limitations of one source over the other.

Access: You have to be extra careful when using online data about other cultures and people. Along with a **digital divide**, there is also a language gap. From journals and books to Wikipedia, most information is in the English language. Though some of the content may be automatically

180 qualitative research methods

translated into other languages, this does not mean that it has broader cultural, historical, or social sensibilities – it contains the same gaps as the English-language content. Often, the English-language content is produced and framed from a **Eurocentric** or Western view or for a Western audience. It keeps Western academics and scholars in their comfort zone. Even popular theories in criminology that we examine are developed and tested in Western paradigms. This does not mean discarding the Western examination of non-Western settings; it only indicates the need to expand our understanding and contribute to creating original knowledge through more collaborative work.

One way to have a broader perspective is to take a step back and let indigenous or local voices take the lead in telling their stories. One needs to prioritize content and substance over technology. Just because you can go in a space with cameras and all the gadgets, it does not mean that you have a better understanding of how things work or should work. The research tools do not substitute for emotional and cultural canvas and sensibilities. As in the case of using any qualitative method, one has to be willing to learn, and not approach any digital data with a preset conclusion.

Research significance: Researchers can use social media and other platforms to share their research with a larger audience that may not access journal articles or books. However, they must guard against establishing the significance of their work, and sometimes even the validity of their research, based on the number of likes and shares. Just like other public figures, they too then run the risk of online trolling and bullying, and some may feel compelled to pick sides to remain in the cloak of 'digital safety'. But that presents another challenge for social scientists to resist joining – or worse, leading – digital mobs.

- This does not mean not using online platforms, but being mindful of if you are staying in compartmentalized spaces and silos and thus committing errors in reasoning of selective observation or confirmation bias, creating facts by repetition, and so on. The academic space is more insular than the news media, and one may not even catch a lot of the errors for a while. Collectively, these factors impact the relevance, **authenticity**, and overall quality and direction of the research.
- One way to identify these errors is to remain engaged offline, and periodically take a break. Think of it like a qualitative method of field participation where researchers get immersed in the setting – but to maintain objectivity and not lose perspective, they must get out at times or stay connected with people outside of the setting. Use the same logic when engaging through online platforms, using digital data, or conducting research in the online space.

> **BOX 8.3 – Quantitative Analysis of Qualitative Data**
>
> Natarajan (2006) analyzed 2,048 wiretap conversations that were gathered in New York City in the 1990s during the prosecution of a group dealing in heroin. This represents a quantitative analysis of qualitative data. It involved a five-step analysis: counting the number of people that each individual was in contact with; determining the major tasks performed by each individual; using a coding guide to assess the relative status of each individual; using the UCINET VI software program for social network analysis; and examining geographical locations using the addresses of the outgoing phone calls. The study found that the core consisted of 38 individuals, and that the group was loosely structured around 294 individuals. The wiretaps did not confirm a large network as many individuals did not interact with others in the group. This supported the assertion that most drug traffickers worked in smaller groups rather than being part of one large or highly structured syndicate (Natrajan, 2006).

Gatekeepers: Many researchers using qualitative methods rely on gatekeepers who help them access the setting – online or offline. This automatically means that the researchers' view of the setting may be shaped by what the gatekeepers see as relevant. If possible, researchers should not rely on a single source and should try to cultivate contacts from across the sociocultural spectrum.

In many settings and for many topics, the qualitative approach may be more demanding of the researcher and also require greater interaction between the researcher and the research subjects. It allows the examination of unique experiences, but for the same reason, it also has limited opportunity for replication, and that invites criticism. The researcher's **subjectivity** may also be impacted due to the nature of interaction and decisions made in the field about how to navigate the space. Due to the **interpretive** and **constructivist** approaches (Leedy and Ormrod, 2014), it is argued that the same phenomenon may be studied differently by different researchers. As an aside, the same could also apply to surveys and the way the questions are framed.

Both approaches – quantitative and qualitative – would deliver interesting and useful data, albeit requiring a different kind of analysis. To sum it up, once again, choose the research approach that best serves your research topic and setting.

Though I have used examples of complex topics of study in this chapter, even for relatively simple topics such as feedback on a food item, you can either use a scale (quantitative) and ask people to rate the taste or quality, or engage in a discussion (qualitative) about what they liked and how it made them feel.

Figure 8.11   Quantitative Data and Qualitative Data

For a long time, there has been an artificial hierarchy that places quantitative research above qualitative research. The primary argument has been based on the higher generalizability in quantitative methods and the ease of obtaining and presenting quantified information. However, many human experiences and behaviors cannot be studied in-depth through numbers. When asking a question to rate items on fear, trauma, pain, worry, happiness, thrill, and so on, the numerical scales or the numbers may very well mean different things to different respondents. On a scale of 1 to 10, one person may rate his toothache at 10 while another may rate his at 2. What does this really mean? It is difficult to gauge certain items on quantified scales. Some scales could be too restrictive simply because the researcher cannot anticipate the wide range of experiences in certain settings or on certain topics. When done right, qualitative methods allow the respondents to be placed at the front and center of research, which helps to create a wider understanding of real-life situations, experiences, perceptions, and attitudes. Qualitative research allows us to construct and reconstruct theories when necessary.

qualitative research methods   183

Further Reading

- Hopper, Columbus B., and Johnny Moore. (1990). Women in Outlaw Motorcycle Gangs. *Journal of Contemporary Ethnography.* Vol.18(4), pp.383–87.
- Ebbs. C. (1996). Qualitative Research Inquiry: Issues of Power and Ethics. *Education.* Vol.117(2), pp.217-22.
- Ensign, Josephine. (2003). Ethical Issues in Qualitative Health Research with Homeless Youths. *The Journal of Advanced Nursing.* Vol.43(1): 43-50.
- Visual Criminology: Viewing and Thinking About Images. April 30, 2014. Centre for Criminology. Retrieved from https://blogs.law.ox.ac.uk/centres-institutes/centre-criminology/blog/2014/04/visual-criminology-viewing-and-thinking-about

Key Terms

Anonymity
Authenticity
Case study
Cognitive maps
Concerned criminology
Confidentiality
Confirmation bias
Constructivist approach
Covert observation
Deception
Descriptive
Digital divide
Eurocentric
Evaluative
Explanatory
Exploratory
Focus groups
Gatekeepers
Grounded theory
Hypothesis
Hypothesis myopia
Illogical reasoning
Inductive approach
Informed consent
Intensive interviews
Interpretive approach
Narrative analysis
Neophobia
Normative argument
Objectivity
Overgeneralization
Phenomenology
Qualitative research
Reactive effect
Relationship diagrams
Structured digital data
Subjectivity
Thematic content analysis
Unstructured digital data
Visual fieldwork
Voluntary participation
Weed and Seed Program

Class Activity

1. Divide the class into two groups. Pick one general research topic and design one qualitative and one quantitative research approach to examine it. Pick a simple topic that can be studied using the class as a sample. After collecting data, examine the difference in the nature of data and conclusions about the topic.

2. Divide the class into smaller groups where students can work in pairs. Give each pair 12 Lego pieces – 2 pieces each of 6 different colors. That is, the pair should have the same sizes and colors of Lego pieces. The students should sit with their backs against each other. In the first instance, Student A would make a design using the six Lego pieces. Student B will try to make the same design without looking at the design by Student A. Student B will ask questions that can be answered by 'yes' or 'no' only. If the question cannot be answered in a 'yes' or 'no', Student A will ask Student B to rephrase the question. Give them about 5–7 minutes to work on it. After that, they can see how similar or dissimilar the designs were.

Next, they will again sit with their backs against each other and Student B will make a design. This time, Student A will try to make the same design; however, Student A can ask open-ended questions and Student B can explain it in as much detail as they want to. Student A can also ask Student B to explain or elaborate further. That is, it will be a conversation without any structured questions or response options. Give students about 5–7 minutes to work on it. After that, they can see how similar or dissimilar the designs were.

Engage students in a discussion about which design was easier to understand and create and why. At the end of the discussion, inform the class that Part 1 of the activity is an example of quantitative methods, and Part 2 is an example of qualitative methods.

Works Cited

Clarke A. 2006. "Qualitative Interviewing: Encountering Ethical Issues and Challenges." *Nurse Researcher*, Vol.13(4), pp. 19–29.

Cohn, Ellen S., and Kathleen Doyle Lyons. 2003. "The Perils of Power in Interpretive Research." *American Journal of Occupational Therapy*, Vol.57(1), pp. 40–48.

Cornwall, A., and R. Jewkes. 1995. "What Is Participatory Research?" *Social Science and Medicine*, Vol.14, pp. 1667–1676.

Hopper, Columbus B., and Johnny Moore. 1990. "Women in Outlaw Motorcycle Gangs." *Journal of Contemporary Ethnography*, Vol.18(4), pp. 383–387.

Krueger, R. A., and M. A. Casey. 2000. *Focus Groups: A Practical Guide for Applied Research*. 4th ed. Thousand Oaks, CA: Sage Publications Inc.

Leedy, P., and J. E. Ormrod. 2014. *Practical Research Planning and Design*. 10th ed. Edinburgh: Pearson Educational Inc.

Leverentz, Andrea 2012. "Narratives of Crime and Criminals: How Places Socially Construct Crime Problem." *Sociological Forum*, Vol.27(2), pp. 348–371.

Natrajan, M. 2006. "Understanding the Structure of a Large Heroin Distribution Network: A Quantitative Analysis of Qualitative Data." *Journal of Quantitative Criminology*, Vol. 22(2), pp. 171–192.

Peled, E., and Ronit Leichtentritt. 2002. "The Ethics of Qualitative Social Work Research." *Qualitative Social Work*, Vol.1(2), pp. 145–69.

Richards, H. M., and L. J. Schwartz. 2002. "Ethics of Qualitative Research: Are There Special Issues for Health Services Research?" *Family Practice*, Vol.19(2), pp. 135–139.

Sinding, C., and Jane Aronson. 2003. "Exposing Failures, Unsettling Accommodations: Tensions in Interview Practice." *Qualitative Research*, Vol.3(1), pp. 95–117.

Tight, Malcolm. 2017. *Understanding Case Study Research: Small Scale Research with Meaning*. Thousand Oaks, CA: Sage.

Tillmann-Healy, L. 2003. "Friendship as Method." *Qualitative Inquiry*, Vol.9(5), pp. 729–749.

"Visual Criminology: Viewing and Thinking About Images." 2014, April 30. Centre for Criminology. Retrieved from https://blogs.law.ox.ac.uk/centres-institutes/centre-criminology/blog/2014/04/visual-criminology-viewing-and-thinking-about

Voorde, Cecile Van de. 2017. "The Concerned Criminologist. Refocusing the Ethos of Socially Committed Photographic Research." In Michael Brown and Eamonn Carrabine (eds.), *Routledge International Handbook of Visual Criminology*. London: Routledge, pp. 427–441.

chapter 9

Data Organization, Report Writing, and Presentation

This chapter explains data organization, data analysis, and data ethics. It includes a brief discussion on data manipulation through images, graphs, colors, and so on. The chapter explains the step-by-step process of report writing and presentation.

At the completion of this chapter, students will be able to understand and explain:

- How to organize data
- Descriptive and Inferential statistics
- Data ethics
- Report writing and presentation

Introduction

After doing all that research work, you need to be able to convey the findings to the target audience. Implicitly, you will need to know the audience in order to best communicate the findings. The format, length, and nature of the written material will vary according to the target audience. Writing a journal article is very different from writing a column in the local newspaper, even if both are based on the same work. Many researchers produce technical reports for agencies that fund research work on a very specific issue. The audience for such reports is much smaller than that for a journal article or a book.

Even the intelligence community produces many reports and follows many principles of research – developing a research question; defining a problem; linear and non-linear approaches; deductive, inductive, and abductive models; identifying target vulnerabilities; resources needed, including experts or contributors; resource allocation (time, funds, staff); and so on. Such reports cater to law enforcement, courts, lawmakers, businesses, and so on. It is important to know the consumer of the final product. Even when studying the same topic, an intelligence analyst would produce a different type of report for the customer. For example, a business entity would generally get the detailed report, while lawmakers are generally given shorter memos or briefs along with the detailed report.

Some research is available to the public through news and other portals; some may be available to a select population, such as faculty and students, through academic and research institutions; some may be available to the larger public but placed behind a paywall; and some may be produced for an organization's internal use only. Many research reports are available online to the public without any subscription or payment.

Let's have a quick look at some of the common issues to consider while writing a report.

Data Organization

After data collection, it is important to describe it in detail. Every aspect and element should be noted followed by coding, identifying patterns, establishing correlations, and so on. Though you can explain data in detail through text, you will also need to consider if certain data can be best represented through tables, charts, and graphs. At this stage, you will need to start thinking in terms of how to make data readable or easy to understand.

Frequency table: also called a **t-chart**, this shows the number of times something occurs in the sample. A frequency distribution could show one variable and its values (**univariate**), interaction between two variables (**bivariate**), or interaction among more than two variables (**multivariate**). Bivariate and multivariate tables are also called **contingency tables**. In the introductory statistics course, you will learn about more key terms and concepts. In this chapter, I will keep the focus on readability, writing, and presentation only.

The tables can contain raw values, percentages, or both. To improve readability, it is suggested to include both raw values and percentages. It can show grouped or ungrouped data. When a variable has too many values, it is best to group data or create categories.

Organizing Data

Age	Tally Marks	Frequency
18 - 27	|||| ||||	9
28 - 37	|||| |||| ||||	15
38 - 47	|||| |||| ||||	14
48 - 57	||||	4
58 and above	|||| |||	8

Frequency Table

Age	Number of Respondents
18 - 27	9
28 - 37	15
38 - 47	14
48 - 57	4
58 and above	8
Total	50

Figure 9.1   Organizing Data

data, report writing, and presentation

Pie chart: This shows values of one variable that must add up to 100 percent.

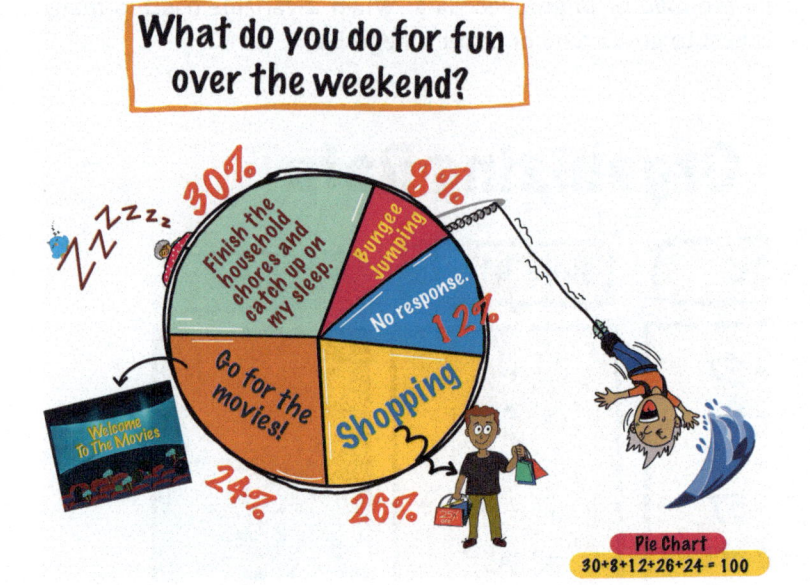

Figure 9.2 Pie Chart

Bar chart: It is best to use a bar chart to display a **nominal variable** the values of which have no overlap. These variables do not have any precise mathematical interpretation such as eye color, religion, location, marital status, sex, and so on. A bar chart is used to display one variable and its values. However, it does not mean that you need to create a bar chart for every nominal variable in your study. For example, you do not have to create a bar chart to 'display' that there were 15 men and 25 women in your sample. You can write that in one short sentence. That is, think about what variable(s) and their values would benefit from a bar chart or any other visual representation.

Histogram: This looks like a bar chart except there are no spaces among bars that represent the values of a variable. It is used for a continuous variable, such as age, income, years of education, and so on, while a bar chart is used for a discrete variable. Histograms can be used to display data on a **Likert-type scale** as well.

Word cloud: This is particularly useful for displaying qualitative data. Online word cloud generators can process large amounts of text in seconds in order to display which words occur most often.

Line chart: Also known as a **line graph** or **line plot**, this is a graph that uses a line to connect the individual data points or values of a variable. It is a simple visualization of patterns or trends over time.

Area graph: This is similar to a line chart and shows the development of values over time, but the area between the axis and line is filled with color.

Scatter plot: This is used to show a correlation between variables and is particularly useful for a larger dataset. It quickly and easily helps the reader to visualize the relationship or trend. The '**line of best fit**' or **trend line** is drawn using the closest data points and shows the correlation, trend, or prediction.

DRY-MIX: This stands for Dependent, Responding y-axis, Manipulated, Independent x-axis. That is, it is best to use the y-axis (vertical) to display the dependent variable and the x-axis (horizontal) to display the independent variable. The x and y axes cross at a point where the coordinates are 0,0.

Depending on the level of measurement (Chapter 4), there are several ways to visualize or display data (measures of central tendency and variability, also discussed in Chapter 4).

Data Analysis

Data analysis involves describing and interpreting data. Is there a meaningful correlation among variables? As discussed in Chapter 4, an increase in crime sometimes may also reflect increased trust in police due to higher crime reporting of previously unreported crimes. Similarly, the absence of data may not reflect an absence of crime. Use the same caution about data validity and reliability when analyzing data taken from online sources, especially crowd-funded platforms.

Figure 9.3 If It's Online …

data, report writing, and presentation

Interpreting data is not just a mathematical operation. Instead, various factors are taken into account to explain what data means or conveys. For example, *does a large prison population reflect a more effective criminal justice system?* When reading data, you will also need to figure out what specific piece of data you need to examine and why, and what variables to cross-tabulate. You need to wear dual hats to read and describe the data that you have collected (or it may be the secondary data that you may be using) as well as what it connotes or means.

Correlation essentially tells us if two or more variables are correlated. It is not the same as causation.

- **Causation** is based on the assumption that two or more *variables are related*.
- **Correlation** explains the *degree of that relation* – that is, how strong or how weak the correlation is between variables.

Regression explains how variables influence each other. It helps us to understand if the variables have a positive association or inverse association (Chapter 2). **Simple or linear regression** shows an interaction between one independent and one dependent variable. **Multiple or non-linear regression** shows interaction among multiple dependent and independent variables. It may even include multiple independent variables as in the case of the Minneapolis Domestic Violence Experiment (Chapter 2), which contained three independent variables – arrest, separation, or advise/counseling – while the dependent variable was the recidivism rate for domestic violence.

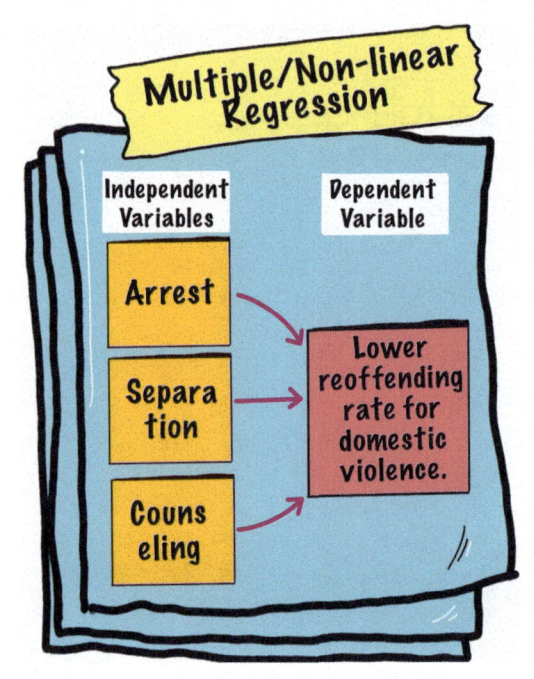

Figure 9.4 Multiple Regression

In sum, while interpreting data, it is important to guard against errors in reasoning and limit interpretation to what can be logically and systemically explained while ensuring authentic reporting of the findings.

Data Ethics

A quick note on data ethics to keep in mind when visualizing and presenting information.

- **Raw data and percentages:** If a study says that last year, 60% more women shopped online for sports equipment in location X, it would seem that there is a huge gap between men and women in their propensity to shop online for sports equipment. However, what if the raw numbers show that the sample size was 13, which included 8 women and 5 men, in a city of 200,000 people? Therefore, always include raw numbers and percentages to avoid misleading or misinterpretation about the sample size.
- **Colors and pictures:** Many people use the color red to show danger, risk, or fear. Many use pictures to get an emotional response. Some may use images for shock purposes. Some may manipulate the thickness of graph lines and text to get the audience to focus on one or the other part of the study or presentation. It is one thing to use these tools to highlight the most important findings or aspects of the study that need the most attention, but these must be avoided to oversell ideas, force-fit conclusions, or create sensationalism.
- **Apples and oranges:** Do not compare what is not comparable. Far too many people in the news and social media make extreme statements based on one or two elements across systems, cultures, or social realities that are fundamentally different. One must guard against this and identify what is truly comparable. For example, the more you study, the more you will learn that it is not possible to compare countries as 'units'. You may be able to identify specific systems within a country and compare them. Even within a country, you would find it challenging to compare different states. For example, New York is very different from Idaho, and Montana is very different from Texas. Despite taking courses in comparative politics, comparative religions, comparative criminal justice systems, and so on, you will realize that it is a very challenging task to compare values, systems, or behaviors outside of their historical, cultural, or social context. This does *not* imply a) rationalizing criminal behaviors within a context and normalizing it, or b) not learning anything from each other. It just means that one has to be mindful of the context and explain and understand behaviors and systems within that. For example, the criminal justice system in the United States may not be comparable to the one in Japan, but researchers in the United States could certainly use elements of the Japanese koban system to examine how community policing works

in that part of the world, and evaluate if it could work in smaller cities or towns, or specific neighborhoods in the United States.
- **Sampling and research methods:** While planning research, you will know what type of sampling and research methods have lower generalizability. It is important to bear that in mind even when analyzing data and reiterating the limitations of the study based on the sampling and research methods. Explain how the study achieved the sample or cross-population generalizability, or what factors compromised generalizations that the study had expected to achieve.

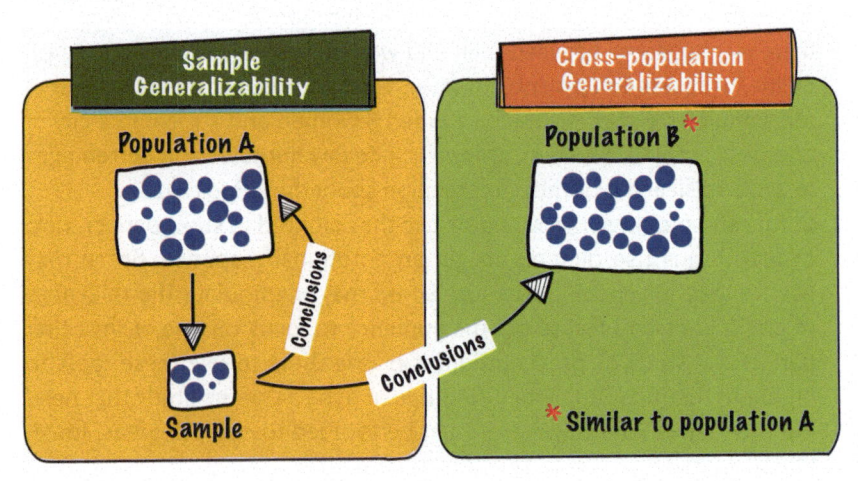

Figure 9.5 Generalizability

Software programs such as Excel, SPSS, Atlas ti., and so on can help you to analyze different types of data, but it cannot 'think' on your behalf about what variables to look for or analyze. That is why critical thinking and the clarity of the research question, sampling method, and research method are important at each step of the research process, including analysis and writing. Always have an awareness of what you are doing, how, and why. Software programs such as Atlas ti. or HyperRESEARCH can help quantify qualitative data and increase its readability, but that should not be confused with increased generalizability. One must remain true to the limitations of the study – sampling and research methods – and not present the findings as more than what they are.

Report Writing

Format and Structure

The basic research report can be divided into the following sections.
   Title page [separate page]
"The student title page includes the paper title, author names (the byline), author affiliation, course number and name for which the paper is

being submitted, instructor name, assignment due date, and page number, as shown in this example" ("Title Page Setup.").

APA title page, https://apastyle.apa.org/style-grammar-guidelines/paper-format/title-page

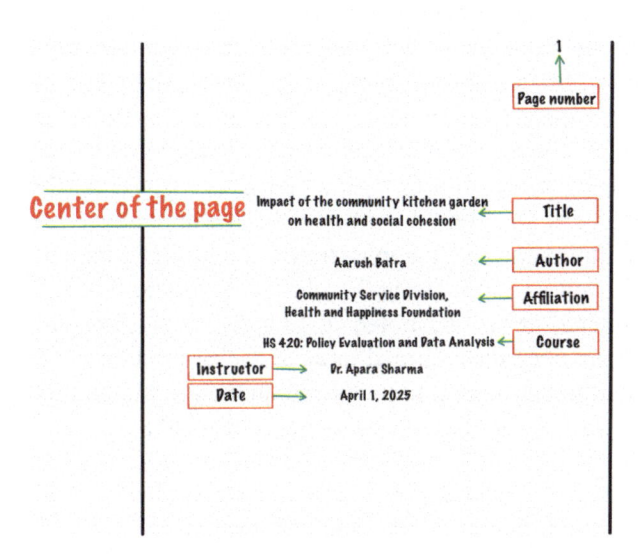

Figure 9.6 Title Page

Abstract [separate page]

The abstract appears right after the title page, but it is suggested to write it after writing the full report. When you have finished writing the report, you will have a better grasp of the key findings. In the abstract, you should include the overall purpose and research question or thesis statement, the sampling and research methods used, and the major findings of the study. It is best to not include any external sources or references to other works in the abstract. Below the abstract, list between three to five keywords that best describe your research work. This will help others to find the paper.

Main body [introduction, literature review, research method (including sampling method), findings, discussion, and concluding comments/recommendations]

Introduction: Give a clear and specific introduction to your research question. Explain it by giving context and background. The introduction should also indicate any specific factors such as recidivism rate, program funding, age group, and so on that your paper focuses on. You can also explain the variables of interest in the introduction. Let us assume that you are evaluating the policy of 'Stop and Frisk' in New York City and are focusing on racial and gender bias. In the introduction, give an overview of the variables and values of interest. This helps the reader to grasp the key points in the literature review and the subsequent data analysis and discussion. From a writing perspective, it can serve as a guide to organize the content as per the variables of interest.

Literature review: See Chapter 2 to read about the literature review. Remember that you would have reviewed the literature before conducting research. Approach the literature review as leading from general information about the topic to a very specific question and/or hypothesis. The literature review is not a summary of one article after the other. It is a synthesis of information from across sources. For example, let's say two articles by two different authors – Swann (2019) and Camacho (2014) – are making the same argument. In that case, you should not type the same argument twice and cite one author at a time – instead, paraphrase and combine (synthesize) information from both sources and cite both sources in one go, like this – (Swann, 2019; Camacho, 2014). As noted in Chapter 2, the literature review involves four main categories – broad topic or background, research categories, studies more closely relevant to your research question, and the hypothesis. At the very least, a literature review serves a two-fold purpose:

a. Learning about the topic, including how others have studied it, findings, and directions for future research – including yours.
b. It helps to develop a sound hypothesis as it is rooted in the 'education' about the topic – a hypothesis is an educated guess.

Limited or a lack of literature on a specific topic would prompt a researcher to use qualitative methods. That is, there is not enough information available for the researcher to propose and test a specific hypothesis. The literature review, even if not on the exact topic, can help to explain how the researcher arrived at the question(s) of interest in their study.

Research method: This gives a detailed overview of the sampling and research methods used in the study, the reason for using them, and their strengths and limitations. Many researchers address ethical considerations in this section as well, while many place them in the end matter.

Findings: In this section, include the major findings – quantitative and qualitative. Consider using data visualizations as needed. In some reports, the tables, figures, and charts are included in the main body while in others they are placed in the end matter.

Discussion: This is the analysis of the findings. You will not only explain, examine, and critically analyze the data that you have gathered, but also make connections back to the literature review, including any theoretical connections. If testing a hypothesis(es), you will explain what was proven and to what degree, what the surprise elements were, and so on.

Concluding comments/recommendations: It is suggested to bring everything together in the last section, which should highlight the most critical findings, make recommendations (if applicable), suggest the line of future research (if applicable), and so on. It is best to not include any external sources or references to other works in this section.

Starting from the introduction to the end of concluding comments/recommendations, the text flows without a page break.

End matter [References, Tables/figures/charts, and Endnotes]

References [separate page]

This section is called references, works cited, or bibliography. It contains a list of all the external sources used in the paper. All entries are in alphabetical order and should not contain bullets or numbers. See the APA guidelines (or the method suggested by the professor) for listing sources and format.

Tables/figures/charts [separate page]

Every figure, chart, or table should have a number and a name or a title. That number should be mentioned in the main body where it applies. Any table, chart, or graph that is placed in this section but not mentioned anywhere in the paper would be irrelevant. Whether it is charts and graphs or text, do not use a 'throw it all, something's gotta stick' approach. Know your topic and include only what is relevant to your work.

Some publications include tables, charts, or figures in the main body and may require you to indicate a placeholder for each item. In that case, follow the same method – Table 1.1 here; Figure 1.4 here; and so on.

Endnotes [separate page]

Some reports and papers may also include endnotes. These are used for descriptive and explanatory comments. The reader may be given additional information in this section that may obstruct the flow of information in the main body. Sometimes endnotes also include an acknowledgment.

Some reports may also include the research data collection tools, such as a blank survey/list of questions and an ethics statement. Some reports may also include an excerpt of the policy, law, or program that the study evaluated.

The citation methods also indicate line spacing, font size, placement of page numbers, section headings and levels, and so on. As many of these methods are updated every few years, it is best to use online resources to check the most recent editions.

APA, 7th Edition, Student Paper Setup Guide, https://apastyle.apa.org/instructional-aids/student-paper-setup-guide.pdf

Your professor would give you specific guidelines about Dos and Don'ts. Here are a few common tips to get used to:

- Do not write in the first person.
- Do not use abbreviations and acronyms without first using the full form. Even then, use acronyms only if necessary.

- The key to good writing is explaining one idea in one paragraph, or one set of paragraphs. Finish one thought before starting another.
- Proofread for grammatical, typographical, punctuation, and citation errors.
- Do not italicize, bold, or use quotes for emphasis or highlight unless it is permitted in the method of writing and organization, or instructured by the professor.
- Preferably, do not use contractions – instead of *don't, won't, they're, haven't*, write *do not, will not, they are, have not*, and so on.
- Each table, figure, or chart placed in the end matter must be referred to in the main body.
- Each table, figure, or chart must have a number and title.
- Do not use any automatic or online citation programs. Learn to use APA guidelines, or whichever method is required for your paper. APA, https://apastyle.apa.org/
- Do not try to memorize APA or any other method of writing, organizing, and citing. As you continue to use them, you will become more familiar with them. It is a matter of practice and habit, not memorization.
- Every aspect of research is time-consuming. Respect the process and its complexity.

> **Helpful Hint:** When you write a report, think back to any aspects of sampling and data collection that could have gone better, hurdles that you ran into, or ethical dilemmas that you faced. This information will be useful for your next project and for other researchers using similar methods or studying similar topics.

Presenting Findings

Though this section is not included in many research guides, as a student you may be asked to present your research in class, or you might get an opportunity to present at a conference. Typically, most academic presentations should include the research question, an overview of the method (sampling and research), and the key findings. Depending on the allocated time, the presentation can be elaborate on specific areas of interest. Here are a few useful tips.

- **Timeline:** Find out how much time you will get as a speaker. Practice speaking so that you stay within the given timeline. This conveys professionalism and respect for your own and other people's time.

- I once attended an event where the keynote speaker was supposed to speak for 45 minutes. After the 2-hour mark, he was still talking and more than half the audience members had left.
- At another event, I was at a panel discussion where I was told that each panelist would have 12–15 minutes. I prepared my presentation for 14 minutes. The other two panelists went on for 35 and 48 minutes, respectively. By the end of it, the audience did not have any time left to ask questions.
- At most conferences, back-to-back sessions are scheduled and you will not be allowed to go over time. The panel chair will give you an indicator to wrap it up, and you should.
- Therefore, while making any presentation, abide by the timeline. If you have a very short session, just share the most important point. Anyone interested in learning more about your work will reach out to you.
- **Presentation tools:** PowerPoints are omnipresent now and not very interesting. Still, they are a good way to stay on the most important points. For the most part, follow the 6 × 6 rule. Avoid having more than 6 bullet points on the slide, and avoid having more than 6 words in each bullet point.
  - Do not write everything on slides. If the audience can read everything on the slides, why would they listen to you?
  - Do not stand and read everything from the slides – use the bullet points as a guideline to stay on topic or cover all the major points.
  - If possible, mix text with imagery.
  - Do not use every special audio-video and animation effect included in the PowerPoint program.
  - Many PowerPoints include external links – in that case, reach the location early and test the Internet.
  - Include your contact information on the last slide.
  - Carefully plan color contrast for slides and text.
  - Do not be overrehearsed, but practice speaking – you should know the material.
  - Technology might fail, so have a backup plan: bring a couple of printouts of your presentation, bring a copy of your presentation on a USB or any other external drive, check clicker batteries, and so on. Often presenters email the presentation to themselves. That sounds like a good idea until you run into a poor Internet connection. Therefore, it is useful to have a copy on an external drive. It also saves time in a setting with multiple presenters.
- If you are chairing a panel, request all presenters to email you copies of their presentations ahead of time.

- Maintain eye contact across the room. Do not get fixated on just the front row.
- Try to use a conversational style of presentation.
- Humor can go a long way in making a connection with the audience, but remember a) humor is cultural or subjective; b) humor should not take away from the sanctity of your research.
- Be on time and be prepared. It is never exciting to attend an 8:30 am session where the speaker opens the presentation by saying, 'I just put it together' or reaches the venue at 8:40 am and starts setting up the equipment. If the audience has put in the time to be there, you should also come prepared to share your work.

Figure 9.7 Be Prepared

- I have learned these techniques and tips through trial and error over the years. It is never too early to start practicing.

Question and Answer Sessions

- If you have more than one panelist or presenter, do not hog all the questions. Answer what is specifically directed at you. It is fine to add a short comment or sentence or two, but do not take over the Question and Answer session.
- Some may ask questions that include multiple items. Keeping a pen and paper handy may be useful so that you do not lose track of what you have been asked and what you have answered.

- If you do not know the answer, just say so.
- If the question is outside the realm of your research, just say so.

That is pretty much it! Knowing these basic aspects of the research should be useful for anyone taking a research methods course for the first time. As you read more and do more research, you will continue to learn more. Do not overthink. Proceed one step at a time, and soon you will see it all come together. It is easy to complain about everything around the world; it is more challenging and useful to identify topics of interest in your immediate or local setting, examine them, and find solutions. Now you know how to go about it! All the best!

Further Reading

World Happiness Report, https://worldhappiness.report/

Key Terms

Abstract
Area graph
Bar chart
Bivariate frequency table
Causation
Contingency table
Correlation
DRY-MIX
End matter
Endnotes
Frequency table
Histogram
Introduction
Likert scale
Line chart
Line graph
Line of best fit
Line plot
Literature Review
Minneapolis Domestic Violence Experiment
Multiple regression
Multivariate frequency table
Nominal variable
Pie chart
Regression
Scatter Plot
Simple or linear regression
t-chart
Trend line
Univariate frequency table
Word Cloud

Class Activity

1. Invite two or three faculty members from your department or school to share one of their research works. Assign 15 minutes to each presenter. The presentation should include the research question, an overview of the method, and the key findings. Allocate points to students for asking at least three questions to each presenter (one student, one question). If it is a large class, students can sit in groups and ask questions on behalf of their group. After the presentations, engage students in a discussion on what aspects of the research and the presentations stood out the most for them and why.

2. If students are involved in doing research, organize a research day for your department or school. Organize multiple panels for students to share their research work. Assign 15 minutes to each presenter. The presentation should include the research question, an overview of the method, and the key findings. Set aside time for the audience questions. If it is a large class, organize a research poster session showcasing student research. The visitors/audience can walk around and ask questions.

Work Cited

"Title Page Setup." APA Style. Retrieved from https://apastyle.apa.org/style-grammar-guidelines/paper-format/title-page

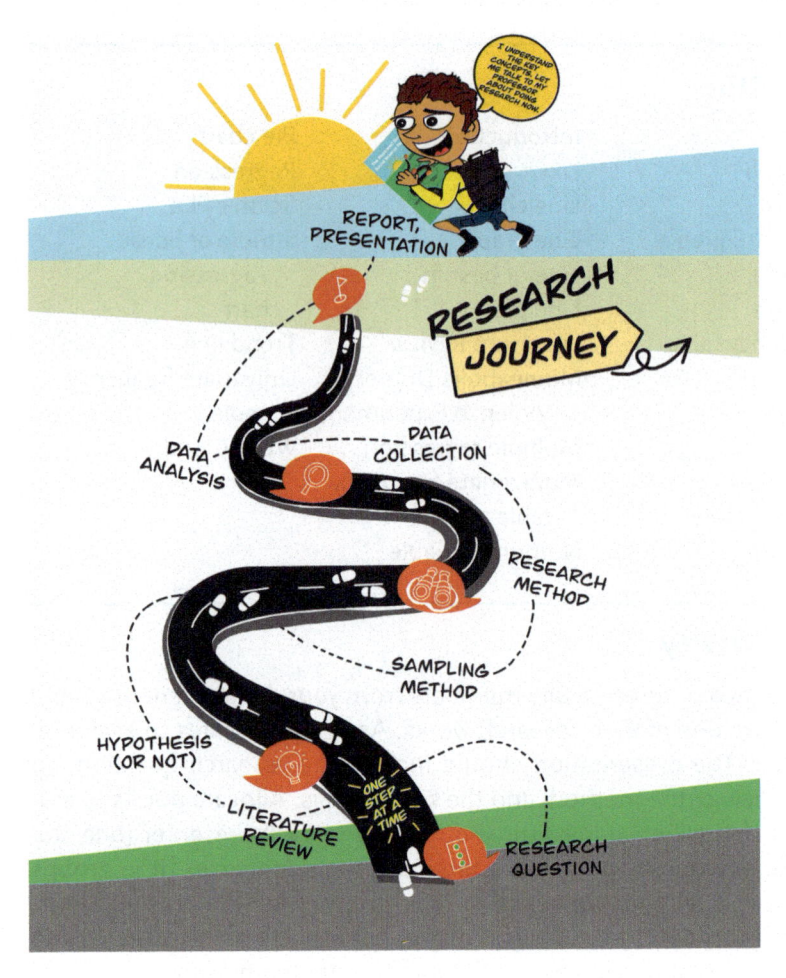

Figure 9.8   Research Journey

Glossary

Chapter 1

Anecdotal fallacy – using personal experiences as evidence for the topic of study.

Authenticity – collecting and presenting information in an unbiased manner; presenting the views of the research subjects without tainting them with personal ideologies or filtering information as per preset views.

Causal validity – the ability to establish a verifiable, evidence-based correlation between cause and effect.

Census – collecting data from everyone in the population.

Citation loop – framing the issue using the same previous sources, authors, and perspectives while adding nothing new; only reproducing the already published work and adding little to no new value or perspective.

Confirmation bias – a type of logical fallacy where one selectively searches, interprets, and documents only the information that suits one's beliefs.

Content validity – assesses whether or not all aspects of the subject can be measured using the research method that one has selected. It relates to fully understanding the concept and having the appropriate method(s) to study it.

Construct validity – achieved when the variables or factors explained in a study are logically strung together. It establishes the correlation among variables and systematically explains the cause(s) and effect(s) in a broader context or theoretical framework.

Correlation – a connection between independent and dependent variables.

Correlation research – also known as exploratory research, this explains causal relationships between variables.

Criterion validity – testing one measure against the other and assessing results on both to see how similar or dissimilar they are.

Cross-population generalization – taking a sample from one population, and applying to findings to multiple similar populations without taking a sample from every population.

Cross-sectional study – collecting data from the sample at one point in time and analyzing it.

Cultural analytics – helps to identify what is a pattern or a regular occurrence (i.e. this happens all the time or is happening quite frequently) as against what is an individual experience, an outlier, or a one-time occurrence.

Dependent variable – the effect or the outcome.

Descriptive research – describes the subject of the study.

Deterrence – discouraging an action or reaction by fear of its repercussions. In criminal justice, this is largely conveyed through the fear of punishment.

E-tailing fraud – a type of e-commerce fraud involving fake receipts, goods purchased through stolen cards, selling stolen goods online, and so on.

Ethnocentrism – evaluating or perceiving other cultures through the values, customs, and standards of one's own culture, often resulting in stereotypes, a false sense of superiority, and overlooking cultural nuances and frameworks.

Ethnological research – a study of how people interpret their behaviors and environment.

Evaluation research – a systematic inquiry aimed at evaluating a program, policy, or law.

Explanatory research – also known as correlation research, this explains causal relationships between variables.

Exploratory research – also called generative research, this is often used to gain an understanding of a setting, phenomena, concepts, or events that may not be clearly defined; they may carry subjective meanings and manifest differently for different people.

Face validity – a judgment-based method where one is sure that on its surface, the measure correctly measures what it is intended to measure.

General deterrence – punishment given to offenders that sends a message to the larger community that crime does not pay. This is measured through overall crime rates.

Generalization – also called generalizability, this refers to the ability to generalize findings from a sample to the larger population from which the sample is taken.

Generative research – also called exploratory research, this is often used to gain an understanding of a setting, phenomena, concepts, or events that may not be clearly defined.

Hypothesis myopia – also called selective observation, this is an error in reasoning where one only looks at the information relevant to one's preset ideas and beliefs.

Illogical reasoning – occurs when the very basis of an argument or information is illogical.

Impact evaluation – an assessment of whether the program has achieved the desired outcome.

Incapacitation – punishment that aims to incapacitate the offender for a specific time by removing them from society, thus removing the opportunity to commit a crime. Incarceration is one of the most common ways to achieve the goal of incapacitation.

Independent variable – is the cause.

Inter-observer reliability – also called inter-rater reliability, this is achieved by having more than one researcher study and interpret the findings.

lex talinois – the law of retaliation.

Logical fallacy – an error in reasoning where one believes that a single event will result in a chain of events in the future.

Longitudinal study – a study in which the researcher analyzes data from or about the same individuals over time to closely examine correlations. The data is collected at several points in time to identify patterns and achieve better predictability.

Measurement validity – the reliability and validity of the tool of data collection.

Neophobia – fear of change or anything new, which can make researchers resistant to change.

Normalcy bias – a state of mental paralysis where one ignores the imminent grave danger and does not believe that it could happen.

Overgeneralization – an error in reasoning, it is the tendency to look at a small unpresentative sample or a handful of cases and assume that it applies to a much larger population.

Ponzi scheme – also called a pyramid scheme, this is a scam in which unsuspecting clients are lured to invest money on the pretext of unusually high returns. The initial investors are paid with money from newer clients. When there are no new clients, the pyramid collapses.

Process evaluation – an evaluation of whether the program is implemented as planned or not.

Rehabilitation – a sentencing goal rooted in the medical model that views crime as a disease.

Restorative justice – a sentencing goal that aims to restore the offender, victim, and society to a pre-crime state.

Retribution – a sentencing goal that argues that the punishment should match the crime. This type of punishment is an end in itself.

Selective observation – also called hypothesis myopia, this is where one only looks at the information relevant to one's preset ideas and beliefs.

Specific deterrence – punishment given to an offender that sends a message that crime does not pay. This is measured through recidivism rates.

The slippery slope – a type of logical fallacy where one believes that a single event will result in a chain of events in the future.

Test-retest reliability – achieved by measuring a phenomenon twice (or more); if the results are similar, the measure can be considered reliable.

Chapter 2

Annotated bibliography – a list of sources available on the topic of research that contains a short paragraph about each source.

Baader–Meinhof phenomenon – a type of cognitive bias about one's tendency to observe or notice something more often and to wrongly believe that it occurs more often than it actually does.

Boolean operators – using AND, OR, NOT, AND NOT; quotation marks " "; and parentheses ( ) to search relevant sources in databases.

Citation loop – framing the issue using the same previous sources, authors, and perspectives while adding nothing new; only reproducing the already published work and adding little to no new value or perspective.

Content analysis – a study of structured and unstructured information including text, photos, videos, and so on. Researchers will generally focus on a list of keywords and examine content to identify patterns or trends.

CRAAP test – evaluating a source by rating it according to Currency, Relevance, Authority, Accuracy, and Purpose.

Deductive approach – involves deducing or extrapolating a specific hypothesis from a theory, collecting data, and analyzing the findings to see if the hypothesis is proven.

Dependent variable – the effect or the outcome.

EBSCO – a database of journals, magazines, e-books, academic libraries, and so on.

Global Terrorism Database – an open-source database including information on domestic and international terrorist events around the world from 1970 through 2020.

Grounded theory – a theory grounded in the data collected in the study.

HyperRESEARCH – software programs for organizing and analyzing qualitative data.

Hypothesis – often called an educated guess, this is a tentative statement that specifies an association between independent and dependent variables that the researcher aims to prove or, in some cases, to disprove.

Independent variable – is the cause.

Inductive approach – a method that starts with a specific question or an observation, followed by data collection and data analysis.

JSTOR – a database of academic journals, e-books, and primary resources.

LexisNexis – a database of legal, government, business, and technology sources.

Literature review – an examination of scholarly sources to contextualize and frame the research question(s) and hypothesis(es).

Minneapolis Domestic Violence Experiment – an experiment evaluating police response to domestic violence to examine which approach would reduce domestic violence.

Monitoring The Future Survey – 'A nationally representative sample of survey participants report their drug use behaviors across three time periods:lifetime, past year, and past month' ('Monitoring The Future').

National Crime Victimization Survey – a self-report longitudinal survey on crimes that are not reported to police.

Negative correlation – also called an inverse correlation or negative association, this is when the value of one variable increases and the other decreases.

Positive correlation – also called a positive association, this is when the increase (or decrease) in the value of one variable results in an increase (or decrease) in the value of the other variable; variables change in the same direction.

Primary data – data collected by the researcher firsthand.

ProQUEST – a global database of academic, government, technology, corporate, newspapers, audio and video content, libraries, and other sources.

Qualitative methods – used to produce qualitative data and are generally used when there is not enough information available to develop a specific hypothesis. Observation, focus groups, and intensive interviews are considered qualitative methods.

Quantitative methods – used to produce quantitative data and are generally used when there is enough information available to develop a specific hypothesis and plan all aspects of research ahead of time. Experiments and surveys are considered quantitative methods.

Secondary data – data that already exists; that is, others have collected it for various studies or databases and the researcher can use it.

SPSS – a software program for quantitative data analysis.

Theory – a systematic study of facts based on evidence and helps to explain things – behaviors, systems, processes, cultures, and so on.

Uniform Crime Reports – a crime data source that contains information from law enforcement agencies in the United States. It is published by the Federal Bureau of Investigation.

Chapter 3

Administrative safeguards – put in place to identify who can or cannot access the data.

Charity patients – the subjects of harmful experiments often carried out on the poor or 'charity patients'; researchers believed that they were doing respondents a favor as, during the experiment, they would get free food.

Chicago Baby Project – an example of an unethical experiment, this involved cremating newly deceased infants and analyzing residual radioactive material in their ashes.

Confidentiality – an ethical guideline for researchers to protect personally identifiable information about the people involved in the study.

Digital data – information shared in electronic format and online.

Digital ethnography – an approach to understanding communities, cultures, and communication in the digital space.

Ethnocentrism – evaluating or perceiving other cultures through the values, customs, and standards of one's own culture, often resulting in stereotypes, a false sense of superiority, and overlooking cultural nuances and frameworks.

Helicopter researchers – researchers whose only concern is to get data for their research without any sincere interest in examining the question, exploring the context, or, for that matter, recording data from the respondent's perspective.

Informed consent – a principle according to which respondents participate in the study of their free will and are free to leave the study at any time without any repercussion or explanation.

Institutional Review Board – also called an ethics committee, this board will review, suggest changes, or approve a research proposal before one can collect data. Its primary responsibility is to ensure that the researchers follow ethical guidelines and that the research subjects are protected.

Milgram experiment – an experiment to study why ordinary people obey authority often without question, even when it is illegitimate or harmful to follow orders.

Netnography – the study of how people create online interactions and relationships.

No harm to subjects – an ethical guideline for researchers to ensure that no physical, emotional, psychological, or any other type of harm is caused to research subjects or participants.

Physical safeguards – safeguards relating to the actual storage of information: where respondents can collect and drop forms, the location of the interview (group or individual), the protocol for locking the cabinets, and so on.

Reductionist view – interpreting other peoples, cultures, and so on through a preset simplistic and often stereotypical lens.

Reflexivity – can create a heightened awareness for researchers as they acknowledge and realize that their personal experiences, beliefs, assumptions, and attitudes, as well as their environment, may influence their research process.

Research ethics – ethical guidelines that the researchers must follow when doing research. These include guidelines such as voluntary participation, a 'no harm to subjects' approach, maintaining confidentiality and anonymity, avoiding deception, and ensuring that the benefits of research outweigh its risks.

Stanford prison experiment – an example of an unethical experiment that was designed to study the prison environment, situational factors, and interactions between guards and prisoners.

Tearoom trade – an example of an unethical experiment about men having sexual encounters with anonymous men in public restrooms.

Technical safeguards – safeguards relating to computer passwords, data sent through email (personal or official), data encryption and coding, and so on.

Tuskegee experiment – an example of an unethical experiment, this was carried out to study the impact of untreated syphilis on African-American males.

Voluntary participation – an ethical guideline according to which respondents participate in the study of their free will and are free to leave the study at any time without any repercussion or explanation.

Chapter 4

Bar chart – denotes a categorical variable where there is no overlap and continuity between the values reflected through separate bins or bars.

Bell curve – also called normal distribution or a sampling distribution, this shows how values of a variable(s) are dispersed. It does not have any skewness. In a bell curve, 68 percent of data falls within plus or minus one standard deviation of the mean; 95 percent of data falls within plus or minus two standard deviations of the mean; and 99 percent of data falls within plus or minus three standard deviations of the mean.

Chicago Alternative Policing Strategy (CAPS) – a community policing approach that involves five steps: identifying and prioritizing problems, analyzing problems, strategizing designs to deal with problems, implementing a plan, and evaluating effectiveness.

Community policing – a policing approach whereby police work in collaboration with the community, resulting in greater mutual trust, understanding, and respect.

Concept – a rough, abstract, or open-to-interpretation idea that the researcher will refine to make it measurable.

Frequency distribution – a good way to organize data to show descriptive as well as explanatory (cross-tabulations) information.

Interquartile range – pertaining to the second and third quartiles when the data set or all the values of the variable are divided into four equal parts.

Interval level – variables that have finite numbers or values, but in which the zero is not fixed.

Likert scale – provides a range of options on a scale indicating responses from one end to the other. For example, a question about the quality of yogurt may contain responses from extremely agree to extremely disagree while also providing a neutral option. Some researchers may decide to exclude the neutral option as they want the respondent to think about the issue at hand instead of picking the 'middle option'.

Measurement validity – the reliability and validity of the tool of data collection.

Median – the middle value or 50th percentile for a date set. It divides the values in half, with 50 percent of values greater than the median and 50 percent placed lower than the median.

Mode – the most common category or value of a variable.

Nominal level – variables that do not have any precise mathematical interpretation or meaning.

Normal distribution – also called a bell curve or a sampling distribution, this shows how values of a variable(s) are dispersed. It does not have any skewness. In a bell curve, 68 percent of data falls within plus or minus one standard deviation of the mean; 95 percent of data falls within plus or minus two standard deviations of the mean; and 99 percent of data falls within plus or minus three standard deviations of the mean.

Ordinal level – variables that can be placed in an order, but where the difference in the values or categories is not mathematically precise or quantifiable.

Outlier – an extremely high or extremely low value that may cause abnormal skewness.

Physical incivilities – physical breakdown of a neighborhood that gives the impression that no one cares about that place.

Primary data – data collected by the researcher firsthand.

Range – the difference between the highest and the lowest values in a distribution.

Ratio level – variables that are mathematically the most precise as there is an absolute zero, and there is a quantifiable difference between values of a variable.

Secondary data – data that already exists; that is, others have collected it for various studies or databases and the researcher can use it.

Social cohesion – a sense of mutual interest and support among members of a community.

Social surveillance – the natural ability of people in a community to look out for each other due to social cohesion.

Standard deviation – also a measure of the dispersion of data, this is the square root of the variance.

Underreporting – failure to report all crimes.

Uniform Crime Reports – a crime data source that contains information from law enforcement agencies in the United States. It is published by the Federal Bureau of Investigation.

Variance – a measure of the dispersion of all data points in a data set. It is the averaged squared deviation from the mean and shows how the data points are spread or deviate from the mean.

Chapter 5

Availability sampling – also called the convenience sampling method, this is a non-probability sampling method. The respondents are selected based on their availability and willingness to participate in the study.

Census – instead of drawing a sample, data is collected from or about everyone in the population.

Cluster sampling – also called multi-stage sampling, this is a probability sampling method. It is most useful when dealing with a very large population across a large geographical area. Naturally occurring clusters are identified and subsequent sampling frames are created at each stage, while ensuring random selection.

Cross-population generalizability – involves taking a sample from one population and applying to findings to multiple similar populations without taking a sample from every population.

Generalizability – also called generalization, this refers to the ability to generalize findings from a sample to the larger population from where the sample is taken.

Hawala brokers – part of the informal banking system in several parts of the Indian subcontinent independent of religion. Also, part of the Islamic banking system in many parts of the world.

Non-probability sampling – methods used when there is no sampling frame or the researcher does not want to use a sampling frame. By doing so, every element or sampling unit in the population does not get an equal chance of being selected in the sample. That is not a negative trait as it serves the purpose – research question, setting, and purpose.

Overgeneralization – the tendency to look at a small sample or a handful of cases and assume that it applies to a much larger population.

Periodicity – an error that may occur while using the systematic random sampling method. Though the researcher tries to select sampling units from across the population using a sampling interval, certain elements may periodically occur at those intervals and thus, skew the sample.

Population – the setting or the group being studied.

Probability sampling – methods that ensure that every element or sampling unit in the population has an equal chance of being selected in the sample. The researcher must ensure random selection based only on equal chance.

Purposive or judgment sampling – a non-probability sampling method used when the researcher can identify the people in the population who would have the relevant information about the topic of study and thus purposively selects them in the sample.

Quota sampling – a non-probability sampling method in which a researcher sets a quota for each element that must be included in the sample. Once that quota is reached, the sample is complete.

Random selection – ensuring that every element in the population has an equal chance of getting selected into the sample. In an experiment, it means ensuring randomly assigning elements from a sample to the experiment, control, and comparison groups.

Random selection error – occurs when certain elements may be over or underrepresented in a sample randomly drawn from the population. In an experiment, it may occur when randomly assigning elements from a sample to the experiment, control, and comparison groups.

Sample – part or sub-set of the population that is studied to make generalizations about the population from which it is taken.

Sampling error – occurs when the results (whether fully or partially) based on a sample do not apply to the population. This may be due to inadequate samples or even non-response.

Sampling frame – a list of all the sampling units in the population. In order to use any probability sampling methods, the researcher must first ensure that there exists a sampling frame of the population from which they will draw a sample.

Sampling interval – an important step in using the systematic random sampling method. It is calculated by dividing the sampling frame by the sample size.

Saturation point – a reference point in data collection by which the researcher has received adequate repeat information but is not getting any new information.

Simple random sampling – a probability sampling method. The preconditions for choosing this sampling method are a clearly defined population and a sampling frame, that is, the list of everyone in the population from which you plan to take a sample. The elements are randomly selected from the sampling frame.

Snowball sampling – a non-probability sampling method in which the researcher identifies one or two members of the population who would have information about the topic of study. That respondent will then refer the researcher to other potential respondents, and so on. The sample is built over time. This is also called a respondent-driven sampling method.

Stratified random sampling – a probability sampling method. Its preconditions are a clearly defined population and a sampling frame. It is the best method to use while studying a diverse population and to adequately represent that diversity in the sample. It requires dividing the population into multiple strata or sampling frames as per the characteristic of interest and then drawing the eventual sample while taking respondents from each separate sampling frame. To ensure randomness or equal chance within each stratum, remember to use the simple random or systematic random sampling method to select respondents from each stratum or sampling frame.

Systematic random sampling – a probability sampling method. The preconditions for choosing this sampling method are a clearly defined population and a sampling frame. In the sampling frame, the first element is selected randomly, and then every nth element is selected until the desired sample size is achieved. The nth element is selected based on a sampling interval.

Theoretical sampling – a non-probability sampling method. It includes following the same steps as snowball sampling except that the researchers modify sample traits as they find new information. For example, while collecting data from informal bankers, if a researcher came across a female banker and was using theoretical sampling, the researcher would be required to actively also look for women involved in the informal banking system. This helps to get a more diverse sample that is modified based on the information that one encounters in the field.

Chapter 6

Closed-ended question – also called the forced-choice or fixed-choice question, this is when the respondent is required to pick a response from options listed by the researcher.

Cover letter – briefly explains the purpose of the research and includes the contact information of the researcher and an ethics statement.

Dichotomous question – a two-point question that includes yes or no as a response.

Digital divide – inequalities between demographics or regions in terms of access to digital tools of communication and information.

Double-barreled questions – contain two questions in one that may confuse the respondent.

Double-negative questions – contain two negative words that can create confusion or mislead.

Drop-off surveys – also called door-to-door surveys, these are delivered to the respondents at the target location. The respondent can either complete the survey while the researcher waits or the researcher can ask questions and note down answers for the respondents. The completed survey can also be collected in a matter of a few hours or a day or so.

E-mail surveys – a survey that is delivered by email as an attached file that the respondents complete and return to the researcher.

Ethics statement – includes information for respondents on voluntary participation, where and how the data will be kept and for how long, issues of privacy and confidentiality, the researcher(s) involved in the project, and their contact information.

Exhaustive responses – in which, in a closed-ended question, all the potential response options are listed for the respondent to choose from.

Face-to-face surveys – surveys that include one-on-one face-to-face interaction between the researcher and the respondent.

Fence sitters – respondents who may know about the topic, but have not made up their minds one way or the other or may be neutral about it.

Floaters – respondents who may not know about the topic, in which case the researcher should give the option of 'Don't know'.

Generalizability – also called generalization, this refers to the ability to generalize findings from a sample to the larger population from where the sample is taken.

Group survey – a survey completed by respondents assembled in a group. The response rate is usually very high in group surveys as the sample is in a controlled setting.

Likert-type scale – provides a range of options on a scale indicating responses from one end to the other. For example, a question about the quality of yogurt may contain responses from extremely agree to extremely disagree while also providing a neutral option. Some researchers may decide to exclude the neutral option as they want the respondent to think about the issue at hand instead of picking the 'middle option.'

Monitoring The Future Survey – 'A nationally representative sample of survey participants report their drug use behaviors across three time periods: lifetime, past year, and past month' ('Monitoring The Future').

Multiple-choice questions – questions that include numerous response options that the respondent can select from.

Mutually exclusive responses – in a closed-ended question, ensuring that the response options do not overlap; one response appears in one category only.

National Crime Victimization Survey – a self-report longitudinal survey on crimes that are not reported to police.

Open-ended questions – questions to which the respondents can give any response; they can write as much or as little as they want to. There are no preset response options listed by the researcher.

Pilot survey – in which a smaller sub-set of the respondents in a sample are asked to complete the survey. This helps to identify if the respondents are reluctant to answer any questions, do not understand a particular question, feel that response options do not include what they want to say, feel embarrassed to answer certain questions, and so on.

Postal surveys – a survey delivered to the targeted sample by post. The respondent is requested to complete the survey by a set date and mail it back.

Questionnaire – a survey that the respondents complete themselves.

Schedule – also called an interview schedule, this is the survey that the researcher completes for the respondent by asking questions.

Semantic scale – involves questions that can also be used to measure attitudes, opinions, and so on. These may seem similar to a Likert-type scale, but the slight difference is that they may not contain a scale that shows a gradual increase or decrease in agreeability or likeability, and so on. Instead, they may only contain contrary response options at the opposing ends while only including the numerical scale between the extreme options.

Telephone survey – a survey in which researchers collect data over the phone and record the respondents' answers.

Text surveys – surveys carried out via text messages on mobile phones. These are generally very short surveys that are used for quick feedback. In the United States, pharmacies, doctors, retail stores, phone and internet providers, postal services, and so on often send a quick text message to the user for immediate feedback on the service provided.

Web survey – a survey delivered as a link that the respondent clicks on. While the terms email, internet, and web survey are often used interchangeably, an email survey is delivered as an attached file that the respondents complete and return to the researcher; the link to a web/internet survey, however, opens an online survey in a new window that the respondent completes and submits.

Weed and Seed program – a neighborhood restructuring program aimed at identifying and weeding out problems and seeding something positive in its place. For example, a dilapidated building may be repaired and converted into a community center.

Chapter 7

Between-subjects factorial design – according to which each research subject is tested in only one condition. For example, each subject can be tested for either eating pizza for lunch or dinner or not eating pizza for lunch or dinner.

Case study – in-depth understanding of a unique event, system, process, or event.

Causal association – for which a researcher must be able to prove an association between variables: the independent variable and the dependent variable must change together.

Causal framework – helps establish the specific situation or case to which that causal explanation applies.

Causal validity – the ability to establish a verifiable, evidence-based correlation between cause and effect.

Classical experiments – also called true experiments, these include at least two groups, randomization, and pretest and post-test.

Comparison group – in an experiment, the group that receives treatment other than the actual treatment or intervention.

Contamination – in which research subjects in the comparison or control group may become aware of the experiment group and realize that they are being treated differently. Even if they do not know the nature of treatment or intervention, this realization may cause them to change their behavior – positive or negative – independent of the experiment.

Control group – in an experiment, the group that does not receive any treatment or intervention.

Debriefing – an important additional guideline for experimental research, this occurs after the experiment is complete. The researcher engages with the research subjects – in a group or individually – and debriefs them about the nature and purpose of the experiment, the points of deception, and stressors, and also identifies if the research subjects may need additional information or assistance of any kind. It gives the research subjects an opportunity to ask questions and get clarity on any aspect of the experiment that they were part of.

Dependent variable – the effect or the outcome.

Experiment/treatment group – in an experiment, the group that receives the actual treatment or intervention.

Expost facto experiment – meaning after the fact, this starts after the event has occurred and, therefore, does not need intervention by the researcher. Instead, it examines the causes to present possible explanations.

Extraneous variable – the third variable that may be influencing independent, dependent, or both types of variable. If the researcher fails to identify the extraneous variable, the causal association would be considered false or not genuine.

Factorial surveys – also called factorial experimental designs, these are used to study a wide range of hypothetical situations by asking research subjects what they would do in a certain situation. The researcher can test several causal explanations involving multiple independent and dependent variables. This helps to identify how variables or factors interact with each other.

Field experiments – opposed to lab experiments, the experiment is conducted in a natural, real-world social setting.

Generalizability – also called generalization, this refers to the ability to generalize findings from a sample to the larger population from which the sample is taken.

Hawthorne effect – a type of error in experiments. In the 1920s, National Research Council researchers studied the impact of work conditions on productivity levels. The expectation was that the poor lighting would lower productivity levels. However, it did not significantly impact productivity levels as the research subjects had become aware of being observed or being part of a study. As a result, the actual impact of the intervention or treatment (poor work conditions) could not be measured.

Idiographic explanation – a causal explanation concerned with a narrower subject of study. It focuses on an individual or an individual or unique event.

Independent variable –the cause.

Informed consent – a principle according to which respondents participate in the study of their free will and are free to leave the study at any time without any repercussion or explanation.

Irrefutability – It is a basic condition of causality. An irrefutable relationship between variables means that the correlation is genuine or not false.

Negative association – also called a negative or inverse correlation, this is when the value of one variable increases and the other decreases.

Nomothetic explanation – a causal explanation concerned with providing a general explanation or more broad causal statements.

Non-randomized groups design – a type of quasi-experiment where the researcher may not be able to or want to randomly assign research subjects to groups.

Placebo – a source of invalidity in an experiment where respondents may think that they are receiving the actual treatment or intervention and thus change their behavior because of that rather than the actual treatment or intervention. As a result, the actual impact of the intervention or treatment cannot be measured.

Ponzi scheme – also called a pyramid scheme, this is a scam in which unsuspecting clients are lured to invest money on the pretext of unusually high returns. The initial investors are paid with money from newer clients. When there are no new clients, the pyramid collapses.

Positive association – also called a positive correlation, this is when the increase (or decrease) in the value of one variable results in an increase (or decrease) in the value of the other variable; variables change in the same direction.

Post-testing – in an experiment, measuring the change in the variable after the treatment or intervention.

Pretesting – in an experiment, measuring the change in the variable before the treatment or intervention.

Quasi-experiments – experiments that do not involve randomization.

Random assignment – ensuring that every element in the population has an equal chance of getting selected into the sample. In an experiment, this means ensuring elements from a sample are randomly assigned to the experiment, control, and comparison groups.

Sample attrition – in a field experiment, the effect of some people dropping out of the experiment or stopping participating for any reason, thus changing the composition of the sample.

Subject fatigue – in which research subjects stop participating in the study because they have become tired of it.

Theory of causality – knowledge of relevant causes.

Time order – in which the researcher must be able to establish which variables are independent and which are dependent. The change in the dependent variable must occur after the change in the independent variable and must be related to it.

Time series experiment – a type of quasi-experiment in which the researcher does not divide the sample into experiment, control, or comparison groups. Instead, the whole sample is pretested, receives the treatment or intervention, and is post-tested.

Unequal benefits in experiments – according to which research subjects in the experiment or treatment group receive the actual treatment while the ones in the control group will not, due to the very nature of the experimental design. This is an ethical dilemma for researchers.

Voluntary participation – an ethical guideline according to which respondents participate in the study of their free will and are free to leave the study at any time without any repercussion or explanation.

Within-subjects factorial design – a more complex design than a between-subjects factorial design, this allows the manipulation of independent variables within subjects.

Chapter 8

Anonymity – an ethical guideline for researchers to maintain the anonymity of respondents in their study.

Authenticity – collecting and presenting information in an unbiased manner; presenting the views of the research subjects without tainting them with personal ideologies or filtering information as per preset views.

Case study – in-depth understanding of a unique event, system, process, or event.

Cognitive maps – mental impressions and perceptions.

Concerned criminology – highlights a wide-ranging topics, including selective coverage of socially constructed crises (constructed here does not mean fake, but how the crisis is presented).

Confidentiality – an ethical guideline for researchers to protect personally identifiable information about the people involved in the study.

Confirmation bias – a type of logical fallacy where one selectively searches, interprets, and documents only the information that suits one's beliefs.

Content analysis – the study of structured and unstructured information including text, photos, videos, and so on. Researchers generally focus on a list of keywords and examine content to identify patterns or trends.

Constructivist approach – understanding and examining phenomena from the respondent's perspective.

Covert observation – also called covert participation, this is a form of observation in which research subjects do not know that they are being observed.

The researcher immerses in the setting and observes and interacts with people without revealing their actual identity or the purpose of the research.

Deception – an ethical guideline that argues against any deception in studies.

Descriptive research – describes the subject of the study.

Digital divide – inequalities between demographics or regions in access to digital tools of communication and information.

Eurocentric – the tendency to examine and interpret various phenomena in cultures around the world from a European lens and perspective.

Evaluative – also called evaluation research, this is a systematic inquiry aimed at evaluating a program, policy, or law.

Explanatory – also known as correlation research, this explains causal relationships between variables.

Exploratory – also called generative research, this is often used to gain an understanding of a setting, phenomena, concepts, or events that may not be clearly defined. They may carry subjective meanings and manifest differently for different people.

Focus groups – participants engaging in a discussion on the topic and answering questions as moderated by the researcher.

Gatekeepers – people who help the researcher in gaining access to a setting.

Grounded theory – a theory grounded in the data collected in the study.

Hypothesis – often called an educated guess, this is a tentative statement that specifies an association between independent and dependent variables that the researcher aims to prove or, in some cases, disprove.

Hypothesis myopia – also called selective observation, this is an error in reasoning where one only looks at the information relevant to one's preset ideas and beliefs.

Illogical reasoning – occurs when the very basis of an argument or information is illogical.

Inductive approach – starts with a specific question or an observation, followed by data collection and data analysis.

Informed consent – a principle according to which respondents participate in the study of their free will and are free to leave the study at any time without any repercussion or explanation.

Intensive interviews – an interview in which the researcher has the topic and a general understanding of what to ask. It is considered a semi-structured tool as the questions are open-ended and flow from the conversations. Even if the researcher asks similar questions on the topic, each respondent may give different answers and thus have varied conversations.

Interpretive approach – understanding and examining phenomena from the respondent's interpretation of the same; different people may interpret the same situation differently.

Narrative analysis – an approach in which the researcher focuses on individual stories and highlights the key points. It allows understanding and presenting the construct from the individual respondent's perspective.

Normative argument – construction of meaning or making a judgment about the person/s, situation, and so on without always knowing the context or even checking the facts.

Neophobia – fear of anything new; fear of change.

Objectivity – unbiased observation, analysis, and reporting of information.

Overgeneralization – the tendency to look at a small sample or a handful of cases and assume that it applies to a much larger population.

Phenomenology – the science of experience.

Qualitative methods – these methods result produce qualitative data; generally used when there is not enough information available to develop a specific hypothesis. Observation, focus groups, and intensive interviews are considered qualitative methods.

Reactive effect – a respondent's behavior influenced by the presence of a researcher, camera, or the knowledge of being observed or being in a study.

Relationship diagrams – describing the inter-connectedness of various factors in a setting or event.

Structured digital data – numbers organized into tables, graphs, charts, and so on.

Subjectivity – based on one's personal opinions, feelings, and perceptions.

Thematic content analysis – an approach in which the researcher focuses mainly on identifying and categorizing common themes and patterns.

Unstructured digital data – images, videos, audio, and so on.

Visual fieldwork – training and techniques needed to scientifically collect and analyze visual data such as photos, videos, documentaries, and films.

Voluntary participation – an ethical guideline according to which respondents participate in the study of their free will and are free to leave the study at any time without any repercussion or explanation.

Weed and Seed program – a neighborhood restructuring program aimed at identifying and weeding out problems, and seeding something positive in its place. For example, a dilapidated building may be fixed and converted into a community center.

Chapter 9

Abstract – text presenting the overall purpose and research question or thesis statement, the sampling and research method used, and the major findings of the study. It should be placed on a separate page by itself before the introduction page.

Area graph – similar to a line chart, this shows the development of values over time, but the area between the axis and line is filled with color.

Bar chart – used to display one variable and its values.

Bivariate frequency table – shows the interaction between two variables. Bi-variate and multi-variate tables are also called contingency tables.

Causation – based on the assumption that two or more variables are related.

Correlation – tells us if two or more variables are correlated. It explains how strong or how weak is the correlation between variables.

DRY-MIX – stands for Dependent, Responding Y-axis, Manipulated, Independent X-axis. That is, it is best to use the y-axis (vertical) to display the dependent variable and the x-axis (horizontal) to display the independent variable. The x and y axes cross at a point where the coordinates are 0,0.

End matter – in a report, journal article, or book chapter, this typically includes references (works cited), tables, figures, charts, and endnotes.

Endnotes – used for explanatory comments. The reader may be given additional information in this section that may obstruct the flow of information in the main body. Sometimes endnotes also include an acknowledgment.

Frequency table – also called a t-chart, this shows the number of times something occurs in the sample.

Histogram – used for a continuous variable, in contrast to a bar chart, which is used for a discrete variable.

Introduction – a clear and specific introduction to a research question. It explains the question by giving context and background.

Likert scale – provides a range of options on a scale indicating responses from one end to the other. For example, a question about the quality of yogurt may contain responses from extremely agree to extremely disagree while also providing a neutral option. Some researchers may decide to exclude the neutral option as they want the respondent to think about the issue at hand instead of picking the 'middle option'.

Line chart – also known as a line graph or line plot, this is a graph that uses a line to connect the individual data points or values of a variable. It is a simple visualization of patterns or trends over time.

Literature review – an examination of scholarly sources to contextualize and frame the research question(s) and hypothesis(es).

Minneapolis Domestic Violence Experiment – an experiment evaluating police response to domestic violence to examine which approach would reduce domestic violence.

Multiple or non-linear regression – shows interaction among multiple dependent and independent variables.

Multivariate frequency table – shows interaction among more than two variables. Bi-variate and multi-variate tables are also called contingency tables.

Nominal variable – a variable the values of which have no overlap. These variables do not have any precise mathematical interpretation such as eye color, religion, location, marital status, gender, and so on.

Pie chart – values of one variable that must add up to 100 percent.

Regression – explains how variables influence each other. It helps us to understand if the variables have a positive association or inverse association.

Scatter plot – used to show a correlation between variables. These are particularly useful for a larger data set. It quickly and easily helps the reader to visualize the relationship or trend. The 'line of best fit' or trend line is drawn using the closest data points and shows the correlation, trend, or prediction.

Simple or linear regression – shows an interaction between one independent and one dependent variable.

Univariate frequency table – a type of data that shows values of one variable only.

Word cloud – particularly useful for displaying qualitative data, online word cloud generators can process large amounts of text in seconds to display which words occur most often.

Index

abstract 33, 50, 195
ad hominem 18
Addington, Lynn A. 26, 29
administrative safeguards 73
Allen, J. J. 58, 60
Allen, Scott 66, 80
Alvi, Shahid 75, 80
American Psychological Association (APA) 50, 67, 68, 78, 79, 195, 197, 198
Anderson, C.A. 58, 60
anecdotal fallacy 17
annotated bibliography 48
Aronson, J. 176, 186
Ash, S.M. 58, 60
atavism 54
Atkinson, R. 110, 113
Atlas.ti 57, 178, 194
authenticity 20, 23–24, 62, 74, 181; see also research goals
Avico, U. 111, 114

Baader–Meinhof phenomenon 45
Ball, David 140, 159
Ball, K.K. 140, 159
bar chart 86, 87, 190

Beccaria. C. 8, 51
Becker, Howard 53, 60
bell curve 90; see also normal distribution
Bellet, Thierry 142, 159
Beneito-Montagut, R. 76, 80
Bentham, J. 8, 51
Berk, R.A. 58, 61, 144, 154, 159
between-subjects 153
Biderman, A. 26, 29
Biernacki, P. 111, 114
Blakeslee, Sarah 46, 60
Blitz, Lisa V. 75, 81
Boissoneault, Lorraine 65, 80
Boolean Operators 41–42
Bornard, Jean-Charles 142, 159
Braithwaite, John 8, 29
Brousse, Cécile 122, 137
BRUSO 133
Bureau of Justice Statistics (BJS) 29, 44, 117

Campbell, D.T. 143, 159
Cantor, D. 25, 29
Carey, S.M. 38, 60
case study 46, 148, 166

Casey, M.A. 163, 185
causal explanation 4, 21, 147, 149, 153; idiographic 147–149; nomothetic 147–148
causal framework 149
causal validity 20–21, 154; see also research goals
census 21, 95–96, 100
Champion, D. J. 101, 114
Chicago Alternative Policing Strategies (CAPS) 84
Chicago Manual of Style (CMS) 50
Chowdhury, S. 123, 138
citation loop 19, 49
CITI Program 68
Clarke, A. 175, 185
Clarke, Ronald V. 53, 60
A Class Divided Experiment 144
classical experiment 149–152
classical thought 51
Cohen, Jerry S. 66, 81
Cohen, Jodi 63, 79
Cohen, Lawrence E. 53, 60
Cohn, Ellen S. 176, 185
community-collaborative approach 19
concept 82–85; conceptualization 83
conditions of causality 147–149, 154
confirmation bias 17, 180–181
conflict of interest 67, 122, 162–163, 167
construct validity 22
content analysis 46, 57, 78, 176–177
content validity 22
contingency tables 188
control group 150, 155, 157
Converse, Jean M. 134, 138
Cook, Thomas D. 143, 159
Cornish, Derek B. 53, 60
Cornwall, A. 163, 185
correlation 51, 54, 145, 149–149, 154, 188, 191–192
cover letter 120–123, 126
Cox, Anton 38, 60
CRAAP test 46, 60
criterion validity 23

cross-population generalization 100, 194
cross-sectional study 25–26, 59; see also prevalence study; transverse study
Crowe, N. 77, 80
cultural analytics 19

debriefing 157
deductive 9, 34, 48, 54, 188; see also rationalism
descriptive research 11–12
deterrence 7–8, 27, 51, 58, 154; see also classical thought; sentencing goals
digital data 62, 76–78, 174, 178–179, 181
digital divide 45, 77, 126, 165, 180
Dissertations and Theses 45
distracted driving 10, 140–141
drug courts 27–28, 38; see also Multnomah County Drug Court, drug laws
drug laws 41-42, 83,
Duffee, D. 29
Dugan, L. 25–26, 29

EBSCO 41
Elizabeth, H.J. 138
empiricism 34, 149, 153
end matter 196–198
endnotes 32, 33, 197
e-tailing fraud 9
errors in reasoning 45, 77, 107, 180-181, 193
ethics 62, 64, 74, 76–78, 116, 120–122, 126, 150, 166, 171, 193, 197; anonymity 73, 78, 163, 166–167, 174; confidentiality 70, 73, 78, 120, 125, 128, 163, 166–167, 174; consent 62–64, 68–73, 77, 121, 126, 128, 155–157, 176; deception 64, 68–69, 73, 155–157, 171, power dynamics 22, 66–67, 122, 162, 166–167; voluntary participation 64, 67–68, 70, 120–121, 123, 128,

Index 229

155–156, 166–167, 171, 176; *see also* informed consent
ethics committee 9, 36-37, 56, 67, 79, 115, 156, 171
ethics statement 120–121, 126, 197
ethnocentric 19, 24, 74, 75; *see also* ethnocentrism
ethnocentrism 24, 74,
ethnological 12
European Commission Publications 44
European Union 44
evaluation 13–15, 25; *see also* evaluative, impact evaluation, process evaluation
evaluative 9, 13, 15, 161
experiments 33, 34, 56, 65–66, 68, 72, 116, 140, 142, 146; classical 150–151; ethics 155–157; field 154–155; generalizability 154; quasi 152–153; validity 154
explanatory 12–13
exploratory 11–12, 84, 161; *see also* generative, ethnological
expost facto 152

face validity 22
factorial design 153–154; *see also* between-subjects, within-subjects
Farrington, D.P. 23, 30
Federal Bureau of Investigation 44
Federal Bureau of Prisons 44
Felson, M. 53, 60
fence-sitters 130
Fine, P.R. 140, 159
Finigan, M.W. 38, 60
fixed-choice 128
Flint, J. 110, 113
floaters 130
focus group 161–165, 168; conflict of interest 167; data analysis 165; ethics 165–166; generalizability 165; moderator 165; notetaking 165–166; sample 164
forced-choice 128

Franklin, C.A. 140, 159
frequency distribution 86, 188

Garner, Annie A. 140, 159
gatekeepers 24, 77, 110–111, 182
General Social Survey 44
generalizability 20–21, 23–26, 46, 55, 59, 77, 95, 149; cross-population 21, 100; experiments 149, 153–154; focus groups 166; qualitative methods 176; sample 21, 99, 100, 108–109, 111; survey 120, 124, 128, 134; *see also* generalization
generalization 20-21, 57, 77, 95, 149
generative 11
Ginsberg, P. 114
Global Terrorism Database 44
Google Scholar 47
Goring, C. 54, 60
GPS 104
Griffin, R. 140, 159
grounded theory 55, 161, 173
Gruyer, D. 141, 159

Hagan, F. E. 96, 114
Hawala 19, 110; *see also* informal banking systems
helicopter researcher 74
Hopper, Columbus B. 174–175, 184
Humphreys, Laud 64, 80
HyperRESEARCH 57, 178, 194
hypothesis 7, 33, 39–40, 53–56, 150–151, 161, 196; myopia 16

illogical reasoning 18, 45, 179; *see also* errors in reasoning
impact evaluation 13
incapacitation 7–8; *see also* sentencing goals
incentives 120, 163–164
incivilities 51, 84–85
inductive approach 9, 34, 48, 55, 57, 161, 173, 176, 188; *see also* empiricism
informal banking systems 9, 19, 99, 101, 109-111, 174

informed consent 63-64, 68-70, 77-78, 155-156, 176
Institutional Review Board (IRB) 9, 36–37, 56; see also ethics committee
intensive interviews 33, 57, 72, 128, 161, 168–169, 175–177
International Monetary Fund 45
interquartile range 88–89
inter-observer reliability 23
inter-rater reliability 23; see also inter-observer reliability
interview schedule 118, 128

Jacobs, K. 77, 80
Jessica's Law 133
Jewkes, R. 163, 185
Jones, J.L. 140, 159
JSTOR 41

Kaplan, Abraham 83, 94
Kaplan C. 111, 114
Kelling, George L. 52, 61, 146
Kelly, J. 123, 138
Korczak, D. 111, 114
Kozinets, R. 77, 80
Krueger, R. A. 163, 185

Lamb, R. 77, 80
Lavigueur, H. 141, 159
Lee, Gary 66, 80
Leedy, P. 182, 185
Leichtentritt, R. 176, 186
levels of measurement 86–87; interval 89; nominal 86–87, 91, 190; ordinal 87–89; ratio 87, 89, 91
Leverentz, A. 179, 185
Levitt, Steven D. 154, 159
Lewis, Abbey B. 60, 61
lex talinois 8
LexisNexis 41
linear 187, 191
List, John A. 154, 159
literature review 15, 22, 32–33, 39–41, 49, 53–54, 56, 195–196

logical fallacy 17–18; see also errors in reasoning
Lohr, S.L. 25–26, 30
Lombroso, C. 54
longitudinal design 25-26
longitudinal study 6, 25–27, 116; see also longitudinal design
Lynch, J.P. 25–26, 29
Lyons, K.D. 175, 185

MacPheran, Karen 66, 80
Malpass, R.S. 141, 159
Masoga, Mogomme Alpheus 75, 81
Massé, Emmanuel 137
Mastrofski, S.D. 29
Maxfield, M.G. 23, 29
Mayenobe, P. 141, 159
Mazerolle, L.G. 29
McDowall, D. 29
McKay, H.D. 51, 61
MDVE methodology 143
mean 89–90
measurement validity 20, 22–24, 91, 116, 119, 128; see also research goals
median 88–89
Mertens, Donna M. 114
Merton, Robert 52, 61
Meter, K. Van 111, 114
Michigan 650-Lifer Law 42
Milgram experiment 64, 147, 156
Minneapolis Domestic Violence Experiment 58, 142, 154–155, 192; see also MDVE methodology
Mintz, M. 66, 81
Mitford, Jessica 66, 81
mode 86, 88
Modern Language Association (MLA) 50
Monitoring The Future (MTF) survey 118
Moore, J. 174–175, 184–185
Multnomah County Drug Court 27, 38
Murphy's Law 173

National Crime Victimization Survey (NCVS) 25, 44, 116–117
National Criminal Justice Reference Service (NCJRS) 44
Natrajan, M. 182, 186
neophobia 18, 180
netnography 76–78
news sources 45–46
non-linear 188, 192
non-probability sampling methods 101, 107, 128; availability 107–108; purposive 109–110; quota 108; respondent-driven 110; snowball 110–111; theoretical 111
non-randomized groups 152
normal distribution 90; see also bell curve; sampling distribution
normalcy bias 17; see also errors in reasoning
notetaking 165, 168, 171, 174

objectivity 171, 181
observation 33, 57, 72; covert 170–171; data analysis 173; ethics 174–175; field 169; grounded theory 173; overt 171–172; reactive effect 172; steps 168; see also generalizability, qualitative methods
Open Access Theses and Dissertations 45
Open Library 45
Ormrod, J.E. 182, 185
outlaw motorcycle gangs 174–175, 184–185
overgeneralization 15–16, 45–46, 77, 94, 179; see also errors in reasoning

Paris, Jean-Christophe 141, 159
paywall 44, 47, 188; see also subscription
Peled, E. 176, 186
periodicity 103
Peruche, B.M. 143, 159
Peterson, R. A. 133, 138
Philliber, S. G. 94, 114

physical safeguards 73
pie chart 190
pilot survey 134
placebo 155
plagiarism 50
Plant, Ashby E. 143, 159
Planty, M. 25, 29
policy questions 38
Ponzi schemes 10, 39, 149
post-test 151–152
Presnall, Landon 138
Presser, Stanley 134, 138
pretest 151
prevalence study 26
probability sampling methods 55, 101–107; cluster 104; periodicity 103; random selection error 102–103; sampling frame 98–99, 101–105, 107–108, 110–111; sampling interval 103; simple random 102; stratified random 105–107; systematic random 103
process evaluation 13
ProQuest 41
public databases 44

qualitative 26, 33–34, 57, 74, 116, 128, 161, 171, 173, 183, 196; approach 76, 182; data 33, 57, 85, 127, 129, 161, 166, 182–183, 190, 194; gatekeepers 182; generalizability 177; see also focus groups; intensive interviews; observation
quantitative 33, 56, 155, 183; data 25, 33, 128, 182; see also experiments; surveys
question format; closed-ended 128; dichotomous 129; double-barreled 131; double-negative 131–132; exhaustive 131–134; filter 136; closed-ended 118, 120, 125, 128–133; Likert-type 129, 136, 190; multiple-choice 129; mutually exclusive 133–134; open-ended 118, 128, 129–130, 175, 185; semantic scale 129; skip

pattern 124–125, 136; see also fixed-choice; forced-choice
questionnaire 71, 118, 136

random assignment 149–152
range 89–90
rationalism 34
reactive effect 118, 154, 156, 172
reductionist error 19, 75
reflexivity 75
refugees 24, 173, 176
regression 192; see also linear, non-linear
rehabilitation 8, 27, 84; see also sentencing goals
relationship diagrams 166, 173
report writing 24, 178, 194–198
research goals 20
research question 36–37
research report 33, 194–195
restorative justice 8; see also sentencing goals
retribution 8; see also sentencing goals
Richards, H. M. 176, 186
Rochère, Bernadette Guiot de la 138
Rockefeller Drug Laws 42

safeguards 73; see also administrative safeguards; physical safeguards; technical safeguards
sample attrition 155
sampling distribution 90
saturation point 111
schedule 118, 128; see also interview schedule
Schneider, Keith 66, 81
Schwab, M.R. 94, 114
Schwartz, L.J. 176, 186
Scopus (Elsevier) 41
searchFast 43
secondary data 15, 34, 55, 115, 192
selective observation 16, 45, 79, 181; see also errors in reasoning
Senese, J. D. 101, 114
sentencing goals 8

Sharma, D. 19, 30, 81, 111, 114
Shaw, C.R. 51, 61
Shei, J. 138
Sherman, L.W. 144, 154, 159
Shokane, Allucia Lulu 75, 81
Sinding, C. 176, 186
Sisiopiku, V.P. 140, 159
slippery slope 18
Sloss, S.G. 94, 114
Smith, A. C. T 77, 81
social cohesion 54, 84, 149
social media 7, 10, 12–13, 18, 45, 54, 59, 76–78, 112, 115, 178–179, 181, 193
social surveillance 84
standard deviation 89–90
Stanford Prison Experiment 65
Statistical Package for Social Sciences (SPSS) 57, 194
Stavrinos, Despina 140, 159
Stewart, B. 77, 81
subject fatigue 154
subjectivity 182
subscription 44, 47, 188
survey research 115–116, 118–119, 127, 131; door-to-door, drop-off 120–121; face-to-face 127; group 121–122; postal 119–120; telephone 122–123; text 124–125; web, email, Internet 125–126
Sutherland, Edwin 52–53, 61

technical safeguards 73
test-retest reliability 23
theory 8, 51–54, 58, 146; grounded 55, 161, 173
theory of causality 149
Thomas, Tina 138
Thompson, E. 19, 30
Three-Strikes and You're Out law 133
Tight, Malcolm 166, 186
Tillmann-Healy, L. 175, 186
time order 149–149
time series experiment 152, 157
title page 32–33, 194–195
transverse study 26

treatment group 150–151, 157
Turner, Jonathan H. 51, 61
Tuskegee Experiment 63

Uniform Crime Reports 44, 85
United Nations 44; United Nations Office on Drugs and Crime 44
University of Illinois 63
USA PATRIOT Act, 2001 36

variable 13, 21–22, 26, 31, 36, 39, 51, 53–54, 57–58, 98–99, 103, 105, 107–108, 111, 134, 153–154, 188–192, 195–196; bivariate 188; dependent 21, 53–54, 58–59; direction of association 54, 149; extraneous 149; independent 21, 53–54, 58–59; interval 89; multivariate 188; negative association 54, 149; nominal 86–87, 189; ordinal 87–88; positive association 54, 149; ratio 89; univariate 188
variance 90, 141
visual criminology 179
Voorde, Cecile Van de 178, 186

Wagner, P. 76, 81
Waldorf, D. 111, 114
Walia, N. 138
Walker, S. 24, 30
Watts, M. 77, 80
Weed and Seed Program 121, 161, 185
Welburn, S.C. 140, 159
Weldon, D.E. 141, 159
West, D.J. 23, 30
white-collar crime 39, 52–53, 83, 85–86
Widom, C.S. 23, 29
Wilson, James Q. 52, 61, 146
within-subjects 153
Wolter, Kirk 138
works cited 32–33, 197
WorldCat 45

Ybarra, L.M.R. 25–26, 30
Yemma, John 65, 81

Zimbardo, P. 65, 72, 145–146, 157
Zimbardo's Experiment on Vandalism 145